CAPSTONE REFERENCE

THE
ULTIMATE BOOK
OF BUSINESS
THINKING

CAPSTONE REFERENCE

THE
ULTIMATE BOOK
OF BUSINESS
THINKING

HARNESSING THE POWER
OF THE WORLD'S GREATEST
BUSINESS IDEAS

DES **DEARLOVE**

CAPSTONE

First Published 2003 by

Capstone Publishing Limited (a Wiley company)
8 Newtec Place
Magdalen Road
Oxford
OX4 1RE
United Kingdom
http://www.capstoneideas.com

CIP catalogue records for this book are available from the British Library and the US Library of Congress

ISBN 1-84112-440-0

Typeset in 10.5/13 pt Plantin
by Sparks Computer Solutions Ltd
http://www.sparks.co.uk
Printed and bound by
T.J. International Ltd, Padstow, Cornwall

CONTENTS

S

T

V

'Practical men, who believe themselves to be quite exempt from any intellectual influences, are usually the slaves of some defunct economist. Madmen in authority, who hear voices in the air, are distilling their frenzy from some academic scribbler of a few years back.'[1]

John Maynard Keynes (1883–1946),
British economist.

INTRODUCTION

Modern management is a curious mix of the practical and the theoretical. Ask a manager which dominates and he or she will naturally say the former. Management is about getting tasks done. But the reality is more complicated. None of us can afford to ignore the theory entirely. It is tempting to dismiss much of what is published in academic journals as 'irrelevant' to what real managers do on a day-to-day basis. It is easy to assume that they continue to do what they have always done. But the fact is that new ideas and concepts shape how we think about the role of managers in a changing business world.

Today's theory is tomorrow's task

A steady flow of new ideas is redefining what managers should be doing, how they should be doing it, and critically what their performance is evaluated against. For this reason alone, it is important to stay abreast of the latest thinking. Today's theory is tomorrow's task.

Today, a growing number of managers have been to one of the many business schools around the world. For these people, schooled in management theory, the power of concepts is understood. But those who did their management training in the school of hard knocks may ask why they should bother. They might argue, with some justification, that management is fundamentally a hands-on activity, and has little relation to the grandiose or ethereal theories of management gurus. They have a case, but only up to a point. Think about how the job of the manager has changed in the past few decades. What is needed in today's business world, it is almost universally agreed, is a lighter touch on the reins, a more intelligent use of human resources. Today, the manager is seen as a leader and facilitator rather than controller and policeman. At the same time, the sort of environment and organization in which managers operate is changing to fit new conceptions of what a business should look like. Even the fundamental understanding or psychological contract between the manager and the organization is being transformed by redefinitions of the employee/employer relationship. Where do such notions come from? From the management literature, of course. From the thousands of business books, articles, case studies and models that are produced each year. These have a constant drip, drip, drip effect on the consciousness of managers everywhere.

The problem is that in recent years the flow of concepts has become a torrent.

This book aims to make life easier by selecting the ideas and concepts that are significant among the thousands that have emerged. Some of them are new, while others have been around in one form or another for years. I make no apologies for that. Good ideas last long after the fads have evaporated into the hot air whence they came.

A good idea is no guarantee of success in the real world, of course. Most are poorly implemented. But, for all that, the ideas in this book have had, and will continue to have, a fundamental impact on what real managers do. It's not simply that business process re-engineering, or downsizing, are likely to put them out of a job; there is a more subtle process at work. Just as the best theory is (or should be) derived from the real world, so the real world is changed by the promulgation of the theory. The great business school and consulting concepts are theory created out of practice, which is then presented back into the workplace as best practice. Concepts cannot be ignored.

The fact is that even if you chose to reject every new idea put forward, your boss – or whoever conducts your annual appraisal – will not. New management concepts change both the terms of reference by which real managers operate, and the yardsticks by which their performance is measured. The unavoidable conclusion is that ideas, even poor ones, influence what real managers do.

Knowledge is the best protection against fads and fashions. For some managers, reading management literature is an attempt to ensure that when a senior manager drops the latest buzzword into a conversation they can have some idea what he or she is talking about. It allows the manager to penetrate the jargon. But it is also the only way to tell the important ideas, the ones that will change the business world, from the detritus of consultancy fodder and other nonsense peddled by self-promoting ideas merchants.

The Oxford English Dictionary defines a concept as 'a general notion', or 'an abstract idea'. Interestingly, it also provides a colloquial usage – 'an idea or invention to help sell or publicize a commodity'. These definitions apply in varying degrees to business concepts. Some are little more than old ideas neatly packaged to provide a commercial opportunity for their originators (typically a consulting firm or business academic). Others are purer abstractions of universal principles. This book contains some of both. What all have in common is that they have been selected because they exert a powerful influence on the way real managers think, or will think in the future.

A growing problem is the sheer volume of new ideas touted each year as 'breakthroughs', new 'blueprints for success', or some other over-blown claim. Idea after idea is launched with ever-louder fanfare. And the trumpeting gets more strident. A fountain of new books gushes from publishers and from new and established authors. Cynicism is reaching epidemic proportions.

Witness the rise of Buzzword Bingo,[2] which inspired a Dilbert comic strip, and made the front page of the *Wall Street Journal*. Instead of numbers, players use corporate buzzwords, ticking off the latest piece of jargon as it falls from the lips of their unsuspecting boss. Buzzword Bingo satirizes management. It is a sign of the times. Jargon overkill is damaging the status of management as a profession. The buzzwords ring hollow. If anything, the credibility gap is widening. People feel disconnected from the language of management. It can seem surreal. The irreverent observations of Dilbert and Dogbert have already made their creator Scott Adams the best-selling business author in the world. The excessive use of buzzwords undermines serious business ideas. The people who use them are often fashion victims.

'It's part of the fad cycle,' notes MIT's Peter Senge, whose book *The Fifth Discipline* spawned the buzzword 'learning organization'. 'People consume then drop fads and ideas all the time and corporations are no different.'

Such is the cynicism that now exists among some parts of the business press that there is little real attempt to decipher those with something important to say from the merely mellifluous. Until now, there has been no quality control.

As a result, managers have been deluged with ideas. In a business world where information overload is already a major cause of stress, the choice is either a desperate attempt to read and assimilate everything – or ignore it altogether.

Most managers are caught in the middle, reading what they can when they can and trying to sort the nuggets from the rest. This book is an attempt to help them in that task.

The ideas in this book are noteworthy – either because they provide truly useful thinking frameworks and tools or because they have the potential to change people's lives in other ways. Forewarned is forearmed. Not everyone will agree with all of the selections, or their interpretation.

Some will argue that some entries are simplistic, naive or unnecessarily scathing. That is the nature of ideas. What one observer finds helpful, another finds to be a waste of time. In a business world riven with fads and fashions, a degree of subjectivity is vital.

We have tried to pick ideas that will last. What distinguishes a lasting concept from the flavour-of-the-month flotsam? Hard to say. The take-up among real companies is a major factor. In this regard, timing is important. An idea that fits the corporate context and agenda is more likely to be sucked into the corporate syringe and injected into the patient. What is administered more often than not is not the pure form, of course. Most are either misunderstood or misapplied at some point. Many a benign concept has turned malodorous, too, when administered for some ulterior purpose.

I've tried to select ideas that have delivered, or have the potential to deliver, significant and lasting benefits, or have had lasting impact in other ways. Most have some of the following characteristics:

- *Timely*. They meet an immediate need, or anticipate one that is not yet recognized.
- *Self-contained*. Even though they are built on earlier ideas, the best concepts stand on their own. They can be understood in isolation from what came before.
- *Real world credibility* – either from extensive research or from experience at the sharp-end of business, and preferably both.
- *Intellectual rigour*. The quality of thought and insight is another distinguishing feature of ideas that last. Some ideas are deliberately vague to allow universal application. Great concepts are razor sharp; they have their own internal logic. They are consistent, and provide useful definitions.
- *Simple*. The best concepts are derived from basic and universal principles. They are intuitive. They help us make sense of the world around us.
- *Practical*. Perhaps the real difference between fads and ideas that last is their usefulness to managers – their practical application.

Against these criteria, certain thinkers have an impressively high batting average. They seem to have a knack of anticipating – and even shaping – the future. Scratch the surface of many of the concepts included in this book and you find the same names just beneath the surface. People like Peter Drucker and Douglas McGregor have had a profound and lasting influence on the way managers – and other management thinkers – understand the world. Go back even further and the names of Henri

Fayol, Mary Parker Follett and even Frederick Taylor echo down the years.

Curiously, however, surprisingly few of the ideas are directly attributed to these people. In part, this is because most of the truly original thinkers have a wide range of interests, which makes it difficult to label them with a single concept. Rather, they contribute to the general consciousness, informing and influencing many concepts. But it is also because they come from another era, from a time when appropriating ideas for commercial gain was not the main objective.

Today, developing a concept goes hand-in-hand with exploiting the financial potential. Concepts have become a business. This is the age of the guru. There are religious gurus, spiritual mentors, motivational gurus, champions of self-help, financial gurus. Gurus are a phenomenon of our times, peddlers of hope in an age of fear, doubt and anxiety. And the business world is no exception. Its gurus come in smart suits. They are the snake-oil salesmen of our age. Ownership of ideas is the key. Many of the original thinkers gave their ideas more freely. Perhaps it would have been different if they were publishing their first books today. Perhaps they would have branded their concepts more assiduously to maximize the commercial return. Somehow I doubt it. They are not one-idea wonders. Their thinking endures, and influences generation after generation. When all is said and done, they are the great business thinkers. Their ideas form a deep reservoir from which all of us can drink. Above all, their ideas are applied quietly and without fuss by real managers on a daily basis.

A history of business concepts

Trying to place the emergence of important business concepts in context is a fascinating, if ultimately impossible, task. What is clear is that acceptance of ideas by companies has often been driven by what is going on around them and the prevailing view of the world (convenience or ideology, rather than merit alone). It is notable, for example, that Frederick Taylor's *Principles of Scientific Management* was published in 1911, just three years before the start of World War I. In Taylor's business model, individual workers were seen as little more than cogs in a machine, giving rise to the 'science of manufacturing'. People were seen as industrial cannon fodder. A similar disregard for individuals was enacted on the battlefields of northern France.

In the US after the war, there were new concerns about power. In the first part of the twentieth century, trust-busting became a popular government pursuit, and eventually forced the railroad, steel and oil behemoths to break themselves into smaller units. At an individual level, too, power was being redefined. The period of the 'Roaring Twenties', up to the Wall Street Crash in 1929, brought the first intimations of empowerment, inspired by Mary Parker Follett – a woman, no less – and the rise of the human relations school of thinkers.

In the 1930s, while Europe lurched towards more centralized planning with the rise of fascism and socialism, America veered in the opposite direction. At GM in the 1930s, Alfred P. Sloan organized the company along federal lines, replacing a bureaucracy-riddled system with a number of divisions or operating businesses. Each of the 30 or so divisions had its own clearly delineated responsibilities. In the marketplace, GM's products – including Chevrolet and Cadillac – competed as separate identities and were managed by different divisions, which were given a high level of autonomy by the centre. This structure allowed GM to overtake Ford.

The onset of war brought new purpose to the industrial machines of America and Europe. The struggle for national survival led to new efficiencies, technologies and management techniques including operations research. Operations research involved the application of scientific methods to accomplish an organization's objectives. The military consumed the entire production of some industries as capacity rose to new levels to meet the needs of the war effort. Industrialists grew rich in the process. Peace, when it came, brought a period of prosperity to America and new challenges to the rest of the world.

A self-congratulatory mood among the victorious countries after World War II saw their competitive position gradually eroded. Confident that the systems that had won the war were the best, the victors were uninterested in radical new ideas, preferring to get their inspiration from the success of the armed forces. Management techniques applied to the war effort were brought to business. In the US, the consulting firm Arthur D. Little was one of the first to seek industrial uses for the techniques. (Later, John Adair's action-centred leadership was derived from his teaching at the Royal Military Academy, Sandhurst.)

But the defeated nations of Japan and Germany were more open to new industrial techniques and concepts. Post-war reconstruction led Japanese companies to rebuild manufacturing systems from a blank sheet of paper. In Japan, the ideas of W. Edwards Deming, which were largely disregarded in his home country of America, were embraced. The quality movement he inspired was instrumental in the Japanese economic miracle. By and large, American companies felt they had no need of such concepts. The systems that helped them win a world war

---

A snapshot of post-war business concepts 1950–1979

1950

The Practice of Management by Peter Drucker published	Action-centred leadership
Formation of the Eastern bloc	XY(Z) Theory
1960	Outsourcing
Intel develops the microchip	Knowledge worker
IBM introduces the System 360	The four Ps
1970	Managerial grid
Future Shock by Alvin Toffler published	Adhocracy
Oil embargo	Lean production (Toyota)
Japanese manufacturing miracle builds up steam	Discounted cash flow
	Scenario planning

1979

---

were clearly best. (An interesting footnote here is that although the use of quality circles is usually ascribed to Japanese companies, it has been argued that the practice really started with the United States Army soon after 1945.)

In the 1950s and 1960s, the advent and development of the computer promoted more radical thinking about how the new technology would affect work. This new interest was reflected in the writing of futurists such as Alvin Toffler, who developed the concept of adhocracy in 1970.

Still in self-congratulatory mood, the excellence movement of the early 1980s in America was triggered by Tom Peters and Robert Waterman's *In Search of Excellence*. It was a celebration of America's greatest companies. The celebration was short-lived. Quality and not excellence was the concept that would dominate the business agenda for the next decade. But in one very important regard the book was a milestone. Almost single-handedly, it launched the multi-million dollar business guru industry. The fact that many of the companies showcased by Peters and Waterman as 'excellent' subsequently slid off their pedestals finally alerted corporate America to the new realities of business life.

Awareness of the growth of Japanese manufacturing muscle created an appetite for new thinking. This was followed in the 1980s by the wholesale adoption of Japanese techniques such as TQM, *kaizen* and just-in-time. A period of catch-up followed. The quality agenda dominated manufacturing throughout the 1980s, and moved to the service industries.

With the world economy booming in the second half of the 1980s, production capacity expanded to churn out more of everything. But as the boom turned to bust, and a world recession set in at the start of the 1990s, companies looked to new concepts to squeeze more profits out of existing businesses. Cost-cutting was dressed up in intellectual attire. In some areas, the unrelenting appetite for profits led to cynical asset-stripping. This process was fuelled by junk bond funded mega-mergers followed by savage cost-cutting, to fund the interest and capital on the junk bond debt. A new concept emerged that fitted the times. It was called downsizing.

Downsizing became a mantra. What had started as optimism had turned to greed. On Monday 19 October 1987, the bubble burst when the Wall Street stock market crashed – the Dow Jones plunged 508.32 points in a single day, losing more than 22% of its total value. The fallout from Black Monday led to a cost-cutting frenzy. What had started with optimism had indeed turned to greed, and ended with ignominy.

By the start of the 1990s, right-wing conservatism was on the wane and the balance of power began to shift to semi-socialist, new-labour middle-ground parties in Europe. In the US, the recession helped put a Democrat in the White House. Bill Clinton's election confirmed that Reaganomics no longer appealed to the American electorate. There was a backlash against the hard-nosed materialistic values of the 1980s. The focus in companies began to shift from physical assets to people. The new decade was heralded as the caring, sharing 90s.

In the first part of the 1990s, companies found themselves under paradoxical pressures on the one hand to regroup, slim down and focus to survive in the short term (emerging concepts at this time included core competencies, balanced scorecard, shareholder value, BPR); and on the other hand, to expand to compete in a global market for long-term success. New concepts emerged (the transnational corporation, matrix management, globalization). Meanwhile, the war on bureaucracy continued with the adoption of outsourcing and new, hollowed-out organizational forms (influenced by the ideas such as Charles Handy's shamrock

---

A snapshot of post-war business concepts 1980–1999

1980

ATT is broken up	Porter's five forces
Rise of the junk bond and leveraged buy out	Excellence
Black Monday on Wall St 19 October 1987	TQM/just-in-time Psychological contract
End of the Cold War	Transnational corporation
1990	Core competencies
The Fifth Discipline by Peter Senge published	Downsizing BPR
Democrats win US election	Knowledge management
BCCI scandal	Virtual organization
May 1997 Labour Party wins UK general election	Strategic Inflection Point Emotional Intelligence
Age of e-commerce	Value innovation
2000	
Dotcom crash	
Enron scandal	

---

organization and others). Companies did anything and everything they could think of to strengthen the balance sheet.

The *coup de grâce* came with a series of corporate scandals, including the collapse of BCCI (Bank of Credit and Commerce International) and the missing Maxwell pension funds in 1991. Corporate excesses drew unwanted public attention. Faced with the threat of shareholder revolt and government action, corporate governance issues came to the fore.

As growing public revulsion to downsizing put increasing pressure on companies, more palatable concepts were picked up. Downsizing metamorphosed into the more politically correct 'rightsizing'. The emergence of a new concept – re-engineering – was greeted with enthusiasm, and gave a more respectable and quasi-scientific garb to redundancies.

As the 1990s wore on, companies tried to repair the damage caused by the corporate bloodletting. New concepts were required to make sense of the carnage. The psychological contract was revisited and the concept of employability surfaced at this time. The learning organization was seen as a way of ensuring that corporate memory is not lost in the future and mistakes were not repeated. The other significant trend of the decade was the growth in use of the computer and the advent of the internet. With it came the move away from tangible assets to the ethereal (intellectual capital). With a new breed of businesses springing up based around the new technologies, big business was forced to look at radically different business models and organizational structures (virtual organization, channel management).

Overnight, Amazon.com and other upstart internet start-ups were creating whole new markets where none existed before – and stealing markets from under the nose of big business. Meanwhile, the mood of big business was summed up in the book by the head of Intel, Andy Grove, called *Only the Paranoid Survive* (which introduces the concept of strategic inflection points). Large companies, fearful now, frantically tried to spot the next big change. Senior managers were desperately trying to make sense and formulate strategy in an increasingly volatile business landscape. Scenario planning and crisis management moved up the corporate agenda.

To make sense of the new business order, companies began to focus on human capital as never before (key concepts are knowledge management and emotional intelligence). By the late 1990s, companies had fought to a stalemate in the war for market share. As the century, and the millennium, drew to a close, companies were looking for something new with which to deal the competitive knockout blow. New concepts such as thought leadership, value innovation and relationship marketing were gratefully received.

At the start of a new century, companies are now turning their attention as never before to the human dimension. In time, it may be possible to look back at the twentieth century as the high tide of machine bureaucracy and its oddly mechanistic view of management. Already new organic metaphors are finding a place in the language of business (witness the success of Arie de Geus's book *The Living Company*, for example). One thing is certain: as the new millennium gets under way there will be plenty of new ideas to think about.

The concepts of the future will radically redefine how business-people think. They will help focus the lens through which we look at the world of work – and understand ourselves in relation to it. For professional managers, it will be more important than ever to keep an eye firmly pressed to the telescope. Increasingly, it resembles a kaleidoscope.

Life cycle of a concept

Inevitably, many of the ideas presented as great leaps forward are simply repackaged versions of hardy theoretical perennials. Little that is written, published or unearthed by diligent business school researchers is truly original. Similarly, little that consultants encounter is truly unique or universally applicable. And yet few would disagree with the notion that ideas are important.

Research at the Massachusetts Institute of Technology suggests that management fads follow a regular life cycle. This starts with academic discovery. The new idea is then formulated into a technique and published in an academic publication. It is then more widely promoted as a means of increasing productivity, reducing costs or whatever is currently exercising managerial minds. Consultants then pick up the idea and treat it as the universal panacea. After practical attempts fail to deliver the impressive results promised, there is realization of how difficult it is to convert the bright idea into sustainable practice. Finally, there follows committed exploitation by a small number of companies.

Nothing better exemplifies this pattern than the rise and inevitable fall of business process re-engineering (BPR). The concept was brought to the fore by James Champy, co-founder of the consulting company CSC Index, and Michael Hammer, an electrical engineer and former computer science professor at MIT. The roots of the idea lay in the research carried out by MIT from 1984 to 1989 on Management in the 1990s. Champy and Hammer's book, *Reengineering the Corporation*, was a bestseller which produced a plethora of re-engineering programmes, the creation of many consulting companies, and a deluge of books promoting alternative approaches to re-engineering. (Thanks to the popularity of re-engineering, CSC also came from nowhere to become one of the largest consulting firms in the world.)

Unfortunately, re-engineering became doublespeak for redundancy and downsizing. By the mid-1990s, Champy and Hammer were lamenting that their concept had been misapplied in a large number of companies. The fashion for BPR abated, leaving the true re-engineering believers to continue their mission more quietly.

And so it is with concepts. Those that burn the brightest are often short-lived, while those that are put forward with minimal fuss and fanfare often turn out to be the ones that endure.

This is not the final word on business concepts. Given their remarkable proliferation it never could be. Nor is it a definitive listing of the greatest 50 business ideas of the twentieth century. That will always be a contentious debate. Rather, it is a personal view. The concepts featured here have been selected because of their impact and influence – past, present and future – on the lives of real managers.

A note to the revised edition

After publication of the first edition of this book, the feedback we received suggested that the selection of concepts for the book had provoked more debate than we might have imagined. With this in mind, the revised edition not only contains a number of additional concepts to the main book, but also the addition of an appendix. In this appendix we have included several concepts that, while deserving a mention, possibly do not merit quite such substantial consideration as those in the main body of the book. There will, no doubt, be further feedback.

Des Dearlove, July 2002.

Notes

1   Keynes, J.M., *The General Theory of Employment, Interest and Money,*
2   Dearlove, Des, 'Buzzword Bingo', *The Times*, 25 November 1999.

ACTION LEARNING

I nvented by British management thinker Reg Revans, action learning is a deceptively simple idea. So simple, in fact, that its power
was overlooked for years. The basic idea is that managers learn
best when they work on real issues in a group, rather than in the
traditional classroom. According to Revans, 'Action learning harnesses
the power of groups to accomplish meaningful tasks while learning'.

Revans is a former Olympic athlete who worked at the Cavendish
Laboratories and for the National Coal Board (alongside E.F. Schu-
macher of *Small is Beautiful* fame). He developed his approach in the
1940s, but it was his 1971 book *Developing Effective Managers* that
sparked international interest in the concept.

Although largely ignored in Britain, Revans is highly regarded
in countries as far apart as Belgium and South Africa. Fans of action
learning include Jack Welch, General Electric's celebrated CEO, whose
Work-out programme is a form of action learning, and Herb Kelleher,
head of Southwest Airlines, another American company that has been a
trailblazer for the concept.

To explain action learning, Revans created a simple equation: $L = P + Q$. Learning (L), he says, occurs through a combination of programmed knowledge (P) and the ability to ask insightful questions (Q).
In essence, action learning is based around releasing and reinterpret-
ing the accumulated experiences of the people in a group. Working in a
group of equals (rather than a committee headed by the chief executive
or a teacher), managers work on key issues in real-time. The emphasis
is on being supportive and challenging, on asking questions rather than
making statements.

While programmed knowledge is one-dimensional and rigid, the
ability to ask questions opens up other dimensions and is free-flowing.
The process is a continuous one of confirmation and expansion. The
structure linking the two elements of knowledge and questions is the
small team, or set, defined by Revans as a 'small group of comrades in

adversity, striving to learn with and from each other as they confess failures and expand on victories'.

Action learning is the antithesis of the traditional approach to developing managers. It is only now, belatedly, being embraced by many business schools as a way to ensure that the neat classroom theory is accompanied by a modicum of useful learning. (Revans correctly argues that many educational institutions remain fixated with programmed knowledge instead of encouraging students to ask questions and roam widely around a subject. He is contemptuous of business schools and of the flourishing guru industry.) Business schools are only now catching on.

Until quite recently, most executive education programmes were packed with concepts and ideas. Content was king. Business schools crossed their fingers and hoped that when participants returned to their jobs some action would arise. It was the learning equivalent of shooting arrows in the air: shoot enough and you just might hit something. Today, that approach is no longer adequate. Companies want learning that's targeted to hit the spot – their spot.

Modern organizations want executive education to do more than fill managers' heads. They want it to transform the way they work. Firms want to see connections between the concepts business schools communicate and their own internal issues. There is a movement away from traditional formats – chalk and talk – toward new approaches, including action learning. It asks managers to focus on their own experiences, not dissect dead cases.

'In the past there was an idea of a business school as knowledge factory, where knowledge is handed to participants. Now we want to bring participants inside the knowledge factory. We're moving towards co-creation of knowledge with our customers,' explains Vijay Govindarajan, professor at the Amos Tuck School of Business Administration in New Hampshire. He continues: 'In the traditional model – learning – the

Ideas into action

Asking questions and listening to answers is an increasingly important managerial skill. Action learning encourages both. Contrast this with executives being 'forced' to go on training courses. The potential benefits of action learning, however, cannot disguise the challenge it presents. Action learning is no quick fix. It requires a fundamental change in thinking.

'The essence of action learning is to become better acquainted with the self by trying to observe what one may actually do, to trace the reasons for attempting it and the consequences of what one seemed to be doing,' says Revans.

Unused to concentrating on their own development, it takes time – and effort – for managers to understand fully and to utilize action learning. Many are handicapped by a mental model that insists that learning is a passive activity. Also, most top managers are used to displaying their self-confidence and competence rather than admitting they feel insecure, vulnerable or anxious. Most are good at parading their strengths and rarely have the opportunity – or willingness – to discuss their weaknesses with people who understand the pressures but have no direct business relationship with them.

All action learning shares a number of features. It:

- uses a genuine current problem or issue as a learning vehicle (not a past case study);
- takes a group approach (peers working together provide support and different perspectives);
- accepts that there are no experts (naive questions illuminate the issues);
- requires commitment from the sponsoring organization and management; and
- focuses on asking questions rather than providing solutions.

Action learning provides benefits for both individuals and organizations. The key benefits available for the learner from action learning include moving beyond the limits of thought, behaviour, and belief, putting behaviour in line with beliefs and values, and making individual behaviour more effective.

The following benefits have been attributed to action learning:

1 reducing the time between learning and application;
2 concentrating the learner's attention on results and process;
3 focusing on the present and the future;
4 reducing costs;
5 providing feedback to group members on performance;
6 delivering innovative solutions;
7 increasing organizational commitment; and
8 enhancing organizational learning.

arrow goes from learning to action; in action learning, the arrow goes from action to learning'. Executives, Govindarajan says, learn more when they do things.

Action learning currently appears to be attracting greater attention. There is now a Revans Centre for Action Learning and Research at Salford University in the north of England. Business schools now utilize action learning – the UK's Ashridge Management College, for example, has an action learning programme for chief executives.

But the most substantial and sustained example of action learning in practice took place, somewhat strangely, in Belgium. In the late 1960s, Revans led an experiment launched by the Fondation Industrie-Université with the support of Belgium's leading business people and five universities. The Belgians responded to the idea of action learning with enthusiasm. Top managers were exchanged between organizations to work on each other's problems. People from the airline business talked to people from chemical companies. People shared knowledge and experience. With minimal attention from the rest of the world, the Belgian economy enjoyed a spectacular renaissance – during the 1970s, Belgian industrial productivity rose by 102%, compared with 28% in the UK.

Work-out at General Electric

When Jack Welch first took over as CEO of General Electric, the company was stumbling. He lit a bomb under its unwieldy cost structure – a move that earned him the nickname of 'Neutron Jack'. But having proved that he could tear the company apart, Welch moved on to stage two: rebuilding a company fit for the twenty-first century.

Central to this was the concept of *Work-out*, which was launched in 1989. This came about, it is reputed, after a chance question was asked by Professor Kirby Warren of Columbia University. Warren asked Welch: 'Now that you have gotten so many people out of the organization, when are you going to get some of the work out?'[1] At this stage, 100,000 people had left GE. Welch liked the idea of getting the work out. The idea turned into a reality. With typical gusto, Welch brought in twenty or so business school professors and consultants to help turn the emergent concept into reality. Welch has called Work-out 'a relentless, endless company-wide search for a better way to do everything we do.'[2]

Work-out was a combination of a communication tool and an action-learning crusade. It offered GE employees a dramatic opportunity to change their working lives. 'The idea was to hold a three-day, informal town meeting with 40 to 100 employees from all ranks of GE. The boss kicked things off by reviewing the business and laying out the agenda, then he or she left. The employees broke into groups, and aided by a facilitator, attacked separate parts of the problem,' explains Janet Lowe in *Jack Welch Speaks*. 'At the end, the boss returned to hear the proposed solutions. The boss had only three options: the idea could be accepted on the spot, rejected on the spot, or more information could be requested. If the boss asked for more information, he had to name a team and set a deadline for making a decision.'[3]

Work-out was remarkably successful. It helped begin the process of rebuilding the bonds of trust between GE employees and management. It gave employees a channel through which they could talk about what concerned them at work and then actually to change the way things were done.

Key texts and further reading

Marquardt, Michael J. (1999) *Action learning in action: transforming problems and people for world-class organizational learning*, Davies-Black, Palo-Alto.

Dotlich, David and Noel, James L. (1998) *Action Learning: How the World's Top Companies are Re-creating their Leaders and Themselves*, Jossey-Bass, San Francisco, CA.

Mumford, Alan (ed.) (1997) *Action Learning at Work*, Gower, London.

Pedler, Mike (ed.) (1997) *Action Learning in Practice* (3rd edn), Gower, London.

Revans, Reg (1979) *Action Learning*, Blond & Briggs, London.

Notes

1 Vicere, Albert and Fulmer, Robert (1998) *Leadership By Design*, Harvard Business School Press, Boston, MA.
2 General Electric Annual General Meeting, 1990.
3 Lowe, Janet (1998) *Jack Welch Speaks*, John Wiley, New York.

ACTIVITY-BASED COSTING

A ctivity-based costing (ABC) aims to provide a dynamic and realistic means of calculating the true cost of doing business. It precisely allocates direct and indirect costs to particular products or customer segments. Like so many other bright ideas, ABC emerged from Harvard and, in particular, from the work of Robert Kaplan (perhaps best known for his work on developing the balanced scorecard, a strategic management and measurement system).

ABC creates models of the real costs a company incurs in a particular process. It is, in some ways, a financial version of re-engineering (*see* p. 175). The company identifies core processes and analyses the costs at each stage within the process. This enables the company to know how much an activity, such as R&D, costs the business and how much R&D expenditure should be built into the costs of a particular product or service. So, for example, the true cost of developing a new product includes an R&D cost, plus all those costs incurred from all the other functions involved from its inception to its arrival in the marketplace. Properly applied, ABC allows companies to better understand and streamline their cost structures. The drawback is that it requires careful examination of what's actually going on in the business.

ABC could offer an antidote to the sort of indiscriminate cost-cutting that occurred in the late 1980s and 1990s. At that time, cost-cutting became a corporate obsession. In an effort to become more competitive, businesses in industries throughout the world focused their attentions on reducing costs. In the quest to become lean and efficient, systems were overhauled; hierarchies dismantled; processes re-evaluated. Having scrutinized and analysed – or paid expensive consultants to do it for them – many companies simply reduced the number of employees. The biggest overhead of all was the easiest to attack, regardless of the true cost-savings.

Labour costs were an easy target because they were clearly and easily measurable. Every company knows how much employing staff costs. They also know how much their premises cost, and how much money is absorbed by transportation and the like. These basic costs are universally

Ideas into action

According to the consulting firm Booz·Allen & Hamilton, companies typically spend 20 to 25% of sales with third party suppliers for goods and services not directly related to the end product or services of the business. These costs sometimes exceed those spent directly for the end product.

As a result, non-product related sourcing offers increasingly attractive opportunities to unlock hidden value. Most obviously, in many companies an opportunity exists for making significant savings. John Houlihan of Booz·Allen & Hamilton believes that often around 25% of annual non-product related expenditure can be saved, with savings of 15% achievable within two years. This can be equivalent to around 2 to 4% of sales – and may exceed this amount.

Such figures are clearly persuasive. So why don't companies manage their indirect costs rather than cutting numbers? The simple answer is that you can only save money if you actually know how much you spend in the first place, and where you spend it. Companies may acknowledge the enormity of their indirect costs, but often possess little idea, or will, to tame the apparently untameable.

That's where activity-based costing comes in. The logic of ABC is that, if it is to be produced, a product or service – 'cost object' in the language of ABC – requires the input of certain 'activities'. Activities include the traditional business functions (marketing, R&D, production etc.) as well as indirect costs such as maintenance, storage and administration. Taken together, these activities are the processes that form the business. There are a number of factors that influence the costs of a particular activity – such as whether it is premium quality. In ABC-speak these are 'cost drivers'.

In addition, there are 'activity drivers' – measures of the demand placed on certain activities by particular cost objects. One product may, for example, require greater marketing expenditure than another. Clearly, activities require resources – people and machines. 'Resource drivers' are measures of the demands placed on resources by activities.

The better understood the relationship between resources, activities and processes, the more likely it is that the most cost-effective resources will be channelled to the right activities at the right time in the process. This is the underlying logic of ABC.

understood and calculated. The trouble is that these direct costs are often the only costs that are understood and calculated.

Initially focused on cost-accounting and pricing, ABC has been increasingly applied elsewhere. A report by the Gartner Group in the United States estimated that 70 to 80% of companies have experimented with ABC. 'By 2000, companies that have not incorporated ABC into a formal ongoing business transformation programme will be at a severe competitive disadvantage', it concluded.

With a wide variety of software packages available, costing systems now enable companies to measure accurately the profitability of particular product lines, customers, channels and facilities. There are measurement systems that go beyond individual organizations so the manufacturers and retailers can capture supplier and customer profitability.

ABC is increasingly spreading its wings to encompass service organizations – such as banking – so that companies can build up more detailed knowledge of their customers and their interactions with them. With the growing emphasis on customer loyalty, ABC can allow companies to target their most cost-effective customers. Some customers are more expensive to attract and retain than others. One survey found that 20% of customers usually account for the bulk of a company's profits. The majority – 60% – of customers allow the company to break even. Meanwhile, 20% of customers actually lose the company money. If the company can identify the rogue 20%, it can maximize its profitability. To do this requires that the company knows how much each customer is costing it.

ABC, at its basic level, is descriptive. It gives managers a detailed and accurate picture of the costs in their business. Some would suggest that managers should already have such understanding. Traditional accounting methods and the sheer scale and complexity of large organizations mean that this is often not the case, however. ABC does nothing, in itself, to reduce or eradicate costs. Armed with the information, managers then have to translate activity-based costing into concrete managerial strategies. ABC becomes activity-based management.

Key texts and further reading

Cooper, R. and Kaplan, R.S. (1998) *Cost & Effect: Using Integrated Cost Systems to Drive Profitability and Performance*, Harvard Business School Press, Boston, MA.

Cooper, R. and Kaplan, R.S. (1991) *The Design of Cost Management Systems*, Prentice Hall, Englewood Cliffs, NJ.

ADHOCRACY

C oined by leadership expert Warren Bennis in the 1960s and popularized by futurist Alvin Toffler, the term adhocracy is basically the opposite of bureaucracy. An adhocracy is an organization that disregards the classical principles of management, where everyone has a defined and permanent role, in favour of a more fluid organization where individuals are free to deploy their talents as required.

Essentially, the concept was an attempt to answer the question of how companies should create an appropriate organizational model for the future. It addresses the nature of managerial work and the strategy formation process, as well as social issues. (From a historical perspective, the organizational form can be seen as an evolution from simple structure, to machine bureaucracy, to divisionalized form, to adhocracy.)

An adhocracy is a highly organic organizational design, representing the idea of an open, free, flexible, creative, spontaneous enterprise that is the antithesis of traditional big business. It has characteristics of a horizontal or lateral organization, where teams consisting primarily of knowledge workers are used, and where they are both empowered and self-directed.

The concept was explored by Alvin Toffler in his 1970 book *Future Shock*. An adhocracy is a non-bureaucratic, networked organization. 'This form is already common in organizations such as law firms, consulting companies and research universities. Such organizations and institutions must continually readjust to a changing array of projects, each requiring somewhat different combinations of skills and other resources. These organizations depend on many rapidly shifting project teams and much lateral communication among these relatively autonomous, entrepreneurial groups,' notes Toffler.

Toffler has gone on to assert that the organizations and institutions that currently exist have become unwieldy and outdated. The problem, he claims, is a lack of flexibility. 'Why is it that all our institutions seem to be going through a simultaneous crisis?' he asks. 'Why is it that the health system's in crisis, the justice system's in crisis, the education system's in

Ideas into action

Henry Mintzberg distinguishes between two types of adhocracy. The *operating adhocracy* works on behalf of its clients (for example, a creative advertising agency or consulting firm), while an *administrative adhocracy* serves itself. The latter offers a model for a wide range of companies.

Along with the benefits of a more fluid organizational form, Mintzberg observes, are some potential drawbacks. One problem, he notes, is that managers in an adhocracy may spend too little time on making strategy. The danger is that managers may be sucked into just responding to problems rather than proactive analysis and formulation of radical, corrective programmes.

The classic dichotomy between operational and strategic decision can easily become blurred. Operationally, managers of adhocracies may too easily become embroiled in resolving conflicts between options – reacting to existing problems rather than looking for radical new directions. Thus decisions may be reactive, rather than proactive. An effective adhocracy, he says, needs to do both – scanning the environment to determine new directions and keeping up with the products or services needed by that environment. In other words, it must balance the need for action in the short term with the need to take a longer-term view of changes occurring within its environment.

For Mintzberg, however, strategy in the adhocracy arises from a flow of operational, action-centred decisions more than conscious expression by strategy-makers. He observes that action planning can result in strategy-makers becoming caught in an activity trap. Too much concentration on action may actually limit the organization's flexibility and ability to respond creatively to the pressures of its environment. It may prevent strategy-makers from standing back from the immediate problem to identify and remedy the underlying cause, or take advantage of a new opportunity. Fast action may stop the bleeding but it may give too little attention to the long-term health of the patient – who may need to go on a diet.

Allied to adhocracy is the notion of 'pockets of good practice'. This recognizes that rather than starting at the top, change is often best coming from the grass roots – through so-called 'pockets of good practice' within the organization.

Companies that have experimented with this approach include the timber and builders' merchant Jewson, Mitsubishi Electric, and BP Marine.

'As organizational structures become more loose, the power of individuals increases', says Dr David Butcher of Cranfield School of Management in the UK, who has championed the idea. 'The question then becomes how to ensure that what is exercised is principled power. This refers specifically to differentiating between good and bad politics.

'Politics is all about competing interests and competing value systems. We don't like politicians when they seem to be in it for themselves. The same applies in business. When people think of politics in their company, they usually mean bad politics.'

Under this model, change isn't aligned with a recognizable or senior-management sanctioned initiative. It calls for pockets of internal activists to challenge the *status quo*, using whatever political tools they have at their disposal. These pockets could represent the equivalent of 'covert operations'.

In an adhocracy, the concept of what is a worthwhile activity is crucial. Once managers see that unofficial activity is useful, they will start to ring-fence and support these pockets. But to be effective, pockets of good practice often have to be kept covert at first. Their creators have to act subversively.

If their motivation is in the long-term interests of organization, then this is justified. 'We're talking about a political model of change', Butcher says. 'It involves making a sharp distinction between those who are doing worthwhile activities. Management should encourage these useful, but possibly subversive, groups. Official approval too early can be the kiss of death.'

What Butcher is advocating is a framework that is inherently messy. He acknowledges that it is guaranteed to offend some people's sense of corporate neatness. In its most extreme form, the pocket of new practice could transform the whole business. Under this model, senior managers should be more hands-off, and flexible. Part of their role is to nurture new ideas unofficially. This creates the opportunity for change to build from grass-roots activists close to customers and flow up through the organization – what has been called 'micro-strategy'.

Successful companies such as Virgin and Asea Brown Boveri (ABB) are living examples of this style. Both have highly devolved decision-making processes centred on the individual companies within the group, which are given licence to create change. The role of senior management in the corporate centre is to set the culture, articulate aims and a brand identity for the group.

> A useful side-effect is that it releases the top management team from the collective responsibility for creating strategy. Given that top management teams, like cabinets, are in reality rarely teams anyway, this is no bad thing.

crisis, the value system's in crisis – you name it – why? There must be something that cuts across all of these. … And why is it happening in Tokyo and London and Italy and so forth? Why is there a political crisis throughout all the political countries? The answer is that we have sets of institutions that were designed either for agrarian life … as parliaments were, or … the Industrial Age, but no longer meet the requirements of today. The problem used to be that it took three months for a message to get from Ohio to Washington, and vice versa. And the idea was the Senate would be a chamber for leisurely deliberation for the major issues. Well, come on! Nobody has two minutes of uninterrupted time. So the external conditions are radically changed.

'So the question is how flexible are the existing institutions themselves. We're fortunate, the Americans are lucky, because our system is generally more flexible and certainly more decentralized than the other industrial states, which gives us a better shot. But I don't believe that the system can continue in its present form.' What is needed, Toffler suggests, is a wholesale move to adhocracy.

The concept was further developed in the work of the strategy theorist Henry Mintzberg, for example, in *Strategy-making and the Adhocracy*. Mintzberg's adhocracy represents smaller scale, fluid, often temporary structures. Typically a group of line managers, staff and operating experts come together in small product-focused, customer-focused or project-focused teams. Informal behaviour and high job specialization are typical characteristics of these adhocracies. Teams rely on liaison methods and mutual adjustment between themselves and other teams. Teams have their terms of reference (decentralization) provided by more senior management and a team's scope for action and membership may run counter to the command structure of the rest of the organization (the classic machine bureaucracy).

Key text and further reading

Waterman Jr, Robert H. (1990) *Adhocracy: The Power to Change*, Whittle Direct Books.

AGILITY

L ike the idea of an adhocracy, the concept of corporate agility is a response to the need for companies to be more adaptive to changing market conditions. It recognizes that speed of response to market opportunities and threats, plus flexibility, are what distinguish many successful companies from their lumbering rivals.

The emergence of agility was influenced by a string of books and articles examining how large companies could become faster on their feet. This idea is implicit in some of the more memorable business book titles, including Rosabeth Moss Kanter's *When Giants Learn to Dance* and James Belasco's *Teaching the Elephant to Dance*.

But the concept was first presented coherently in a report published by Lehigh University's Iacocca Institute in the Autumn of 1991. It was called 'Twenty-first Century Manufacturing Enterprise Strategy: An Industry-Led View,' and was prepared in response to a Congressional request to identify the requirements for US industry to return to global manufacturing competitiveness. By 1992, the Agile Manufacturing Enterprise Forum (AMEF) had been created within the Iacocca Institute. By mid-1994, Agile Manufacturing Research Institutes for the machine tool, aerospace and electronics industries were in operation at the University of Illinois, the University of Texas, and the Rensselaer Polytechnic Institute.

Sometimes linked with the emergence of virtual organizations (*see* p. 256), a number of writers and academics have since written about agility. Tom Peters and Richard Pascale are among those who have propounded it in recent years. But if the movement has a principal architect, then he is probably Dr Roger N. Nagel, the internationally recognized competitiveness expert.

Trained as a computer scientist, Nagel is the Harvey Wagner Professor of Manufacturing Systems Engineering at Lehigh University, and deputy director of the university's Iacocca Institute, a strategic resource centre founded in 1988 to help American industry deal with the challenges of international competition. The author of more than 50 research papers and a frequent lecturer on the subject of competition, Nagel's

Ideas into action

Nagel, Goldman and Preiss present agile competition as a system, with four strategic dimensions:

1 *Organizing to master change and uncertainty*. An agile company is organized in a way that allows it to thrive on change and uncertainty. (There is no single, right structure or size; it can support multiple configurations.)

2 *Leveraging the impact of people and information*. In an agile company, management nurtures an entrepreneurial company culture that leverages the impact of people and information. People are seen as an investment in future prosperity.

3 *Co-operating to enhance competitiveness*. Co-operation – internally and with other companies – is an agile competitor's operational strategy of first choice.

4 *Enriching the customer*. An agile company is one that is perceived by its customers as enriching them in a significant way, not just itself.

The first principal says that companies need to be able to survive in an atmosphere of change and uncertainty. In that environment, both large and small organizations need to be entrepreneurial, and by that we mean quick-reacting and proactive with their customers. Companies need to make decisions rapidly and effectively.

The second principal says that all organizations sell the skills of their people, their knowledge base and the information that the organization has accumulated explicitly or implicitly. As the product life cycle gets shorter and shorter, it becomes much more obvious that what companies really sell are the skills of the people who work for them, their knowledge and the information that the organization has accumulated. In that kind of environment, it makes the most sense for the organization to invest in and increase the impact of its people and information. It suggests that to remain competitive, companies should be investing, not necessarily in capital equipment, but to increase the impact of their people and information.

The third principal states that co-operation enhances competitive capability. Therefore, companies should use the virtual-company model inside and outside the organization. In other words, the aim should be to create a network of skills and information which maximizes the value to the customer – regardless of where those people are located or even whether they work directly for the company.

The fourth principal is that, in an agile world, customers either pay a fee for your skills and the materials used to make products when they don't know their value; or they pay you a percentage of their perceived value for solutions whose value they do know. Solutions are easier for customers to value. Therefore companies need to work to transform their products and services into solutions for their customers.

This gives rise to the 'value-based product strategy' or 'value-based solution strategy'. The question becomes, how do you transform what you make from being products into solutions? Product here is a synonym for service as well.

'In the current mass-production environment, we are in a silly situation. People don't like to admit it, but it's true. You differentiate your product by how few defects you make, how rapidly you can get the product to me and the way you manufacture it', Nagel observes. 'In fact, if you ask how General Motors lost business, it's because Toyota made better cars, not cars with better features.'

So the question is, when everybody makes high-quality, low-cost, rapid products, how do you differentiate yourself? And the answer is determined by what the product does for you, the features it has, the way it meets your needs. It becomes a solution as opposed to a product.

Agility has another great advantage over product-based competition. It allows companies to migrate from one business to another. Nagel illustrates his argument with the example of an electric utility. Most people assume that the cable TV company and telephone company are going to be the paths for information into the consumer's home because they're wired to send information now. But, the electric utility company has been wired to homes for much longer and it is possible to send information over those kinds of lines as well. Modulated energy is how you transmit information. This raises the prospect that agile electric utilities could end up being the information services company as well.

In Nagel's view, agility is more than simply speed of action; the ability to adapt and make lateral moves is more important. 'If electric utilities are going to stay solely in the business of providing me energy, they're in danger of being wiped out by solar technology', he says. 'Maybe we're going to go to transmitted energy. I just don't understand what the future is going to be like, and the electric utilities have to tell me what they're selling. You need to find out what is it your customers think they buy from you. For an electric utility company it's power, but what might it be ten or fifteen years from now? I don't know.'

views on competitiveness issues have been sought by both houses of Congress, and the White House.

Nagel focuses on agile manufacturing and agile competition, and co-authored the 1995 book *Agile Competitors and Virtual Organizations* with Steven L. Goldman and Kenneth Preiss. The book defined agility at the organizational and individual level:

> For a company, to be agile is to be capable of operating profitably in a competitive environment of continually and unpredictably changing customer opportunities.
> For an individual, to be agile is to be capable of contributing to the bottom line of a company that is constantly reorganizing its human and technological resources in response to unpredictably changing customer opportunities.

Beyond these definitions, however, the trio of authors observes that agile competition demands that the processes that support the creation, production and distribution of goods and services be centred on the customer-perceived value of products. This is very different from building a customer-centred company.

Key text and further reading

Goldman, Steven L., Nagel, Roger N. and Preiss, Kenneth (1995) *Agile Competitors and Virtual Organizations*, Van Nostrand Reinhold, New York.

Note

1 Leemputte, Patrick J. and Benda, Peter, *High-Velocity Approach Places Premium on Opportunities*, AT Kearney, Executive Agenda II, Fourth Quarter 1998.

High-velocity companies

The agility concept has also influenced others to examine the characteristics of highly responsive organizations, and given rise to the term 'high-velocity companies'. These are businesses that are able to 'pounce on opportunities' note Patrick J. Leemputte and Peter Benda of the consulting firm AT Kearney.[1] A high-velocity approach to business refers to the need for greater speed of decision-making, execution and implementation to exploit new opportunities that arise.

'Both large and small companies are turning away from sluggish habits to join a high-speed track to growth (and profitability). Adopting a high-velocity approach, they are taking a fresh look at strategy, structure and organization,' they observe.

The ability to move swiftly, they say, owes much to the emergence of two ubiquitous trends, which are related to Nagel's five principles of agility:

- *Outsourcing*: the use of contract resources to provide high-quality service at a competitive cost. High-velocity companies manage no core functions and rely on partners for complementary expertise.
- *Alliances*: the creation of what they call an 'extended enterprise' or integrated market approach. This dramatically changes the notion that every business is an island fending only for itself. (Alliance-building, they claim, is rampant, and has doubled or trebled in the last decade.)

Walt Disney, for example, maintains alliances with Coca-Cola Co., Microsoft, Intel, and General Electric, among others. Leemputte and Benda outline five steps for managing speed:

1 Manage the business portfolio – i.e. view the business as a portfolio of business opportunities at different stages.
2 Focus on value first and costs second – high-velocity companies cannot be created simply by cutting costs.
3 Embrace change management – change is a given, get good at it.
4 Empower managers to seek opportunity, take risks and operate flexibly.
5 Use sophisticated management tools.

BALANCED SCORECARD

T he balanced scorecard is a strategic management and measurement system that links strategic objectives to comprehensive indicators. It recognizes that companies have a tendency to fixate on a few measurements, which blinkers their assessment of how the business is performing overall. The balanced scorecard focuses management's attention on a range of key performance indicators, to provide a balanced view.

The concept was originally put forward by David Norton, co-founder of the consulting company Renaissance Solutions, and Robert Kaplan, the Marvin Bower Professor of Leadership Development at Harvard Business School. This duo developed the balanced scorecard concept at the beginning of the 1990s in research sponsored by KPMG. The result was an article in the *Harvard Business Review* ('The balanced scorecard,' January/February 1993). This had a simple message for managers: what you measure is what you get.

Kaplan and Norton compared running a company to flying a plane. The pilot who relies on a single dial is unlikely to be safe. Pilots must utilize all the information contained in their cockpit. 'The complexity of managing an organization today requires that managers be able to view performance in several areas simultaneously', said Kaplan and Norton. 'Moreover, by forcing senior managers to consider all the important operational measures together, the balanced scorecard can let them see whether improvement in one area may be achieved at the expense of another.'

The dilemma of what to measure is as old as business itself. In the twentieth century, measurement became an almost obsessional pursuit. The balanced scorecard sought to answer a long-running debate.

The man who put the measure into the hands of managers was Frederick Taylor, the inventor of scientific management (*see* p. 188). Taylor's approach involved measuring the performance of workers against predetermined optimum times. Managers have been actively seeking new things to measure and more sophisticated means of measurement ever since. At times, measurement has appeared to be the central function of management. Every manager knows the mantra 'what gets measured gets done'.

The most fruitful area for this mania for quantification has been finance. Managers once simply talked of sales and profits. But over the years a complex array of ratios, measures, analytical tools and software packages have evolved. Every penny a company spends or produces can be analysed in an infinite number of ways. Such are their powers of persuasion that entire companies can be driven by such financial measures. The most famous instance of this was ITT in the 1960s, under the control of Harold Geneen. Geneen took management by financial measurement to its limits, creating an elaborate system of financial reporting. When he left the company, the whole deck of cards collapsed.

The obvious conclusion to be drawn from Geneen's approach was that if you concentrated solely on financial measures, you could achieve short-term, even medium-term success, but such narrow constraining measures were unlikely to yield long-term prosperity. The trouble was that financial ratios and performance were the easiest things to measure. Other elements of corporate performance – such as customer loyalty or employee satisfaction – were more abstract issues and measurement appeared to raise more questions than answers.

At the same time as companies were considering how to measure 'softer' elements of their performance, they became increasingly addicted to managerial fads and fashions. Throughout the last twenty years in particular, there has been a steady stream of bright ideas which have all been seized upon by companies as the Holy Grail. Most have disappointed.

So, organizations are faced with the dilemmas of unwieldy financial measurement systems; few reliable means of measuring other elements of their performance; and a predilection for short-lived fads whose impact is rarely measured in any way whatsoever. This was fertile soil for a new approach.

Ideas into action

The balanced scorecard made an important contribution to the measurement debate, helping companies cope with more complex market conditions. In many ways, it is simple common sense. Balance is clearly preferable to imbalance. The balanced scorecard is now widely championed by a variety of companies. Its argument that blind faith in a single measurement or a small range of measures is dangerous is a powerful one. However, effective measures remain elusive.

Kaplan and Norton suggested that four elements need to be balanced:

1 *the customer perspective*: companies must ask how customers perceive them;
2 *the internal perspective*: companies must ask what it is that they must excel at;
3 *the innovation and learning perspective*: companies must ask whether they can continue to improve and create value; and
4 *the financial perspective*: how does the company look to shareholders?

According to Kaplan and Norton, by focusing energies, attention and measures on all four of these dimensions, companies become driven by their mission rather than by short-term financial performance. Crucial to achieving this is applying measures to company strategy. Instead of being beyond measurement, the balanced scorecard argues that strategy must be central to any process of measurement – 'A good balanced scorecard should tell the story of your strategy'.

Identifying the essential measures for an organization is not straightforward. One company produced 500 measures on its first examination. This was distilled down to seven measures – twenty is par for the course.

According to Kaplan and Norton, a 'good' balanced scorecard contains three elements:

1 it establishes 'cause and effect relationships': rather than being isolated figures, measures are related to each other and the network of relationships makes up the strategy;
2 it should have a combination of lead and lag indicators: lag indicators are measures, such as market share, which are common across an industry and, though important, offer no distinctive advantage. Lead indicators are measures which are company (and strategy) specific; and
3 an effective balanced scorecard is linked to financial measures: by this, Kaplan and Norton mean that initiatives such as re-engineering or lean production need to be tied to financial measures rather than pursued indiscriminately.

Key texts and further reading

Kaplan, Robert S. and Cooper, Robin (1998) *Cost and Effect: Using Integrated Cost Systems to Drive Profitability and Performance,* Harvard Business School Press, Boston, MA.

Kaplan, Robert S. and Norton, David P. (1996) *The Balanced Scorecard: Translating Strategy into Action,* Harvard Business School Press, Boston, MA.

BENCHMARKING

Benchmarking became a buzzword of the 1980s and 1990s (although it actually relies on techniques developed by the quality movement). The idea is to benchmark performance against other companies or other departments. Benchmarking involves the detailed study of productivity, quality and value in different departments and activities in relation to performance elsewhere.

The principle behind benchmarking (or best-practice benchmarking as it is also sometimes known) is very simple. If you want to improve a particular aspect of your organization or the service it provides, find others who are good at the activity you want to improve and use them to provide a benchmark to raise your own standards. In effect, it's a way of pulling up performance by the bootstraps.

Typically, a database of relevant performance measures is drawn up from looking at similar activities in other parts of the firm and in other firms. The information obtained is then used to compare the performance of the unit being reviewed with the range of experience elsewhere.

There are three different techniques that can be used in benchmarking:

1 **Best demonstrated practice** (BDP): this technique, used successfully for the last fifteen years, is the comparison of performance by units within one firm. For example, the sales per square foot of a retail outlet in one location can be compared with the same statistic for a store in another, within the same chain, as can the unit cost of electricity, security, or any other cost item cut any way that is relevant. BDP usually throws up large variances, some of which can be explained by lack of comparability, but much of which is due to superior techniques or simply greater efficiency at one site. That site can then be used as a challenge to lever up performance at all other sites.

2 **Relative cost position** (RCP): RCP analysis looks at each element of the cost structure (e.g. manufacturing labour) per £ of sales in

firm X compared to the same thing in competitor Y. Good RCP analysis is very hard to do but very valuable, as much for its insight into competitors' strategies as for cost reduction.

3 **Best related practice**: this is like BDP, but takes the comparisons into related (usually not competing) firms, where direct comparisons can often be made by co-operation between firms to collect and compare data.

Companies that take benchmarking seriously, like the Xerox Corporation, have a web of benchmarking partners both within the organization and with outside partners across a wide spectrum of activities. So, for example, a manufacturing company might benchmark its transport and delivery performance against other business units it owns and against a transportation specialist such as one of the courier companies. The same company might also benchmark its accounting systems against a financial services company, and so on.

Ideas into action

Benchmarking is not about trying to clone other organizations, or industrial espionage. Nor should it be measurement for measurement's sake. Rather it is based on simple logic: why waste time and effort trying to reinvent the wheel, when you can have a look at someone else's wheel and refine its applications to fit your own needs. Benchmarking typically involves:

- establishing what improvements would make an important contribution to competitiveness;
- identifying other organizations, or business units, with superior performance in the key area;
- approaching those organizations to form benchmarking partnerships, enabling the study of internal processes;
- determining meaningful measures of performance (metrics);
- setting new targets in the key areas based on those observed in the benchmark organizations; and
- applying best practice from the benchmark organizations to meet and if possible exceed the new targets.

Key texts and further reading

Camp, Robert C. (1989) *Benchmarking: The Search for Industry Best Practices that Lead to Superior Performance*, ASQC, Quality Press, New York.

Boxwell, Robert J. (1994) *Benchmarking for Competitive Advantage*, McGraw-Hill, New York.

Bendell, T., Boulter, L. and Goodstadt, P. (1997) *Benchmarking for Competitive Advantage*, Pitman, London.

BOSTON MATRIX

So influential was the Boston matrix – one of the tools developed by the Boston Consulting Group (BCG) – that a whole generation of senior managers grew up with cows, dogs, stars and question marks as a way to classify their businesses. The Boston matrix became an icon in an era of strategic planning.

Until the 1960s, models were the impenetrable domain of economists. The man largely credited with bringing business models into the mainstream was the Australian engineer Bruce Henderson (1915–92). Henderson worked as a strategic planner for General Electric. He was also dismissive of economists – 'Darwin is probably a better guide to business competition than economists are,' Henderson said. From GE, he joined the management consulting firm Arthur D. Little. In 1963, Henderson announced that he was leaving to set up his own consultancy, the Boston Consulting Group (BCG).

At the time, management consulting was beginning to establish itself as a profession. Despite the longevity of other big name consulting firms such as McKinsey & Company, BCG is regarded by some as the first pure-strategy consultancy. While strategy drifts in and out of fashion, it is a cause that BCG still robustly champions. 'Strategy leads to the continuous creation of real value. Real value requires sustained competitive advantage. Leaping at opportunities without strategy consistently produces failure,' it says. BCG quickly became a great success. Within five years it was in the top flight of consulting firms – where it has largely remained. It has been called 'the most idea-driven major consultancy in the world'.

The first model discovered – or rediscovered in this case – by Henderson was something of an antique. In the 1920s, an obscure company called Curtiss Aircraft came up with the concept of the 'learning curve', which also became known as the 'experience curve'. This posited that unit costs declined as cumulative production increased because of the acquisition of experience. This had been applied solely to manufacturing. Henderson applied it to strategy rather than production and found that it still worked and provided a useful practical tool.

BCG went on to originate or develop concepts such as sustainable growth; time-based competition; segment-of-one marketing; value-based strategy; total shareholder value; and, even, disease management. However, the model for which Henderson and BCG are best known is the Boston matrix, which measures market growth and relative market share for all the businesses in a particular firm.

Much admired in the 1960s, the Boston matrix proved a highly popular innovation. From a business point of view, the matrix had the characteristics of any great model: it was accessible, simple and useful. However, it was also limiting. Measuring corporate performance against two parameters is straightforward, but potentially dangerous if these are the only two parameters against which performance is measured. A product of its time, the matrix offered a blinkered view of a world where growth and profitability were all that counted.

The Boston matrix encouraged a preoccupation with market share. Sometimes this bordered on obsession. This was not to the liking of all executives. In a 1974 speech, David Packard, co-founder of Hewlett-Packard, warned his staff: 'If I hear anybody talking about how big their share of the market is or what they're trying to do to increase their share of the market, I'm going to personally see that a black mark gets put in their personnel folder.'

Not surprisingly, other consulting firms were quick to respond with their own variations on the Boston matrix. The most credible response came in the form of the General Electric and McKinsey matrix. This measured performance against two variables – industry attractiveness and business strength – and was effectively a dandified version of the original.

As a business tool, the Boston matrix had a significant and long-term impact. It provided a useful way of looking at the world. Of equal significance was its influence on the management consulting industry. It spawned a host of imitators. Today, no consultant's report is complete without a matrix of some sort. More importantly, BCG could be said to have introduced the first off-the-shelf consulting product (though it wouldn't see it that way). Companies required the big idea. They wanted to see how they fared on the matrix and how it could shape their strategies. The consulting firm product was born.

Previously, consultants had gone into client companies to solve specific business problems. The success of the Boston matrix marked a change in approach. As well as problem solving, consultancy became concerned with passing on the latest ideas, the frameworks, models and matrices that were in vogue. Problem solvers became peddlers of big ideas. This opened up huge new vistas for the management consultancy profession, which it has been assiduously – and profitably – chasing ever since.

Ideas into action

The Boston matrix, sometimes called the 'dog star' matrix for obvious reasons, actually started life in the 1960s as the growth/share matrix. Still much-quoted, this analysis tool epitomized a sort generic view of strategic decision making.

It is, in fact, a simple two-by-two matrix (a format popular with management consultants ever since) which measures market growth and relative market share for all the businesses in the company's portfolio. Each business can be placed on the matrix and classified accordingly.

The hypothesis of the Boston matrix is that companies with higher market share in faster-growing industries are more profitable. The further to the left a business is on the Boston matrix, the stronger a company should be. (The matrix can be applied to individual products or entire businesses.)

As with most such models, refinements have been added along the way. On its original matrix, BCG superimposed a theory of cash management, which included a hierarchy of uses of cash, numbered from one to four in their order of priority. This identified the top priority as *cash cows*, characterized by high market share and low

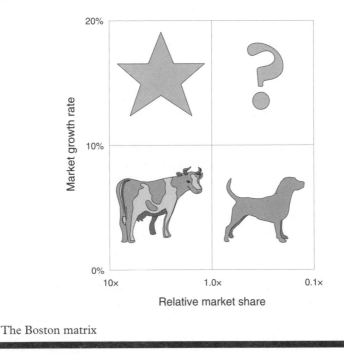

The Boston matrix

growth. Investment in cash cows is easily justified, as they are dull, safe and highly profitable. (BCG itself falls into this category – it has grown every year since its foundation and in the past two decades its growth has averaged 20% per annum.) Next in line are the *stars* (high growth; high market share) though their investment requirements are likely to be significant. More problematic is the third category, *question marks* (problem children or wildcats in some versions) where there is high growth and low share. Any investment in them is risky. The final category is the aptly titled *dogs*, where low market share is allied to low growth. Dogs should not be approached.

The golden age of strategic planning

Although the most famous of its kind, the original Boston matrix was followed by a host of other neat two-by-two matrices. Royal Dutch/Shell, for example, took BCG's original matrix a stage further with its directional policy matrix. There is also Roger's box, which offers a hypothesis on how executives should spend their time, the Ansoff matrix, and Blake and Mouton's 'managerial grid' (*see* p. 147). The list continues to grow. By the end of the 1970s, no self-respecting business journal article would be complete without a conceptual map or framework.

Such models helped to underpin a golden age for business strategists. Strategic planning reached its height in the 1970s. At that time, some companies had planning departments working on detailed strategic plans for up to ten years ahead. Regiments of bright, young graduates were paid large salaries to sit in strategic planning departments removed from the cut and thrust of day-to-day operations and gaze into the future. Meanwhile consulting firms such as McKinsey & Co. and the Boston Consulting Group built multi-million dollar businesses on advising clients about how to shuffle their business portfolios. For a price, business school graduates at McKinsey or BCG would do a company's strategic thinking for it.

But as strategic planning departments mushroomed in the 1970s, so they became more and more disconnected from the reality of what was happening at the sharp end of the business. Strategy had become a purely cerebral activity. Figures fed in from the operating companies at one end were crunched by the planners back at corporate headquarters, and strategic plans emerged at the other end. The strategic planning department was the brain of the body corporate, but it took little or no interest in what messages it received from its eyes and ears in the marketplace.

All that came to an end in the early 1980s as a string of household-name companies were outflanked by more nimble competitors. One after another, the strategists in a string of seemingly unassailable companies were wrong-footed by new competition. Often their market was hi-jacked by a player who arrived from nowhere. Many commentators saw these failures as evidence that markets were changing so fast that it was impossible to plan more than a few months ahead. Strategic planning departments were dismantled, and the strategists replaced by downsizers. The new arrivals – many of them upstarts from Silicon Valley – broke the mould. They seemed to be making up strategy as they went along.

For many commentators, the turning point came in 1983 when General Electric CEO Jack Welch dismantled the company's 200-strong planning department. In the face of fierce competition, Welch found the GE planners so preoccupied with financial and operating details that they failed to realize that the company's strategic position was being eroded.

Other strategic planning departments followed. The best-laid plans of giants – IBM, Sears, Digital, Kodak and General Motors among them – crumbled under a barrage of competition. From what had seemed unassailable strategic positions, many found themselves staring into the abyss. Throughout the 1980s and early 1990s, once-mighty companies were forced to come down from the strategy mountain and engage in a humbling new pursuit called downsizing.

The death of strategic planning

In his 1994 book *The Rise and Fall of Strategic Planning*, the business academic Henry Mintzberg seemed to sound the death knell of the professional strategist. Strategy, he said, cannot be planned but must emerge by 'synthesis' from changes taking place inside and outside the company.

The most effective role for planners, in Mintzberg's view, was the unearthing of 'fledgling strategies in unexpected pockets of the organization so that consideration can be given to (expanding) them'. Under this interpretation, strategy is less concerned with handing down 'big ideas' from on high and much more concerned with identifying and communicating the best of what is already happening within the organization. The role of senior management becomes the identification, interpretation and articulation of ideas bubbling up from below.

Far from signalling the end, however, Mintzberg's book opened a new chapter in the strategy debate. Suddenly, strategy had moved out of the planning department to involve the people closest to the action. There are two important changes taking place in the way companies look at strategy. First, there is a movement away from the dry, paper-based exercises that once dominated, as companies recognize that strategy must be animated by what is actually happening on the ground.

Second, instead of trying to predict what will be happening in your market in five year's time, strategic planning today is about spotting an opportunity to create an alternative future, one that redefines the business you're in. At the same time, a whole new generation of thinkers is redefining the way companies understand strategy, and a host of new and not-so-new tools and techniques are being adopted by strategists. All in all, it's a remarkable recovery for a discipline that just a few years ago seemed to be dead. Today, however, the strategists are back in favour. A recent study by the Association of Management Consulting Firms found that executives, consultants and business school professors agree that strategy is now the single most important issue facing companies and will remain so for the next five years.

'At one company after another, strategy is again a major focus in the quest for higher revenues and profits,' *Business Week* magazine observed. 'Some companies are even recreating full-fledged strategic planning groups … Mainstream consulting firms say their strategy business is booming, meanwhile a new wave of gurus and consulting firms has emerged.'

A flood of new books on the subject is further indication of the renewed interest. But although strategy is back in the driving seat, it is strategy with a difference.

Key texts and further reading

Stern, Carl W., Stalk, George and Clarkeson, John S. (1998) *Perspectives on Strategy: From the Boston Consulting Group*, John Wiley, New York.

Mintzberg, Henry (1994) *The Rise and Fall of Strategic Planning*, Prentice Hall International, Hemel Hempstead.

BRANDING

O ver the last decade, branding has become a critical contributor to a company's bottom line. The value of a brand once accepted as an unquantifiable element of a company's goodwill has in more recent times become a quantifiable monetary amount paraded in a company's roster of intangible assets and assembled in rankings such as the branding consultancy Interbrand's league table of most valuable brands. Brands don't obtain value by magic, however: the value, or brand equity, delivered by the brand is the culmination of the branding process, which consists of many elements and, to be effective, requires the alignment of management behind the brand values. More on these terms later.

At its most basic, branding is the process whereby value is added to a product or service (which becomes the brand) over and above its retail price. This is achieved through a variety of branding strategies, which include creating a psychological and physical relationship between the consumer and the product, a brand identity, and brand values. But to understand branding it is necessary first to understand what constitutes a brand.

One survey of CEOs by the McKenna Group, the firm of the celebrated 'father of high-tech marketing', Regis McKenna, highlights the difficulty of defining 'brand'. The question 'What is a Brand?' was posed to 100 CEOs, many of whom were leaders of high-tech companies in the driving seat of the new economy. The response – 100 different answers.

The opinions of experts offer some clues. The traditional view of what constitutes a brand is summed up by marketing guru Philip Kotler in his classic textbook *Marketing Management*. He writes: '[A brand name is] a name, term, sign, symbol or design, or a combination of these, which is intended to identify the goods or services of one group of sellers and differentiate them from those of competitors.'[1]

Then there is brand defined in terms of relationship. Leslie de Chernatony, professor of brand marketing at the UK's Open University Business School, echoes this perception of brands: 'The brand is, through the staff, an active participant in any relationship, be it between customer and brand, employee and employee, employee and customer, or employee and other stakeholders. Inadequate communication of the corporation's values and individual's roles in delivering them can quickly result in inconsistencies between the brand's espoused values and the values perceived by stakeholders when dealing with staff.'[2]

Another practical and contemporary definition of brands comes from the consultants Booz·Allen & Hamilton: 'Brands are a shorthand way of communicating critical data to the market to influence decisions. Across a multitude of consumer-focused industries, brands are an important means for differentiation and competitive advantage, although they are most influential when customers lack the data to make informed product choices and/or when the differentiation between competitors' versions of the same product are small to non-existent. Additionally, brands take on more significance when consumers place great importance on the decision being made.'[3]

Whatever definition is accepted, the importance of branding in modern business is unquestionable. Whether it is branding the product, the firm, or even the individual, branding is an essential part of business life. Through clever and appropriate branding, companies can add considerable value to their balance sheets. This is a fact borne out by brand consultancy Interbrand's annual most valuable brands survey.

The world's most valuable brands 2001

Rank/(Rank 2000)/Brand	Brand value ($ billion)
1 (1) Coca-Cola	68.95 (72.53)
2 (2) Microsoft	65.07 (70.19)
3 (3) IBM	52.75 (53.19)
4 (6) GE	42.45 (39.05)
5 (5) Nokia	35.04 (38.53)
6 (4) Intel	34.67 (38.13)
7 (8) Disney	32.60 (36.37)
8 (7) Ford	30.10 (33.55)
9 (9) McDonald's	25.29 (27.86)
10 (10) AT&T	22.83 (25.55)

Source: Interbrand

Ideas into action

Like many aspects of business, branding has its own lexicon, which lends it a mysterious air and renders it impenetrable to the layman. In an effort to lift the shroud of mystery, here is an explanation of those terms most commonly encountered in the branding process.

- *Brand architecture* – a corporate structure delineating relationships between different parts of the brand. It explicitly defines the relationship between the master brand, sub-brands, and products/ services.
- *Brand awareness* – the degree to which a consumer recognizes and recalls a particular brand. Brand awareness is not just about recalling a brand's name, but about the reason for which the consumer recalls the brand. Building brand awareness means creating a broad sales base and can involve operating outside the normal media channels – by using events promotion, product placement, guerrilla marketing, and other less conventional methods of reaching the consumer.
- *Brand equity* – the perceived added value that a brand confers on a good or service. There are three distinct components that intertwine to form brand equity. The first is the notion of the financial value of a brand as a distinct asset capable of representation on a company's balance sheet; this can be thought of as 'brand valuation'. The second is the consumer's degree of attachment to the brand, or 'brand loyalty'. Finally, there is the description of the associations and beliefs that a consumer has about a brand, which is sometimes referred to as 'brand description'.
- *Brand extension* – an extension of a brand to products and services not normally associated with the core brand. Producing sub-variants of an existing branded product is line extension; applying a brand to an entirely different product is brand extension. The Virgin brand is the most commonly-cited example of how to extend a brand successfully.
- *Brand image* – the mental perception of the brand in the minds of consumers. This is developed through communications and experience of the brand, and includes the distinguishing 'human' characteristics of brand personality (e.g., warm, friendly, fun, strong, etc.). The concept of brand identity is also closely aligned with that of brand positioning. However, positioning tends to

suggest action on the part of the company in assigning the brand with attributes, as opposed to brand image, which is more about consumer perception.

- **Brand loyalty** – attachment to a particular brand, even if that brand is more expensive than competing brands. Brand loyalty is the target of all marketers. It is hard to win and easy to lose. Brand loyalty is a product of the psychological contract between the brand and the consumer. If the brand moves in a direction that is out of character with its brand identity, betrays its brand values, or extends itself too far, it will breach the psychological contract and lose the loyalty of its consumers.

- **Brand U** – the application of corporate branding strategy to the individual. The concept was outlined by management guru Tom Peters in a 1997 article in *Fast Company*. An individual, argued Peters, should establish his own brand by going through the type of procedures that a company would. This includes identifying his brand identity, determining key differentiating characteristics, and marketing himself at every available opportunity.

- **Brand values** – the essence of the brand, often expressed in key words, such as quality, creativity, luxury, or integrity. Tom Blackett of the media agency Interbrand has suggested that brand values can be divided into three classes: *functional* (what the brand 'does' for the consumer); *expressive* (what the brand 'says' about the consumer); and *central* (what the brand and the consumer 'share' at a fundamental level).

- **Co-branding** – where two or possibly more independent brands, often from different companies, join forces to support a new product or service. This practice is becoming increasingly popular, in order to squeeze the last drop of competitive advantage from a brand. Co-branding enables brands to increase their sphere of influence, enhance the reputation by association, deliver economies of scale, and utilize new technologies more efficiently. It often takes place where the economics of the market do not justify the launch of a new brand or formal joint venture. All brands involved will retain their individual brand names and usually the brands will be roughly equal in terms of public recognition.

Key texts and further reading

Kapferer, Jean-Noel (1994) *Strategic Brand management: New Approaches to Creating and Evaluating Brand Equity*, Macmillan, New Jersey.

Aaker, David A. (1996) *Building Strong Brands*, Free Press, New York.

Coomber, Stephen (2001) *Branding*, Capstone, Oxford.

Notes

1 Kotler, Philip (1993) *Marketing Management: Analysis, Planning and Control*, (8th edition) Prentice Hall, Engelwood Cliffs.

2 Marketing Business, May 1999.

3 Totonis, Harry and Acito, Chris (1998) 'Branding the bank: the next source of competitive advantage', *Insights* series.

BROADBANDING

Broadbanding is seen as an antidote to the demise of regular promotions and salary increments associated with the traditional career ladder. It involves a compression of the traditional hierarchy of pay grades into fewer, wider bands, which provide a more flexible and less hierarchy-driven reward system.

'It's a way of helping people develop their careers without the old strictures of status and hierarchy. It offers a means by which people can be rewarded in flatter organizations where there are far fewer promotions,' explains Frances Cook, managing director of the career consultancy Sidney & Sanders. 'People would once have expected to move up every two years or so – both in terms of salary and grade. But that is no longer possible. So we need new ways of making people feel good about themselves and developing their careers even if they are in the same job as last year.'

Broadbanding originated in the US and was heavily influenced by the pioneering efforts of the General Electric Corporation. It became more established outside GE in the late 1980s as a result of the move to flatter management structures. Indeed, many argue that the switch to broadbanding is a necessary step to support a delayered organization, as a failure to tackle pay will otherwise demotivate employees who have fewer opportunities for promotion.

The aim is to bring compensation in line with the flatter organizational structures introduced in recent years, and to make lateral career moves and additional training more attractive to employees. With fewer opportunities to move upwards in companies, the theory goes, staff can easily become demotivated. If there appears to be no reward for their efforts, there is a risk that people will feel disinclined to develop, expand and innovate. Broadbanding is supposed to mitigate this problem. It allows employees to enjoy salary increases without being promoted to a more senior position. So, for example, a pay increase could result from a sideways move or from developing new skills in an existing job. By focusing attention on career development, continuous improvement and role flexibility, broadbanding encourages a less rigid interpretation of career progression and provides a sense of direction and achievement.

The basic idea is that it is no longer helpful to have several levels in the hierarchy and many different salary brackets. By widening these, broadbanding is meant to free up job mobility and gives individuals more headroom. Like any system, though, it must be properly administered and applied with flexibility. However, some employees are understandably nervous of companies meddling with pay structures. Where it is used to underpin a flatter organizational structure and to support lateral career development opportunities, however, broadbanding can represent a valuable redrawing of the career map. In particular, it can be used to highlight the skills and competencies the organization identifies as important to its future and to reward employees on their efforts to acquire those skills.

Key text and further reading

Ryden, O. *et al.* (1997) *IPD Guide on Broadbanding*, Institute of Personnel and Development, London.

Ideas into action

Multinationals such as Glaxo Wellcome, IBM, and BP have already introduced broadbanding pay systems, and other employers seem likely to follow suit. Just as delayering involves stripping out layers of management, so broadbanding works by collapsing the tiers of traditional pay scales into wider bands. So, whereas the traditional pay structure might have had fourteen or so job grades with pay range spreads – or spans – ranging from 20% to 40%, and 15% differentials between adjacent ranges, broadband grade structure might involve six or seven grades with range spreads of 50% and differentials between bands of 20%.

Advocates claim that broadbanding can be used for a variety of situations.

At IBM, broadbanding was introduced in 1993. The 25 traditional grades were replaced with ten bands. The bands were aligned with 40-plus job families or 'professions' – e.g. marketing, human resources, legal etc. Employees were placed in the bands according to their role and the skills required. Line managers now have more discretion over pay decisions and are issued with market range guidance by the HR department.

In the UK, the RAC introduced broadbanding for management pay scales because the existing system was seen as inappropriate to the organization's present needs. In particular, the old system was felt to emphasize status rather than the contribution or performance of managers and was seen as inhibiting sideways moves. Similarly, an existing pay and grade system that was considered too rigid and costly to maintain and an awareness of declining promotion opportunities were two of the reasons Midland Bank plc, part of the HSBC Group, switched to broadbanding.

At the pharmaceuticals giant Glaxo Wellcome, on the other hand, there were additional reasons for introducing broadbanding. The restructured pay system introduced in 1995 followed the merger between Glaxo and Wellcome and provided a way to harmonize pay scales across the two cultures. It consists of six bands and applies to all staff.

Broadbanding can be a powerful integrating force,' says Oonagh Ryden, policy adviser to the UK's Institute of Personnel and Development and co-author of a 1997 report on the subject. 'It encourages flexibility, teamwork, continuous development and empowerment. It is also a way of focusing the attention of employees on the skills the business needs to maintain its competitive advantage.'

BURNOUT

B urnout is the term given to the physical or psychological condition induced in workers by overwork or overexposure to stress in the workplace. In the US, the phenomenon of career burnout has long been recognized. Employees who work too hard, for too long, can become demotivated, depressed and, in extreme cases, can suffer nervous breakdowns or worse. Comparative figures are hard to come by, but anecdotal evidence suggests that the problem may be getting worse in the UK. The situation in the US is so bad that almost one-third of the workforce feels overworked or overwhelmed by the amount of work they have to do.

Burnout markedly impairs the performance of employees and may even incapacitate them. Some jobs are known by employer and employee to cause burnout and employees only expect to be in such positions for a limited period. This type of job tends to be very well rewarded financially. Traders in financial markets are a typical example. In other industries, burnout is unpredictable and companies take measures to guard against it, such as enforcing vacation time and introducing stress-management programmes.

'Feeling Overworked: When Work Becomes Too Much' is a survey conducted by the non-profit Families and Work Institute, supported by international accountancy firm PriceWaterhouseCoopers.[1] 'Overworked' was defined by the authors of the study as 'a psychological state that has the potential to affect attitudes, behaviour, social relationships, and health both on and off the job.'

The study looked at a sample of 1003 adults who performed paid work for an employer (as opposed to being self-employed). When asked how often they felt overworked and/or overwhelmed by work over a period of three months, over half said that they felt overworked and overwhelmed sometimes and a significant number said they felt that way most of the time.

Professor Andrew Kakabadse of the Cranfield School of Management has also investigated the phenomenon of burnout as part of a worldwide study of executive performance. His data, based on a detailed survey of 6,500 managers from ten countries, suggests that all leaders are prone to burnout, but their organizations are often embarrassed by the phenomenon and don't know what to do about it. 'Corporate life requires deadlines to be met and inevitably workloads are unevenly shared, meaning that organizations generate their share of workaholics irrespective of the wishes of the individual,' he says. 'In addition, organizational chaos is rife, yet most workplaces still implicitly demand employees be "corporate people", living and dreaming about attaining success in organizational life.'

Serious attention, Kakabadse says, should be given to how burnout happens, how to recognize and cope with it, and how to combat it. The symptoms include increasing fatigue, not listening effectively, feeling saturated with work, and feeling unable to participate in routine operational conversations.

What makes the telltale signs hard to spot, however, is that declining morale and feelings of personal vulnerability usually emerge slowly and insidiously. 'Increases in stress, job pressure, competition, higher work complexity, faster pace of life, and the greater likelihood of redundancy all make for an inevitable drip, drip of negativity which leads many top managers to burnout,' says Kakabadse. 'Prolonged demotivation leads to an emotional deterioration which is worsened by a realization that to some extent current lifestyle traps us in our jobs. Age, difficulty in matching remuneration packages, and the continuity needed to support family life contribute to a sense of being trapped.'

It is often worse for those further down in the organization. Evidence suggests that stress is more pronounced among those who are not in control of their own destiny. Employees who are suffering burnout and feeling overworked and overwhelmed by work are detrimental to an organization. According to the Families and Work Institute study, overworked employees are more likely to make mistakes at work, resent their employers for expecting them to do so much, resent colleagues who do not work as hard as they do, and look for a new job.

While these effects are bad for the employers, it gets worse for the employee. The study also found that employees who feel overworked are more likely to suffer from sleep loss, are more likely to neglect themselves, are less likely to report very good or excellent health, feel less successful in personal relationships, experience more work/life conflict, have higher stress levels, and are less able to cope with everyday life.

Ideas into action

Companies of all sizes need to implement systems that detect and prevent burnout. If they fail to do this, they run the risk of burnout becoming endemic. This is something that Japanese industry has found out to its cost.

At 8.30am on 24 October, 1988, Satoshi Nagayama, aged 28, walked out on to the rooftop of the Kawasaki Steel Corporation building in Tokyo, walked over to the edge and threw himself to his death.

In April of that year, Nagayama, a Kawasaki Steel employee with a promising career ahead of him, was asked to take on the development and implementation of an experimental plan. These duties were outside his normal responsibilities. Nagayama worked diligently on his new task. Too diligently. Almost every day he worked until midnight. He worked weekends. He worked holidays – including public holidays. He even stayed at the office overnight. His overtime for the month of October 1988 amounted to 85.5 hours – not including the overnight periods from midnight to 8.00am.

The night before Nagayama hurled himself from the building, he telephoned his mother. He had stayed over on two nights in the previous week and he told his mother that he was exhausted and could not go on.

In some ways, Nagayama's death was not in vain because, in a groundbreaking decision, his death was found to be occupational by the Tokyo Central Labour Standards Inspection Office (LSIO) – one of the main local authorities that promote occupational safety and health. The Japanese have a word for it: they call it *karoshi* – death by overwork. *Karoshi* became a social problem in Japan during the late 1980s. As the country's economic miracle ran out of steam, the number of hours put in by workers increased. As unemployment became a growing concern, the pressure on overworked salarymen intensified. Used to a job for life, workers were burdened by the social stigma attached to redundancy, which meant that they were often unwilling to complain even when their workload had become unbearable. The Japanese government officially recognized *karoshi* as an occupational hazard in 1994. It is a problem that has not gone away. Figures released by the Japanese labour ministry indicate that 90 people died from overwork in 1998 alone.

In June 2000, the Japanese advertising company Dentsu made legal history by admitting responsibility for the *karoshi* of an employee who had committed suicide in 1991. Ichori Oshima worked an average of 80 hours a week, on gruelling shifts, sometimes toiling from 9.00am to 6.00am the following morning. The case against Mr Oshima's employer was pursued by his parents for eight years. The company belatedly demonstrated its remorse to the tune of ¥168 million ($1.65 million). Sadly, however, Mr Oshima is not an isolated case.

The inevitable corporate restructuring of recent years has piled more work on to those who survived the job cuts. 'Service overtime' – or working beyond normal hours without payment – is a growing problem. In May 2000, for example, Karoshi 100, the *karoshi* hotline that offers counselling to overworked salarymen, received more than 200 calls.

Key texts and further reading

Maslach, Christina and Leiter, Michael P. (1997) *The Truth About Burnout*, Jossey-Bass, San Francisco.

Demarco, Tom (2001) *Slack: Getting Past Burnout, Busywork, and the Myth of Total Efficiency*, Broadway Books.

Berglas, Steven (2001) *Reclaiming the Fire: How Successful People Overcome Burnout*, Random House.

Note

1 Galinsky, E., Kim, S. and Bond, J. (2001) *Feeling Overworked: When Work Becomes Too Much*, Families and Work Institute.

CHANNEL MANAGEMENT

C hannel management recognizes that companies no longer compete just on the quality of their products and services. The channels they create to reach customers differentiate their offerings and play an increasingly important role in their competitive positioning. In recent years, a number of companies have utilized effective channel management to secure competitive advantage and add value to their business performance. The most obvious example is the use of the internet to create a new channel to serve a growing segment of customers who prefer to shop online.

Steven Wheeler and Evan Hirsh, two consultants at Booz·Allen & Hamilton and the authors of *Channel Management* define the term as follows: 'Channels are how and where you purchase a product (or service) and how and where you use the product.' A channel, then, they note 'is the essence of how customers and the product interact. It is a business's route to its customer and a business's on-going relationship with its customer.'

Product-based differentiation has traditionally been the cornerstone of corporate competitiveness. Better products led to market dominance. While this was once true, it is no longer the case. Increasing global competition and rapid technological evolution have shortened product life cycles. Products are quickly emulated, copied, matched or outdone, no matter where they are produced and no matter by whom.

But differentiating the business from the competition remains important. Now, in addition to product differentiation, companies are differentiating themselves through the services they offer to their customers. The overall service is made up of purchases, interactions and relationships delivered by a channel. At the same time, companies are using new channels to bypass the middlemen and strengthen their relationship with the end-user. The name of this particular game is channel management.

Channel management, Hirsh and Wheeler argue, is a systematic means of reaching and taking care of your customers wherever they are

Ideas into action

In some industries, effective use of channels has become a competitive imperative – even more important than creating better products. There are two key reasons for this. First, customers are more demanding than ever before and want personalized service. Just putting a product into a mass-market outlet and waiting for the buyer to come and get it works less and less for the busy consumer.

Second, any product, however unique initially, rapidly becomes a commodity, copied and improved by competitors. Companies can no longer rely on just building or creating a better product; they have to get it into the hands of the buyer in a way that serves that buyer's needs.

Service excellence is not bland or ethereal. It is concerned with delivering substantive and measurable benefits to customers; benefits which customers value and are willing to pay for. Managing channels has, as a result, become highly important and is already being utilized by some top performing companies. In delivering such benefits, channels fulfil three roles:

- information flow (inward and outward);
- logistics to deliver products/services to the end consumer; and
- value added services which augment the product or service.

Effective channel management enhances customer service. It offers wider choice for consumers. It creates innovative responses to their needs and aspirations. It may change the fundamental definition of what business a company is in.

Managing channels more effectively is vital to corporate success at a time when product-based differentiation appears to be diminishing as a source of competitive value.

and however they like to be reached. It is about identifying the most important customers to the business. It is how you consummate the relationship with customers. It is how you communicate with customers. It is how you create and capture value from the product after the initial sale.

They use the simple example of grocery shopping. Some customers will always prefer the traditional channel, visiting their local grocery store, or more likely supermarket. But others will welcome the introduction of a home shopping service, *via* the telephone, a cable service or the internet. For both groups of customers the product – i.e. the groceries – is the

Building a better channel

Michael Dell built the $66 billion Dell computer empire (market cap June 2002) on a single, simple business insight. His inspiration was that he could bypass the dealer channel through which personal computers were then being sold. Instead, he would sell directly to customers and build products to order. Dell created a new channel for selling and manufacturing PCs. The new channel meant that the company wasn't hostage to the mark-ups of resellers. Nor was it burdened with large inventories. In fact, it was the ultimate in virtuous circles. Costs were low and profits high. 'You actually get to have a relationship with the customer,' explains Michael Dell, 'and that creates valuable information, which in turn allows us to leverage our relationships with both suppliers and customers. Couple that information with technology and you have the infrastructure to revolutionize the fundamental business models of major global companies.'[1]

Today, other companies are following Dell's example by discovering new and different channels by which to market. In many cases, it is their ability to invent and manage these channels which is revolutionizing the industries they are in. What a growing number of the world's leading companies are realizing is that channel management has the power to change the rules of the game.

With the launch of *Saturn*, its first new marque since Chevrolet, for example, General Motors realized that car buyers were fed up with slick car salesmen and the poor service most dealerships offered, so it created its own dealer network, providing a new distribution channel. The result was a dramatic increase in customer satisfaction and repeat purchases. Rather than view the car narrowly as a product, the new approach recognized that customers wanted a bundle of transportation services. Saturn's brand development focused on the buying experience, service and support, rather than being narrowly focused on the product. It was concerned with people and processes rather than the product.

same; only the channels change. But it is the channel that imbues the relationship with additional value. (At present, much the same applies to Amazon.com. The product is still a traditional book – only the channel has altered. In time, though, innovative products such as electronic books will emerge to meet emerging demands from the new channel. Instead of a book, companies will be selling a reading experience.)

Channel management, then, is not a narrow discipline. It is not merely distribution or logistics – though these are obviously important. Instead, it is a way of thinking. Channel management is a way of making new connections with customers to exploit new commercial opportunities. Think channels, say its supporters, and you should be thinking strategy. Effective channel management offers the chance to reinvent not just your business but the industry you're in. In a nutshell, Amazon.com became the biggest book retailer in the world simply by offering book buyers a new channel – *via* the internet.

Key texts and further reading

Hirsh, Evan and Wheeler, Steven (1999) *Channel Champions*, Jossey-Bass, San Francisco.

Friedman, Lawrence G. and Furey, Timothy R. (1999) *The Channel Advantage*, Butterworth-Heinemann, Boston.

Note

1 Hirsh, Evan and Wheeler, Steven (1999) *Channel Champions*, Jossey-Bass, San Francisco.

CORE COMPETENCIES

I n his influential 1960 article 'Marketing myopia' in the *Harvard Business Review*, Ted Levitt called on companies to identify what business they were in. 'Management must think of itself not as producing products but as providing customer-creating value satisfactions,' he said. Levitt observed that production-led thinking inevitably resulted in narrow perspectives.

Railway companies should think of themselves as being in the transportation business, argued Levitt, rather than confine themselves to railways. Levitt went on to level similar criticisms at other industries. The film industry, for example, failed to respond to the growth of television because it regarded itself as being in the business of making movies rather than providing entertainment.

The concept of core competencies provided a new angle on Levitt's call for corporate clarity. Instead of identifying what business they are in, companies are called upon to identify the distinctive and differentiating competencies that lie at their heart. Identifying core competencies allows an organization to nurture and build from its strengths rather than pursue red herrings for which it does not possess appropriate skills. A clear understanding of core competencies can also help a company to decide which areas of its business are non-core and would be better if they were outsourced, and which are so vital to its competitive position that they must be maintained at all costs.

The champions of the concept of core competencies have been the American academics Gary Hamel and C.K. Prahalad, authors of *Competing for the Future* and a succession of well-received *Harvard Business Review* articles. (Most notable is 'The core competence of the corporation' which is now the most reprinted article in the history of the journal.) Hamel and Prahalad define core competencies as 'the collective learning in the organization, especially how to coordinate diverse production skills and integrate multiple streams of technologies'. Hamel and Prahalad call on organizations to see themselves as a portfolio of core competencies as opposed to business units.

Ideas into action

In practice, actually identifying what a company's core competencies are is fraught with difficulty. Hamel and Prahalad suggest that a core competence should provide potential access to a wide variety of markets, make a significant contribution to the perceived customer benefits of the end products, and be difficult for competitors to imitate. In practice, these are highly demanding tests.

As a result, what tends to emerge is a wish-list of what the company would like to be good at, a compendium of vague aspirations. The helpfulness of stating that R&D excellence is a core competency is open to debate. There is also the temptation to identify a number of core competencies when the reality is that they are few in number. Coming up with 25 core competencies has a similar effect to producing 48 commandments.

Part of the problem is that there is confusion between personal competencies and corporate competencies. The temptation for companies when they set out in pursuit of competencies is to start with personal competencies. These are relatively easy to establish. Companies can then synthesize the skills of their people into generic competencies, which apply to the firm as a whole. This is not what Hamel and Prahalad intended. The end result of the bottom-up approach may be personally beneficial but, from a corporate viewpoint, it is usually confusing.

Instead, Hamel and Prahalad advocate that companies take a much broader view, seeking out links between activities and skill areas. A transportation company, for example, moved into operating private hospitals where it was able to utilize its logistical competence. Similarly, Hamel and Prahalad identify the core competence of Nike as design and merchandising while McDonald's is convenience and Sony's miniaturization.

These are undoubtedly neat summations of what makes up the competitive advantage of these corporate titans. How much awareness of these competencies has played a part in their success is impossible to tell.

For those organizations able to determine a persuasive and useful list of their core competencies comes the next stage: how to develop strategies that are driven by those competencies. Once companies have established their core competencies they can establish the likely source of competitive advantage.

Herein lies what some consider the greatest danger of the neat theory. If a company seeks out markets, mergers and acquisitions in areas where its core competencies would be most advantageous, it may well be entering markets about which it knows nothing.

In effect, the concept of core competencies encourages companies into diversification. They need to go where their competencies would be put to the most effective and profitable use. Sony needs to seek out opportunities to miniaturize; McDonald's needs to maximize its competence in 'convenience'. Unfortunately, corporate history is littered with unhappy experiences of diversification. (Against this, it can be argued that the success of McDonald's lies in maximizing the impact of its core competence – through international expansion – within the business it knows.)

Another weakness to the core competency argument is that the critical competencies and insights of a business often reside among a small coterie of people – not necessarily senior managers. In the knowledge- and information-intensive age, this is increasingly the case. If the people depart, so too do the competencies. If Microsoft's most innovative software design team left, the company would feel the impact. For smaller organizations, the impact could be potentially terminal.

While Hamel and Prahalad led the way, others have followed in their wake. There are a host of alternative definitions and suggested approaches. Core competencies can, for example, be regarded as 'organizational knowledge', the elusive infrastructure of knowledge and behaviour which lies at the corporate heart. Hamel also refers to 'deeper capabilities'.

While there are clear drawbacks to religious adherence to the tenets of core competencies (some of them are discussed above), the concept marks an important development. Once differentiation was regarded as being solely concerned with products. Companies sought to develop their products to compete. Now, differentiation is increasingly identified with the skills, knowledge and aspirations of the organization. Differentiation comes from the 'soft' areas of branding, organizational innovation and service. As a result, differentiation is more human and harder to achieve than ever before.

Key texts and further reading

Hamel, Gary, and Prahalad, C.K. (1994) *Competing for the Future,* Harvard Business School Press, Boston, MA.

Hamel, Gary, and Heene, Aime (editors) (1994) *Competence-Based Competition,* John Wiley, New York.

CORE VALUES

Distinct from the concept of core competencies, core values are concerned with what an organization stands for. The term may be a relative newcomer to the business lexicon, but the notion of a set of values as an important aspect of corporate life is not. It is an area of interest that seems likely to grow.

'Every organization needs values, but a lean organization needs them even more. When you strip away the support systems of staffs and layers, people have to change their habits and expectations, or else the stress will just overwhelm them,' Jack Welch, CEO of General Electric, has observed.

Although not always described as 'values', many companies have long recognized the importance of possessing a set of guiding principles. The evolution of the concept can be traced through some of the most influential business books over the last fifty years. Indeed, the notion of values has had an enduring impact on the development of thought since ancient times.

'Values,' the Greek philosopher Aristotle observed, 'are qualities, human excellence, reflected through our habits, skills and behaviours.' Honesty, integrity, wealth, fairness are all values that we may be able to relate to on an individual personal basis. In recent decades, values have begun to be explored in the context of business and corporations.

In his 1963 book *A Business and Its Beliefs*, Thomas Watson Jr, CEO of IBM, observed: 'Consider any great organization – one that has lasted over the years – I think you will find it owes its resiliency not to its form of organization or administrative skills, but to the power of what we call beliefs and the appeal these beliefs have for its people.'

When Watson talks about beliefs, he is talking about fundamental principles or standards, about what is valuable or important to IBM, the organization. He is talking about values. Similarly, Tom Peters and Robert Waterman thought corporate values important enough to warrant an entire chapter in their 1982 book *In Search Of Excellence*. For them the terms 'beliefs' and 'values' were interchangeable. Other writers touched on the subject with varying degrees of interest.

But the debate took a leap forward in 1994 with *Built to Last*, the influential book by James C. Collins and Jerry I. Porras. These two business academics from Stanford University set out to identify the qualities essential to building a great and enduring organization; what the authors called 'successful habits of visionary companies'. The companies they wrote about had outperformed the general stock market by a factor of twelve since 1925.

For Collins and Porras, 'corporate values' are of paramount importance when building a lasting company; so important, in fact, that the authors craft a carefully worded and precise definition of 'core values'. The interest this section of the book provoked led to an article in the *Harvard Business Review* clarifying their findings. This is one of the most authoritative interpretations to date.

Core values, they say, are: 'the organization's essential and enduring tenets – a small set of guiding principles; not to be confused with specific cultural or operating practices; not to be compromised for financial gain or short-term expediency.'

Values run deep. They are timeless guiding principles that drive the way the company operates – everything it does – at a level that transcends strategic objectives. For Hewlett-Packard, for example, values include a strong sense of responsibility to the community. For Disney they include 'creativity, dreams and imagination' and the promulgation of 'wholesome American values'.

Organizational goals (specific targets that help to realize a vision) are not values; neither are mission or purpose (the fundamental reason for existence); nor should values be confused with vision (a picture of the intended future). All these have their place in a successful company. Values, however, it could be argued, are the precursor, the foundation on which the others are built.

Corporate values, then, are the fundamental beliefs for which a company stands. They are the essence of a company's identity, a corporate DNA if you will. Long-lasting, possibly immutable, values are guiding principles by which a company can chart its course across the business seas. The rougher the seas, the more important it is to have values to navigate by.

The growing recognition of the importance of values by business commentators has led to a better understanding of the nature of corporate values. It has also, however, raised a number of other important associated issues.

John Kotter, professor of leadership at Harvard Business School, makes an important point when he says, 'At a deeper level, corporate culture is about the implicit shared values among a group of people – about what is important, what is good and what is right.'

As he rightly points out, however, the problem with this is 'that values and norms are invisible, and actions to reinforce them occur subconsciously. So people are often not very aware of culture, or of the role that they play in helping to maintain a particular culture.'

In other words, every company has its own culture and its own set of values. In most cases, however, these are not clear either to outsiders or even to many of those within. Messages about values – and even the values themselves – are regularly confused. The solution lies with better understanding and communication. Values-driven businesses articulate their values clearly so that stakeholders are not left in any doubt what the organization stands for – and will not stand for. To do this, however, the organization has to know what its core values are.

Ideas into action

In their widely acclaimed book *Built to Last*, James C. Collins and Jerry I. Porras note, 'Companies that enjoy enduring success have core values and a core purpose that remain fixed while their business strategies and practices endlessly adapt to a changing world.'

This, they say, is a key factor in the success of companies such as Hewlett-Packard, Johnson & Johnson, Proctor & Gamble, Merck, and Sony. Collins and Porras recommend a conceptual framework to cut through some of the confusion swirling around the issues. In their model, vision has two components – core ideology and envisioned future. Core ideology, the Yin in their scheme, defines what the company stands for and why it exists. Yin is unchanging and complements Yang, the envisioned future. The envisioned future is what the company aspires to become, to achieve, to create – something that will require considerable change and progress to attain.

Core ideology provides the glue that holds an organization together through time. Any effective vision must embody the core ideology of the organization, which in turn has two components – core values and core purpose.

1 *Core values*, a system of guiding principles and tenets; and
2 *core purpose*, the organization's most fundamental reason for existence.

Core values are the essential and enduring tenets of an organization. A small set of timeless guiding principles, core values require no external justification; they have intrinsic value and importance to those inside the organization. Some examples of these are well known:

Disney imagination and wholesomeness;

Cadbury Schweppes competitive ability, quality, clear objectives, simplicity, openness, and responsibility to stakeholders;

Merrill Lynch client focus, respect for the individual, teamwork, responsible citizenship, and integrity;

Hewlett-Packard respect for the individual;

Merck corporate social responsibility, unequivocal excellence in all aspects of the company, science-based innovation, honesty and integrity, and profit – but profit from work that benefits humanity;

Sony the elevation of Japanese national culture and status, being a pioneer – not following others, but doing the impossible, and respect for and encouragement of individual ability and creativity;

Ikea innovation, humility, simplicity; looking after the interest of the majority, and will-power;

Reuters accuracy, independence, accountability and openness, speed, innovation, and customer focus;

US army loyalty, duty, respect, selfless service, honour, integrity, and personal courage.

(Source: Coomber, S. and Dearlove, D. (1999) *Heart & Soul: A Study of the Impact of Corporate and Individual Values on Business*, Blessing/White, Maidenhead.)

Key texts and further reading

Collins, James C. and Porras, Jerry I. (1994) *Built to Last*, Random House, London.

Collins, James C. and Porras, Jerry I. 'Building the Vision', *Harvard Business Review,* Sept/Oct 1996.

Coomber, S. and Dearlove, D. (1999) *Heart & Soul: A Study of the Impact of Corporate and Individual Values on Business*, Blessing/White, Maidenhead.

CRISIS MANAGEMENT

W hether they are lawsuits, environmental disasters, financial collapses or accusations of fraud or sexual harassment, crises are a fact of corporate life.

In recent years, this realization has fuelled the creation of a whole field of specialized advisers and crisis management specialists. The American Institute for Crisis Management (ICM) boasts a database of 60,000 business crisis news stories. For the practicing manager it is daunting to note that this database has only been compiled since 1990.

Inevitably, definitions and perceptions about what constitutes a crisis and how it should be managed differ greatly. What can be said is that the word *crisis* originates from the Greek verb meaning *to decide*. In corporate terms, a crisis is a major, unpredictable event with a potentially negative impact on the company's employees, products, services, financial situation or reputation. It is a decisive moment. The ICM defines a crisis as 'a significant business disruption which stimulates extensive news media coverage. The resulting public scrutiny will affect the organization's normal operations and also could have a political, legal, financial and governmental impact on its business.' It is perhaps significant that the modern measure of a crisis is column inches rather than lives lost.

Crises are caused by a multitude of events and factors. Some are pure acts of nature – storms destroying a factory – or the result of mechanical malfunctions, such as when metal fatigue causes an aeroplane to crash. More avoidable are crises precipitated by human error or management. Indeed, the ICM calculates that 62% of business crises can be traced back to management and 23% to employees. As most crises are caused by human frailty, rather than dramatic outside intervention, the profession of crisis management has emerged. Over the last decade in particular, crisis management has become a substantial business. Companies increasingly accept that crises, in whatever form, are inevitable. (Indeed, some regard crises as catalysts for change. This owes more than a little to the macho-management tradition of characters being shaped by crises – 'Great crises produce great men and great deeds of courage,' said John F. Kennedy.)

Ideas into action

While there are a variety of theories and opinions on how best to manage a crisis, some fundamentals are common. First, accurate information is essential. Any attempt to conceal relevant facts and to manipulate the situation ultimately backfires and increases the damage to the company. Perrier's management maintained that its mineral water did not contain any toxic element in spite of persuasive evidence to the contrary. When it finally admitted the failure, the damage to Perrier's public image was already done. Honesty is the best policy – even if there is nothing to report.

For some companies, this is easier said than done. If a company has fostered a culture of secrecy and manipulative behaviour, it cannot simply transform itself. In a crisis the real nature of a company's culture surfaces. Usually, management has only limited control over the situation. It cannot prevent all of its employees from talking to the press, nor prescribe what finally appears in the media. When faced with unforeseen predicaments, employees have to act according to their own judgement rather than to instructions from senior management. (For this reason, communicating with employees is critical.)

Second, the company must react as quickly as possible. Any suggestion that the company is playing for time, is unsure as to what is happening, or is being indecisive is counter productive. In 1989 Exxon CEO Lawrence Rawl waited two weeks before paying a visit to the scene of the Exxon Valdez oil spill. This sent a clear message about where mass pollution figured in his priorities. For all the media clamour, actions speak louder than words. British Airways has a rolling crisis management team that can be assembled within half an hour, day or night, 365 days of the year.

Third, the response must come from the top. Credibility comes from the presence of senior management. Texaco CEO Peter Bijur took control of the company's reaction to a potentially damaging lawsuit. British Midland's Sir Michael Bishop was the company's only spokesman after the Kegworth air crash. The level of response is an indication of the importance management places on the problem.

The fourth fundamental is a long-term perspective. The long-term goodwill the company enjoys from its customers should be kept in mind when considering the short-term costs of corrective measures. Immediately withdrawing all your products from supermarket shelves if there is a suggestion of contamination sends a clear signal that you are taking the problem seriously and are intent on sorting it out.

Fifth, predicting problems requires a coherent strategy. Companies need to be prepared for a crisis. Bombs do explode; planes do crash; products do go wrong; boats do sink; and people sometimes make disastrous mistakes. Companies need to review and rehearse options in advance. Systems need to be in place. Most large organizations now have crisis management plans covering a variety of eventualities. At a government level, crisis management is well-established – much crisis management best practice has its origins in the armed services. The American Federal Emergency Management Agency has 2600 staff, as well as a further 4000 who can be called on in a crisis.

Whatever an organization's level of preparedness, the central problem with crisis management is that most problems are caused by management. As a result, the people charged with resolving a crisis are often the very same people who made – or did not make – the decisions that got the company into the situation in the first place. To resolve this situation demands a degree of decisiveness, humility and public honesty which executives often struggle to muster.

The best decision would often be for certain executives to accept responsibility and, sometimes, for them to leave the company. In reality, however, reactions to an impending crisis are often denial, followed by castigation by the media, by malicious competitors or by unions. Bringing in an outside agency with expertise in crisis management is usually a last resort, a sign that management has finally admitted that it has lost control.

Key texts and further reading

Albrecht, Steve (1996) *Crisis Management for Corporate Self-Defense*, AMACOM Books, New York.

Fearn-Banks, Kathleen (1996) *Crisis Communication: A Casebook Approach*, Lawrence Erlbaum Associates, New Jersey.

Marconi, Joe (1997) *Crisis Marketing: When bad things happen to good companies*, NTC Business Books, Chicago.

Mitroff, Ian I., Pearson, Catherine M. and Harrington, L. Katharine (1996) *The Essential Guide to Managing Corporate Crises*, Oxford University Press, Oxford.

Sikich, Geary W. (1995) *Emergency Planning Handbook*, McGraw-Hill, New York.

DECISION THEORY

'**E**xecutives do many things in addition to making decisions. But only executives make decisions. The first managerial skill is, therefore, the making of effective decisions,' Peter Drucker has observed. How decisions are made, and could be improved, is a topic of major interest to businesspeople and academics alike.

An entire academic discipline, decision science, is devoted to understanding management decision making. Much of it is built on the foundations set down by early business thinkers who believed that under a given set of circumstances human behaviour was logical and therefore predictable. The fundamental belief of the likes of computer pioneer Charles Babbage and Scientific Management founder Frederick Taylor was that the decision process (and many other things) could be rationalized and systematized. Based on this premise, models emerged to explain the workings of commerce which, it was thought, could be extended to the way in which decisions were made.

In general, management literature defines two different types of decision:

- **Operational decisions**, which are concerned with the day-to-day running of the business. Typical operational decisions might involve setting production levels, the decision to recruit additional employees, or to close a particular factory.
- **Strategic decisions**, which are those concerned with organizational policy and direction over a longer time period. So, a strategic decision might involve determining whether to enter a new market, acquire a competitor, or exit from an industry altogether.

Interestingly, Madan G. Singh, chair of information engineering at the University of Manchester Institute of Science and Technology and an acknowledged expert on decision making, prefers an alternative breakdown of decision levels, which recognizes some of the changes taking place within companies. He divides the decision makers in an organization into three levels of decision:

- day-to-day decisions;
- tactical decisions; and
- strategic decisions.

Day-to-day decisions, he says, are those made by front-line staff. Collectively, they make thousands of decisions daily, most of them in a short time frame and on the basis of concrete information – answering a customer's request for information about a product, for example. Their decisions usually have a narrow scope and influence a small range of activities. Tactical and strategic decisions, on the other hand, are both longer-term decisions. The data needed to make them is much broader, extending outside the organization, and the information derived from that data is less precise, less current and subject to more error. Tactical decisions cover a few weeks to a few months, and include decisions such as the pricing of goods and services, and deciding advertising and marketing expenditures.

Strategic decisions are those with the longest time horizon – one to five years or longer. They generally concern expanding or contracting the business or entering new geographic or product markets.

To help managers cope with all these decisions, there are numerous models, frameworks, tools, techniques and software programmes. One of the best known, and most useful, Kepner-Tregoe (K-T) is explained below. What nearly all have in common is the assumption that business decisions are rational. Decision theory is grounded in the notion of the logical manager, and overlooks the role of intuition – or gut feel – in human decision making. This is a very Western view of decisions. Eastern cultures take a variety of different approaches. The Japanese, for example, have traditionally relied on a consensus-building process – *ringi* – rather than a decision-making formula.

Despite the growing body of evidence that many of the best business decisions are not strictly rational, the belief in decision theory persists. Indeed, most management books and ideas are inextricably linked to helping managers make logical decisions. Strategic management, for example, was a model by which strategic decisions could be made. Unfortunately, it was a model that demanded vast amounts of data. As a result, enthusiastic managers turned themselves into data addicts rather than better decision makers. Decisions were perpetually delayed as more data was gathered in order to ensure the decision would be 100% certain to work. 'Paralysis by analysis' became commonplace.

Decision-making models assume that the distilled mass of experience will enable people to make accurate decisions. They enable you to learn from other people's experiences. Many promise the world. Feed in your particular circumstances and out will pop an answer. The danger is in concluding that the solution provided by a software package is *the* answer.

Whether in a software package or buried in a textbook, decision theorizing suggests that effective decision making involves a number of logical stages. This is referred to as the 'rational model of decision-making' or the 'synoptic model', and it involves a series of steps – identifying the problem; clarifying the problem; prioritizing goals; generating options; evaluating options (using appropriate analysis); comparing predicted outcomes of each option with the goals; and choosing the option which best matches the goals.

Such models rely on a number of assumptions about the way in which people will behave when confronted with a set of circumstances. These assumptions allow mathematicians to derive formulas based on probability theory. These decision-making tools include such things as cost/benefit analysis which aims to help managers evaluate different options.

Alluring though they are, the trouble with such theories is that reality is often more confused and messy than a neat model can allow for. Underpinning the mathematical approach are a number of flawed assumptions – such as that decision making is consistent; based on accurate information; free from emotion or prejudice; and rational. Another obvious drawback to any decision-making model is that identifying what you need to make a decision about is often more important than the actual decision itself. If a decision seeks to solve a problem, it may be the right decision but the wrong problem.

The reality is that managers make decisions based on a combination of intuition, experience and analysis. As intuition and experience are impossible to measure in any sensible way, the temptation is to focus on the analytical side of decision-making, the science rather than the mysterious art. (Much of the management consulting industry is based on reaching decisions through analysis.) Of course, the manager in the real world does not care whether he or she is practising an art or a science. What they do care about is solving problems and reaching reliable, well-informed decisions.

This does not mean that decision theory is redundant or that decision-making models such as K-T should be cast to one side. Indeed, a number of factors mean that decision making is becoming ever more demanding. The growth in complexity means that companies no longer encounter simple problems. And complex decisions are now not simply the preserve of the most senior managers but the responsibility of many others in organizations. In addition, managers are having to deal with a flood of information – a 1996 survey by Reuters of 1200 managers worldwide found that 43% thought that important decisions were delayed and their ability to make decisions affected as a result of having too much information.

These factors suggest that any techniques, models or analytical procedures which enable managers to make more-informed decisions more quickly will be in increasing demand. In the past, models were the domain of economists and strategists. Now, there is increasing use of decision support systems. Some show the best types of decisions for a given situation. Typically, these involve how best to use resources. An oil refinery, for example, may use a support system to determine on a daily basis what is the optimum product that it should produce. Airlines run similar programmes to establish optimum pricing levels. Other systems aim to yield increasingly better decisions based on past results. These learning-based models allow companies to take the data they have gathered and any analysis they have undertaken and store them up in one place directly related to the decision.

There is little doubt that decision theory and the use of such models is reassuring. They lend legitimacy to decisions that may be based on prejudices or hunches. But the usefulness of decision-making models remains a leap of faith. None are foolproof, as none are universally applicable. And none can yet cope with the wilful idiosyncrasies of human behaviour.

Key texts and further reading

Baron, Jonathan (1994) *Thinking and Deciding* (2nd edn), Cambridge University Press.

Kepner, C. and Tregoe, B. (1965) *The Rational Manager*, McGraw-Hill, New York.

Drucker, P. (1974) *Management Tasks, Responsibilities, Practices*, Harper & Row, New York.

French, Simon (1988) *Decision Theory: An Introduction to the Mathematics of Rationality*, Ellis Horwood and John Wiley, New York.

Keeney, Ralph L. (1992) *Value-Focused Thinking: A Path to Creative Decision Making*, Harvard University Press.

Kepner, C. and Tregoe, B. (1981) *The New Rational Manager*, Princeton Research Press, New Jersey.

Richards, Max D. and Greenlaw, Paul S. (1966) *Management Decision Making*, Richard D. Irwin Inc., Homewood, IL.

Yates, J. Frank (1990) *Judgement and Decision Making*, Prentice Hall, Englewood Cliffs, NJ.

Ideas into action

One of the more useful and certainly one of the best-known decision models is that developed by Charles H. Kepner and Benjamin Tregoe. In 1958, they founded Kepner-Tregoe Inc., a Princeton-based, international management consulting firm which focused on the critical need for training in problem solving and decision making. In their 1965 book *The Rational Manager*, Kepner and Tregoe identified three main components in effective decision making:

- the quality of the decision about factors to be satisfied;
- the quality of the evaluation of alternatives; and
- the quality of the understanding of what alternatives can produce.

They used this analysis to define the major elements in their decision analysis methodology: construction of a decision statement; identification of the objectives, i.e. criteria which can either be considered to be 'musts' (must be achieved), or 'wants' (desirable but not essential); identification of alternatives; and evaluation of the consequences of the choice outcome.

Thus the Kepner & Tregoe (K-T) technique can be neatly summarized as:

- generate a decision statement, specifying the level of decision making (they suggest that this is best effected in a group);
- generate objectives and classify into 'musts' and 'wants'. 'Wants' are then weighted (values 1 to 10) on an importance scale relative to each other;
- generate and evaluate alternatives. If an alternative does not achieve the 'must' criteria then it is eliminated. Otherwise, the remaining alternatives are rated against 'want' criteria;
- the mark for each alternative is determined by calculating the sum of the rates multiplied by the weights it carries. The alternative with the highest score is the tentative choice; and
- this tentative choice is examined to evaluate the less quantifiable risks associated with it. If such risks seem prohibitive, the choice may be abandoned and the next highest alternative considered.

Today Kepner-Tregoe processes are used by millions of employees and managers in many countries and in seventeen languages, to achieve sustainable results. The firm also claims to have been the first to introduce the 'train-the-trainer' concept – developed as a methodology for transferring Kepner-Tregoe approaches to clients.

The garbage-can model

This is the name given to a pattern of decision making in organizations and was first identified by an American professor of management, James March. In simple terms, it describes an organizational model in which, when faced with a decision, members of the organization generate a constant stream of problems and solutions. These are then in effect 'dumped' into a 'garbage-can', and only a very small percentage of the solutions generated are ever incorporated in the final decision.

Underpinning this model are March's observations on organizational behaviour, which suggest that the people working in organizations tend to develop a preference for certain courses of action. These may be regarded as the 'pet solutions' of their individual champions. The upshot of this, the model implies, is that whenever a problem arises, individuals will seize upon it as an opportunity to implement their chosen solution. This in turn influences both the decision-making process and the final output.

Another way to look at this model is to see organizations as sets of competing solutions waiting for problems to arise. Under the garbage-can model, then, decisions can be regarded as what happens when a set of problems, solutions and choices come together – or collide – at a particular juncture. In a sense, the final decision is no more than the by-product of the alchemy that takes place within the garbage-can.

This fits with another idea put forward by March and another American management academic, Richard Cyert, which saw the way organizations behaved as a form of 'organized anarchy'.

Ringi

An alternative view of decision making is enshrined in Japanese companies. The *ringisei* process used by Japanese companies means that proposals circulate within the organization and are initialled by agreeing participants. This system is a manifestation of the Japanese bottom-up method of decision making, and probably the best-known example of collectivist decision making in business.

The traditional tendency in Japan has been to make corporate decisions from the bottom up rather than from the top down. The Japanese decision making process is that of consensus building, or decision making by consensus. Under this system, any changes in procedures and routines, tactics and even strategies are originated by those who are directly concerned with those changes. The final decision is made at the top level after an elaborate examination of the proposal through successively higher levels in the management hierarchy. The acceptance or rejection of a decision is the result of consensus at every echelon. *Ringi* (requesting a decision) is a written recommendation urging a specific course of action. The *ringi* is submitted upward to superiors and to the relevant departments until it reaches the top decision makers. They then pass down the decision on whether the proposal is finally to be accepted. This system enables all employees to participate in corporate policy decision-making.

When the lower or middle manager is confronted with a problem and wishes to present a solution, a meeting is called in that particular section by the section chief (*kacho*). The members of the section may agree that the idea should be pursued, but they may feel that it needs the overall support of the company. The section chief then reports this to his department head or department manager (*bucho*), and consults with him. If the department head expresses support for the section's proposal, the time-consuming activity of getting a general consensus starts.

In practice, the process of seeking a general consensus in reaching a final decision is known as *nemawashi*, during which many communications and consultations are carried out repeatedly before the formal document or *ringi* is written. First, a general consensus among the persons who will be directly and indirectly involved in the implementation in a department is sought. Then an overall, but informal, consensus in the company is obtained. The department head may arrange a meeting with the other departments concerned.

Normally each department sends one department head, one section head and one or two supervisors (*kakaricho*), as they are the ones who will be involved in the implementation stage. If the opinion of specialists or experts from the shop floor is required, they will be represented. In fact, the meeting is aimed mainly at the exchange of information among the involved persons in order to implement a plan.

Through these discussions, other information and materials may be found to be needed. In that case, the heads go about, formally or informally, from section to section and from department to department to collect the necessary information and to prepare the document to be presented in the next meeting.

After more meetings, when the department considers that it has attained an informal agreement from all other departments concerned, the formal procedures start. First, the initiator and his colleagues, under the section head's supervision, write up a formal document of request, the *ringisho*, which outlines the problem and the details of the plan for its solution. Also enclosed are supportive information and materials. The *ringisho* is then circulated among various successively higher echelons of management for approval. Each responsible manager or executive concerned stamps it with his seal of approval. If a manager finds a fault, or that some points in the document are not in agreement of the consensus reached earlier, it will be returned to the originator for clarification and rectification. The *ringisho* finally goes to the top management for formal authorization for the final go-ahead. Once a proposal is accepted during the *newawashi* stage, it is seldom opposed or rejected at the *ringi* stage.

The *ringi* system is used to confirm that all elements of disagreement have been eliminated at the *newawashi* stage. It ensures that responsibility is assumed by all the persons who have affixed their seal of approval. Only persons in responsible positions have the authority to write a *ringi* because it is considered a recommendation by staff to the top management concerning measures that should be taken not just within a specific workplace, but throughout the company as a whole. This system involves the complete consensus of everyone concerned with the decision.

When a *ringi* has been approved, the conclusions it embodies constitute a supreme decision that the company as a whole is bound to put into effect immediately. Thus, while considerable time is required for the final decision on a *ringi* to be reached, once it is made, it is executed quickly because all those involved in the implementation know the part they are required to play in the plan and commit themselves fully to implementing the decision rapidly and smoothly.

In Japanese companies, the decision-making process will also often suggest the level at which a decision should be made and may even identify the person or people who should make it. Most critical of all, the process eliminates the need to 'sell' the decision later. As such, it actually builds effective implementation into the decision-making process.

US and European companies, on the other hand, typically make rapid decisions and view the decision as entirely separate from implementation. Many Western managers pride themselves on the speed with which they make decisions compared to their Japanese counterparts. It wasn't until management writers such as Peter Drucker and others began pointing it out that Western business people began to realize there was something different about the way decisions were reached in the two cultures. Since then, many others have written about the differences between the Japanese and Western business cultures, but few have improved on Drucker's early observations.

It wasn't simply that the Japanese were slow at making decisions – although it did sometimes seem that way to their impatient Western colleagues and business partners – it was something far more fundamental. Put simply, in the West the emphasis is on finding the right answer and moving on to implementation as speedily as possible. The Japanese, in contrast, tended to place the emphasis on defining the right question. They are especially good at managing a process by which they reach a consensus on the need to make a decision about a particular issue. Once that consensus has been reached, it is possible to move quickly because there is broad agreement that a decision is needed.

In the West, there is a cultural bias towards doing it the other way round. In other words, while Western managers think they are faster at making decisions, what they actually do is decide on a solution – i.e. the right answer – and then attempt to sell it to the organization. (By the time the Japanese decide on the solution the organization is already in agreement that a decision is needed. It's a classic case of 'less haste, more speed'.) What it means in practice is that Japanese companies don't waste as much time on 'the wrong decisions'. This can be said of ineffective and effective decision makers – and organizations.

As Peter Drucker noted: 'Japanese managers may come up with the wrong answer to the problem, but they rarely come up with the right answer to the wrong problem. And that, as all decision makers learn, is the most dangerous course, the irretrievably wrong decision.'

Says Drucker: 'When the Japanese reach the point we call a decision, they say they are in the "action stage". Now top management refers the decision to what the Japanese call the "appropriate people".

By the time the 'decision' or action is finally agreed, it will come as no surprise to the organization, and will meet little or no resistance. As a result, implementation is much faster. His observations of the way that Japanese companies operated compared to US companies also led Drucker to the conclusion that it was the difficulty of selling decisions to others in the organization that was the chief reason for their failure.

DISCOUNTED CASH FLOW

D iscounted cash flow is a sophisticated technique used by financial analysts. It refers to a method of valuing a company used by private company investors and venture capitalists. The concept is used to answer some specific concerns of investors. In particular how they should determine the size of their investments in projects. (Other methods ignore tax benefits and appreciation, which most professional investors consider as part of their return. Moreover, in certain situations, investors are not even looking for cash flow. They expect their entire return to be in tax benefits.)

Unlike the market valuation method, the discounted cash flow method estimates company value without reference to the price:earnings ratios of similar publicly held companies. To that extent, it represents a more individualized calculation of future value. It is used to determine the value of bonds, loans, and other fixed-income investments. For example, venture capitalists use it to predict returns from investments in new companies. It also has a wide range of applications in real estate analysis.

Discounted cash flow analysis takes all benefits (cash flow, tax credits, net sale proceeds, paper losses) into account, not just cash flow. The aim is to assess a projected stream of economic benefits and calculate the maximum equity contribution that an investor should be willing to make. It also enables an analyst to compare an equity amount with a stream of benefits and calculate an overall rate of return. The investor's minimum rate of return is called the discount rate, the rate at which the investor will discount benefits promised in the future. The discount rate converts benefits promised in the future into an equivalent value today, called present value.

Despite its complexity, discounted cash flow analysis is based on a simple idea – that cash today is worth more than cash promised in the future. It assumes that any investment should yield a return over and above current cash value. It makes no sense, for example, to invest $100 today for the promise of only the same amount in the future. If you invest $100 today, you should receive more than that amount back at a later date.

There are a number of factors involved. The first factor is the risk incurred. An investor in a property development, for example, is looking for cash flow and appreciation, but neither is guaranteed. The investor bears significant market risk, and risk demands some compensation. Part of the return on investment is compensation for taking risk. The greater the risk, the higher the rate of return demanded by investors. Treasury bonds are very low-risk investments, so investors may be satisfied with 6% or 7% returns. Venture capitalists take huge risks on unproved companies and may demand a 40% return on their money.

Second, inflation reduces the value of money. An investor needs some return just to preserve the value of the capital. If inflation is proceeding at 4% per year, an investor needs a 4% after-tax return just to get back what he has invested. The other justification of return on investment, then, is compensation for inflation.

Third, there is the opportunity cost of the investment. When an investor places money in an investment, he or she gives up the right to use it for anything else – alternative investments or consumption. Economists call this 'opportunity cost'. You lose the opportunity to use the money for any other purpose. Property investments in particular pose heavy opportunity costs, because they are non-liquid. It's difficult to convert a real estate investment to cash, compared to investments such as stocks and bonds. So, the third part of return on investment is compensation for opportunity cost.

An investor's perception of these three factors – risk, inflation, and opportunity cost – determine his or her desired rate of return, the minimum rate of return required for a particular investment.

For the purposes of venture capitalists, discounted cash flow assumes that the future value of a company can be estimated by forecasting future performance of the business and measuring the surplus cash flow generated by the company. The surplus cash flows and cash flow shortfalls are then related back to a present value using a discounting factor and added together to arrive at an overall valuation. The discount factor used is adjusted for the financial risk of investing in the company. The mechanics of the method focus investors on the internal operations of the company and its future.

Like any other valuation method, the discounted cash flow method has its shortcomings. As Peter Johnson, a lecturer in management studies, notes: 'It is easy to list some of the difficulties associated with any crystal ball view of valuation: predicting events that are far away; deciding over which time horizon to evaluate the performance of the business; choosing appropriate discount rates and terminal values. Besides these inherent difficulties, other subtler assumptions are often made. It is usually assumed, for example, that ownership of the company is constant, which may well not be the case. DCF analysis also often overlooks the strategic degrees of freedom created by good performance, and the constraints imposed by short-term disappointments.'[1]

Since it is only concerned with the generation of future cash flow, it ignores outside factors that affect company value, such as price:earnings ratios. It also ignores asset values and other internal factors that can reduce or increase company value. Since the method is based on forecasts, a good understanding of the business, its market and its past operations is essential.

Key text and further reading

Wright, Maurice G. (1990) *Using Discounted Cash Flow in Investment Appraisal*, McGraw-Hill, New York.

Note

1 Johnson, Peter (1999) 'Beyond EVA: Resource Margin Accounting', FT Mastering Strategy, *Financial Times*, 22 November.

Ideas into action

Discounted cash flow is a commonly used method in venture capital financing because it focuses on what the venture investor is actually buying – a slice of the future operations of the company. Its focus on future cash flows also neatly coincides with a key issue for venture investors: the company's ability to sustain its future operations through internally generated cash flow.

Discounted cash flow analysis has two different uses. The first is to calculate the value of a stream of benefits in the future (present value analysis). The second is to analyse a stream of benefits and to determine what rate of return they represent on a particular investment (internal rate of return analysis).

The discounted cash flow method can be applied in six steps:

1 Develop accurate projections of the company's future operations. This is clearly the critical element in the calculation. The more closely the projections reflect a good understanding of the business and its realistic prospects, the more confident investors will be with the valuation it supports.

2 Quantify positive and negative cash flow in each year of the projections. The cash flow being measured is the surplus cash generated by the business each year. In years when the company does not generate surplus cash, the cash shortfall is also measured.

3 Estimate an end value for the last year of the projections. One common and conservative assumption is the perpetuity assumption. This assumes that the cash flow of the last projected year will continue forever and then discounts that cash flow back to the last year of the projections.

4 Determine the discount factor to be applied to the cash flows. One of the key elements affecting the valuation generated by this method is the discount factor chosen. The larger the factor is, the lower the valuation it will generate. This discount factor should reflect the business and investment risk involved. The less likely the company is to meet its projections, the higher the factor should be. Discount factors used most often are a compromise between the cost of borrowing and the cost of equity investment. If the cost of borrowed money is 10% and equity investors want 30% for their funds, the discount factor would be somewhere in-between.

5 Apply the discount factor to the cash flow surplus and shortfall of each year and to the terminal value. The amount generated by each of these calculations will estimate the present value contribution of each year's future cash flow. Adding these values together estimates the company's present value.

6 Subtract present long-term and short-term borrowings from the present value of future cash flows to estimate the company's present value.

DOWNSIZING

ownsizing is the *bête noire* of management thinking. It reached its height during the recession of the early 1990s. It advocated a wholesale reduction in staffing levels as the key to greater efficiency and improved financial performance. The term has been attributed to Stephen Roach, chief economist at the investment bank Morgan Stanley. But although it was originally intended as the antidote to the growing bureaucracy within large American organizations, downsizing became a flag of convenience for many organizations looking to boost profits by cutting headcount.

Downsizing was a natural extension of the prevailing ideology of the time. In the 1980s, market forces were elevated to the status of elemental forces. The profit motive was suddenly the one true social force, cutting through weak socialist notions of economic equality. Downsizing was pursued with such vigour and disregard for the human cost that its victims and survivors alike came to regard it as little more than a cynical exercise. In many cases where companies downsized, corporate income rose significantly while conditions for many working families continued to stagnate or decline.

In the twelve months ending June 1995, one half of the major US corporations eliminated jobs, averaging 8% of the company workforce. The term 'corporate downsizing' had come to mean the corporate practice of discharging large numbers of regular employees – often to substitute contingent workers, foreign workers, or workers employed by subcontractors.

At the heart of the downsizing movement was the outdated assumption that the sole purpose and *raison d'être* of companies was to increase the wealth of shareholders. Downsizers of the brutal kind included 'Chainsaw Al' Dunlap, who observed on ABC's *Nightline*: '...The reason to be in business is to make money for your shareholders. The shareholders own the company. They take all the risk.'

Confronted by the unpalatable face of capitalism, even Roach himself recanted, claiming that many companies had taken downsizing too

---

Ideas into action

Downsizing was very much in keeping with other changes taking place in the business world in the late 1980s and early 1990s. Probably the most significant is the trend towards *delayering*. Much of the restructuring over recent years has involved cutting out layers of middle management 'fat' to create 'lean' management structures. As a result there is very little spare management capacity to handle unexpected crises, sudden departures, or short-term projects.

That much of the delayering occurred during the recession of the early 1990s is no coincidence, of course. In many companies, the move to flatter structures has been driven by the need to cut costs by making redundancies among their management populations. A number of management theories and ideas have also had a major influence on the move to flatter and leaner structures. Allied to the downsizing trend was another management cure-all: business process re-engineering (BPR).

---

far and used it for the wrong purposes. 'Plant closings, layoffs and other forms of downsizing have certainly had the effect of providing a short-term boost to earnings,' he noted. 'However, whether ... [they] will also drive lasting productivity enhancement is highly debatable ... Labour can't be squeezed forever, and Corporate America can't rely on the "hollowing" tactics of downsizing to maintain market share in an expanding global economy'. Roach's conclusion? 'I'm now having second thoughts as to whether we have reached the promised land.'

On 24 April 1995, Mobil Oil announced quarterly profits of $636 million, 19% above the previous year's level and sufficient to put Mobil on course to break all previous records for profitability in 1995. One week later, the company announced a 9% boost in its dividend pay-out, citing a strong balance sheet, continuing cost initiatives and optimism about future growth opportunities. The following day, on May 2, Mobil announced it would lay off 4700 workers, or 9.2% of its workforce. Mobil Oil gained $3.88 or 4.1% in market value in the trading session following its announcement.

Public anger at seemingly unnecessary corporate bloodletting of this kind led to downsizing being reinvented in the more politically correct guise of 'rightsizing'. No one was fooled. The corporate world had overplayed its hand, generating a backlash. Pro-corporate and free-market purist ideas are unlikely to be displaced from their dominant position in American political life, but they are meeting increasing resistance.

Much of the damage, however, has already been done. The result is that many companies have lost some of their most experienced middle managers, who some commentators believe contain the 'corporate memory'. An optimistic view of the downsizing binge would be that it may have been a painful but necessary step towards the re-evaluation of the fundamental purpose of business in society.

Key texts and further reading

Gordon, David M. (1996) *Fat and Mean: The Corporate Squeeze of Working Americans and the Myth of Managerial Downsizing*, Free Press, New York.

Bamberger, William and Davidson, Cathy N. (1998) *Closing: The Life and Death of an American Factory*, W.W. Norton & Co., New York.

Boyd, Steven W. and Wooldridge, Bill (1996) *The Strategic Middle Manager*, Jossey-Bass, San Francisco.

E-COMMERCE

Generally associated with doing business over the internet, e-commerce is any commercial activity that takes place by means of connected computers. But despite the current hype surrounding the new web technology, e-commerce is no magic bullet. With a few exceptions, most companies are still struggling to create profitable business models based on the internet. As is so often the case, the practice lags some way behind the hype.

Jeffrey Rayport of Harvard Business School provides a framework to understanding the development of different e-business models. First, there was 'the content business' – 'People who supplied content to online services ... got credit for helping keep users online.'[1] Next along was the advertising model. This was driven by measuring the volume of traffic. More volume meant more sets of eyeballs viewing the content and a better selling proposition to advertisers. The trouble with this model was that a few sites dominated – search engines including Yahoo! and the like; and stars such as Amazon.com and CDnow.

The third business model was that of selling things over the internet. The enticing logic of this was that companies could be virtual with dramatically lower overheads than their conventional competitors. The most celebrated example of this is Amazon.com.

This evolves naturally into the fourth e-commerce model: 'never making a profit selling real products for real money.' This basically means establishing a base of customers and then converting their loyalty into money somewhere down the line.

Thankfully, the superficial hype about e-commerce is switching to the nuts and bolts of how you build online customer loyalty. Simply putting .com after the company name is not a strategy. 'Loyalty online comes not from brands but from empowerment,' says David Siegel, the author of *Creating Killer Websites*. 'The key to loyalty online is to empower groups of customers to gang up on your company and take it in new directions. You can't do that unless you are listening strategically. This goes way beyond customer service. This is about the CEO of your company answering e-mail from the front lines and empowering employees to use the internet as easily as they use the telephone today.'

For all the talk about e-commerce, surprisingly little has been written about how to manage the move from a traditional business to an internet-based business.

The internet has the power to change whole industries. It can happen. For some, it will happen. It will not be by luck, but by effective management. There are lessons to be learned from the implementation of IT in the 1980s. The companies that used IT to best effect then were those that approached it with a clear idea of what they wanted to achieve.

As Adrian Slywotzky[2] has pointed out, the question that enlightened organizations asked in the 1980s was, 'What business are we in?' In the early 1990s, that changed as companies such as Dell began asking, 'What is the best business model?' The question is now changing yet again. Today it is, 'How digital is your company?' The key question in the future will be, 'What can e-commerce do for the customer?'

In reality, it is all about applying the new technology to the right part of the business. The point is that it is no good simply creating e-channels for the sake of it. Digital technology is most effective when it is linked to a specific strategic goal.

So, for example, when Intel invested $300 million in CAD/CAM technology in 1986, it did so to achieve a clear objective. CAD/CAM was the digital answer to a purely competitive question: how could Intel create a two-year lead over its competitors? Becoming more digital in the design and production of microchips was key to improving competitive advantage.

Similarly, at about the same time, Wal-Mart invested roughly the same amount in digital technology to support a different business goal, digitizing its logistics system. By installing sophisticated communications and stock management systems to provide real-time-sales-and-ordering information, the company moved from atoms to bits. As a result, the retailer outperformed its competitors.

These two companies were in the vanguard of the digital revolution. The impact of their decisions is clear for all to see. Other companies are making investments today which will create competitive advantage in the future. The hard bit is figuring out where the new technology can make the most difference. The same rigour should be applied to e-channels.

Key texts and further reading

Ghosh, Anup K. (1998) *E-Commerce Security:Weak Links, Best Defenses,* John Wiley & Sons, New York.

Peppers, Don and Rogers, Martha (1999) *Enterprise One-to-One: Tools for Competing in the Interactive Age,* Doubleday, New York.

Shaw, Jack (1999) *Surviving the Digital Jungle: what Every Executive Needs to Know about E-Commerce and E-Business, Electronic Strategies.*

Notes

1 Rayport, Jeffrey F. (1999) 'The truth about Internet business models', *Strategy & Business,* Third Quarter.
2 Slywotzky, Adrian (1999) 'How digital is your company?' *Fast Company,* February.
3 Hirsh, Evan and Wheeler, Steven (1999) *Channel champions:The rise and fall of product-based differentiation,* Jossey-Bass, San Francisco.

Customer relationship management

To date, the move to online businesses has been characterized by a mad scramble to translate existing customer benefits and value to the internet medium. Customer relationship management (CRM – not to be confused with cause-related marketing), many believe, is the vital ingredient to building a successful online business and the key to unlocking the commercial potential of the internet.

Although they invoke the mantra of CRM, most of these crude efforts are merely a preliminary to the more serious and sophisticated next wave. The e-business intelligence company MicroStrategy offers this useful guide:

1 Make it personal!

This is perhaps the most important ingredient for success in e-commerce. Make sure that your online offering is unique in terms of both individualized content and personalization. This may involve allowing customers to stipulate what sorts of information they want and how they want it to be delivered to them. Offering a personal service online is likely to engender loyalty in a channel that is becoming notorious for stimulating customer 'promiscuity'.

A financial services company, for example, may want to offer a financial news information option. The company's 'information portal' should enable the customer to set the parameters for what types of information they would like to receive. Try to build in the ability to communicate with the customer *via* their mechanism of choice (mobile phone, pager etc).

2   Find out how many customers you have and who they are

For many, this is the starting point. Many companies still have no idea how many customers they have, let alone what their preferences are. Start by ensuring that proper systems are put in place to centralize all historical information that you have on existing customers. Then analyse what information you still need to build a complete picture of the customer. E-commerce and CRM project teams should work together to find ways of qualifying and categorizing customers, once all core information is gained and centralized.

3   Keep information relevant and up to date

Corporate web sites should not fall into the trap of looking like electronic versions of the corporate brochure. Web sites must be refreshed with updates daily. They should also provide forums for interaction and feedback. Ideally they should reflect the dynamism and growth of the company in real time. This makes the role of the web master a crucial one to provide these updates.

4   Make it active

Enable customers to subscribe for specific types of information that they are interested in. When new information in their chosen areas of interest becomes available, it should be sent automatically on to the customers' e-mail inbox, or even their pager, mobile phone or other personal digital assistant. The broadcast technology is already available in the UK to do this. The web site could also offer customers access to other valued information such as financial markets information, which may affect their share portfolio.

Triggers could be set up so that customers can be informed when an analyst has produced a report reflecting poorly on one of the shares in their portfolio. A further trigger might alert them if their portfolio has slipped in value more than 5% in a single day of trading. This sort of insightful information will make it easier for people to live their lives and will keep the customers coming back to your site.

5 Integrate CRM and e-commerce plans wherever possible

The web will be successful as a sales channel if it enables companies to understand their customers better. To this end, make sure CRM and e-commerce programmes are fully integrated and pulling in the same direction. The ultimate goal of both is to work towards treating the customer as an individual, not just one element of an amorphous and anonymous mass.

6 Gain board-level sponsorship for the CRM/e-commerce plans

CRM and e-commerce should solve the key corporate business issue of getting closer to customers and offering them more valuable products and services. They may even be critical to the continued prosperity of the company in the wired world. As such, they must involve board-level consideration and support. The board will also need to sign off the budgets to make any e-commerce strategy a reality and are therefore best involved at an early stage.

7 Build a customer-centric database

The key to success is to build systems that put the customer at the centre of the business. All the information on a customer must be stored and updated centrally and be made accessible by all customer-facing personnel. It is critical that information known about customers by a salesperson on the road is also known in the call centre and at all branches.

8 Ease of use is the key consideration for the e-commercially successful web site

Customers must be able to navigate around your site and get what they want in a few short clicks. Avoid long forms and make sure that you do not ask for information they have already given you during a previous transaction.

9 Integrate all 'touch points' with the consumer

Ensure, through implementation of advanced integration systems, that all staff have access to as complete a picture of the customer as they need. A single version of the truth, and an ability to share this information with sales, marketing and other departments right across the business, is critical.

10 Security considerations are critical in e-commerce

Companies must work hard to ensure total security of all personal information and to make customers feel happy about leaving their credit card details or passing other personal information via the company web site. Particular attention should be paid to securing 'sensitive information' like medical records. Failure to do this could also bring companies in breach of the Data Protection Act.

Reinforce customer-focused thinking in all training materials and programmes – stating and restating the importance of building and maintaining good customer relationships with every interface with the customer.

Ideas into action

According to Booz·Allen & Hamilton consultants Steven Wheeler and Evan Hirsh,[3] e-channels can be leveraged by companies at three different levels:

- as an information platform;
- as a transaction platform; and
- as a tool to build and manage the customer relationship.

The impact on the business increases as you move up the levels. Currently, most companies primarily use e-channels as an information platform, although, increasingly, they are experimenting with innovative ways to use them as transaction platforms and to build more sophisticated customer relationships.

The progression from information to relationship platform is a logical one. It might be tempting to try to jump to the third level missing out the first two but, in most cases, this is unlikely to be successful. In time, as customers become more comfortable with e-commerce, this may be possible, but for the time being it is more sensible to roll out e-channels one level at a time. The most effective e-channels involve an evolution from low value to high value platforms.

Level 1: Information platform

E-channels are already used widely as informational platforms. Technological improvements mean that their functionality is rapidly improving. Today, such channels are used to provide customers with instant information on product specifications and features. They also allow the customer to customize features and options – even colours – to make a personalized purchase decision. For example, Dell and Gateway both have web sites which allow the customer to build a PC to his or her own specification, from a list of off-the-shelf components. The site automatically adjusts the price. In future, smart interfaces – which re-configure to meet individual customer requirements – and higher internet speeds will make this increasingly powerful.

Level 2: Transaction platform

At the second level, e-channels provide additional information and a mechanism for making transactions. Such systems are already used to provide quotations, place orders, check availability, and to access additional services – such as applying for finance or insurance.

The stumbling block here remains the security of payment. However, this is unlikely to present a serious problem to the future development of e-channels. Some customers will be more comfortable with a parallel payment channel, preferring to place their orders electronically but pay by more traditional means. Increasingly, however, credit cards and other instant payment methods mean that the e-channel can provide a complete system for transactions. Amazon.com, for one, has shown that this is a workable model.

Level 3: A platform for managing customer relationships

This level incorporates the first two levels. It is here that e-channels have the most potential impact. By creating an ongoing dialogue with customers, they theoretically offer a way to market to segments of one. To date, however, the practice is a long way behind the theory. Some companies are experimenting at this level through interactive entertainment, special offers targeted at customer segments, and even tie-ins with other products. So, for example, internet service providers and magazines use information-push technology to deliver regular updates and advance information via e-mail. Over time, this will become more widespread.

The key attribute of the e-channel is its ability to push as well as pull information. Push too much information at the customer and he will become irritated and pull the plug. The internet is an exciting new frontier. It opens up new business vistas. But it would be foolhardy to assume it is an easy option. Far from it. At present, however, many companies are throwing money at the issue in the blind hope that it will transform their business overnight. Worse still, many are simply running scared that their competitors will crack the e-commerce code before they do. In some sectors, the development of e-commerce is reminiscent of the space race. In the 1950s and 1960s, both the US and USSR pumped money into their space programmes because each feared the other would beat it to the punch.

EMOTIONAL INTELLIGENCE

E motional intelligence (EI) is arguably one of the most important ideas to hit the business world in years. It is based on the notion that the ability of managers to understand and manage their own emotions and those of the people they work with is the key to better business performance. Like so many important management breakthroughs, however, its origins lie outside business.

Rising rates of aggression and depression in US schools led Daniel Goleman to compile the research summarized in his 1995 book *Emotional Intelligence*. He concluded that human competencies, like self-awareness, self-discipline, persistence and empathy are of greater consequence than IQ in much of life. Goleman asserted that we ignore the emotional competencies at our peril, and that children can – and should – be taught these abilities at school.

The ground-breaking book did much to raise awareness of the concept of emotional intelligence in the business community. The new interest is reflected in the growing number of business books and articles on the subject. Goleman himself is now a rising star in the management guru constellation. *Emotional Intelligence* was on *The New York Times* bestseller list for eighteen months, and was translated into nearly 30 languages. The term is now finding its way into management development programmes and on to business school curriculums.

Goleman, a psychologist by training, built on the ideas of the Harvard-based psychologist Howard Gardner – who is credited with the development of the multiple intelligence theory – and the Yale psychologist Peter Salovey. In his book, he adopts Salovey's definition of emotional intelligence. According to Salovey, EI can be observed in five key areas:

- knowing one's emotions;
- managing emotions;
- motivating oneself;
- recognizing emotions in others; and
- handling relationships.

(Salovey subsumes in these categories Gardner's earlier theory of multiple intelligences, including interpersonal, intrapsychic, spatial, kinesthetic, and musical.)

Goleman has gone on to explore the issue of personal and professional effectiveness. In a business world too often obsessed by cold analysis and intellect, he argues, the emotional climate is more important to the success of an organization than previously recognized. His 1998 book, *Working With Emotional Intelligence*, argues that workplace competencies based on emotional intelligence play a far greater role in star performance than do intellect or technical skill, and that both individuals and companies will benefit from cultivating these capabilities.

In particular, he claims that the emotional dimension is critical in determining the effectiveness of leaders, arguing that in demanding jobs, where above-average IQ is a given, superior emotional capability gives leaders an edge. At senior levels, 'emotional intelligence' rather than 'rational intelligence' marks out the true leader. This may explain why someone like Richard Branson, who twice failed his elementary maths exam, makes a better leader than someone with a degree from Harvard Business School. Branson's emotional intelligence – his 'people radar' – is much more keenly developed.

According to Goleman, studies of outstanding performers in organizations show that about two-thirds of the abilities that set star performers apart in the leadership stakes are based on emotional intelligence; only one-third of the skills that matter relate to raw intelligence (as measured by IQ) and technical expertise.

'Our emotions are hardwired into our being,' he explains. 'The very architecture of the brain gives feelings priority over thought.' In reality, it is impossible to separate thought from emotion entirely. 'We can be effective only when the two systems – our emotional brain and our thinking brain – work together,' he says. 'That working relationship, which encompasses most of what we do in life, is the essence of emotional intelligence.'

Ideas into action

The good news is that, according to Goleman, emotional intelligence can be learned. There are five dimensions to this, he says, each of which is the foundation for specific capabilities. These are:

- *Self-awareness.* We seldom pay attention to what we feel. A stream of moods runs in parallel to our thoughts. This and previous emotional experiences provide a context for our decision making.
- *Managing emotions.* All effective leaders learn to manage their emotions, especially the big three: anger, anxiety, and sadness. This is a decisive life skill.
- *Motivating others.* The root meaning of motive is the same as the root of emotion: to move.
- *Showing empathy.* The flip side of self-awareness is the ability to read emotions in others.
- *Staying connected.* Emotions are contagious. There is an unseen transaction that passes between us in every interaction that makes us feel either a little better or a little worse. Goleman calls this a 'secret economy'. It holds the key to motivating the people we work with.

This fits neatly with changes in the business world. Companies are re-evaluating the leadership characteristics they require for the future. Some companies talk about an inward journey. Emotional intelligence is part of that redefinition.

'We're talking about "relationship savvy",' notes Gill Stringer, executive development manager at BT. 'That's how you inspire people. We're looking to develop interpersonal sensitivity and a mindset that is about collaboration, and understanding what others have to contribute, and seeing partnerships as an opportunity to learn.'

In the last twelve months, BT has been through a major rethink of the leadership profile required to support the company's global ambitions. The new leadership profile was presented to the main board earlier this year.

'Our strategy for global expansion includes a high degree of partnering and joint ventures. As boundaries get fuzzier and fuzzier, leadership becomes more and more vital. It's always been a big issue, but the requirements have changed. We don't want people who will sit at the top of their organisational pyramid and say I manage what I control, and I control what I manage.

'The emphasis is on relationship management', notes Stringer. 'The critical issue is interpersonal sensitivity. This ties in with Emotional Intelligence. These issues are converging now for us not because they are nice to do, but because they are being driven by business objectives. We are moving to a more holistic approach.'

Key texts and further reading

Cooper, R. and Sawaf, A. (1997) *Executive EQ*, Orion Business Books, London.

Gardner, Howard, *Intelligence Reframed: Multiple Intelligences for the 21ˢᵗ Century*, Basic Books, New York.

Gardner, Howard, *Frames of Mind: the Theory of Multiple Intelligence* (10th edn), Basic Books, New York.

Goleman, Daniel (1995) *Emotional Intelligence*, Bantam Books, New York.

Goleman, Daniel (1998) *Working with Emotional Intelligence*, Bantam Books, New York.

Kurtzman, Joel (1999) 'An interview with Howard Gardner', *Strategy & Business*, First Quarter.

EMPLOYABILITY

Much beloved of human resources professionals, the concept of employability is meant to provide the basis for a new psychological contract between workers and employers. With companies no longer able to guarantee long-term job security for employees, employability represents a shift to a new deal whereby employers offer shorter job tenure with an undertaking to provide skills development and training which will make staff more employable later.

Employability grew out of the delayering and downsizing exercises that occurred at the end of the 1980s and early 1990s. As the eighties drew to a close and a global recession began to bite, companies took a knife to their cost-structures. Many set about restructuring and re-engineering; a process that shocked a workforce accustomed to the concept of 'a job for life'. The corporate landscape was permanently reshaped. As a result, the world of 'corporate man' is no longer. In the old economy, job security was a given. Employees willingly traded body and soul to the corporation. In return, they received periodic pay rises, regular promotions and a good pension at the end of their career. It was a win-win situation.

Downsizing and delayering changed all that. They represented the unilateral revocation of an unspoken, unwritten contract between corporate man and woman and the company. It is difficult to overstate the effects of this change. Many employees felt the corporation had let them down. The fact that it happened during an economic slump, when they were vulnerable and needed security, made it worse. Employees felt betrayed by the organization they had given their loyalty to. The bond of trust between employee and employer was irredeemably broken.

In the face of change, HR departments were forced to rethink what the company was able to offer in return for a degree of loyalty. The new message from organizations is 'we can't offer you a job for life, but we will add to your employability'. Typically, this involves a move away from the traditional paternalistic approach to career development towards one where the employee is expected to manage his or her own career prospects. Today, loyalty can no longer be taken for granted – by either side. Employability is an attempt by organizations to provide a new basis for trust in the future. As management commentator Charles Handy notes in his book *The Hungry Spirit*: 'The psychological contract between employers and employed has changed ... No longer can anyone expect to be able to hand over their lives to an organization.'

Whether employability is more than simply a conceptual underpinning for the reality of modern working arrangements, however, remains to be seen. Some commentators argue that the next step down this road is to move to explicit employability contracts. This would involve replacing traditional employment contracts, based on ongoing employment, with renewable fixed-term contracts whereby employees negotiate pay and development opportunities on an individual basis.

But not everyone buys into employability as a concept. One of the most vociferous critics is the influential business commentator Richard Pascale, formerly of Stanford Business School. 'A new social contract based on "employability" is the sound of one hand clapping,' he has observed. 'Its impetus is wishful thinking masquerading as a concept – a lived-happily-ever-after ending to replace the broken psychological contract of the past. The hard truth is, there is no painless remedy. In fact, the death of job security, like any death, means that we have to learn to relate to the pain, not escape from it.'[1]

Pascale sees employability as an inadequate response. 'Once upon a time, corporations were like ocean liners,' he says. 'Anyone fortunate enough to secure a berth cruised through a career and disembarked at retirement age. A clear agreement charted the voyage: in return for loyalty, sacrifice, bureaucratic aggravation, and the occasional demanding boss, you received job security for life. In theory, "employability" aims to restore the *quid pro quo* between the ocean liner and its crew. Instead of a lifelong voyage, companies take smaller excursions with crew members who understand that they might change boats after any trip. In exchange for employees making dedicated efforts during these shorter engagements, the company agrees to pay somewhat higher wages and to invest in the employees' development. This makes them more marketable when it comes time to move on.'

But, as he points out, it's not that easy. Employability is a simplistic attempt to shore up rents in the social fabric: 'There is a fundamental flaw with this convenient new arrangement: philosophically, employability is a slick palliative that sidesteps the need to confront our essential humanness.' There are, he says, three interlocking elements to the problem. First, job loss and employment insecurity is an inherently painful experience that triggers a loss of self-esteem and social identity. Second,

Ideas into action

Moving from the theory to the practice has been problematic for companies. As a 1999 report by the Institute of Employment Studies notes:[2] 'Employability is a concept that has joined the mainstream of individual human resources and national policy vocabulary. It has been summoned as the means by which individuals can cope with changing employment conditions, organizations can maintain their ability to adapt and succeed and the nation can enhance its competitiveness. However, despite such grand hopes, pinning down the concept can be elusive and turning the rhetoric into anything that can serve as a firm basis for action can be frustrating.'

The same report goes on to to offer a definition of employability which provides a useful framework for action. Employability is based on four main elements:

1 *Assets*. These comprise an individual's knowledge, skills and attitudes. Here the authors distinguish between *knowledge and skills* – including basic skills such as numeracy, literacy etc., or subject- and occupation-specific knowledge at different levels – e.g. from book-keeping skills through to senior accountancy roles; and *personal attributes and attitudes*, ranging from basic levels of reliability, common sense and integrity through to initiative, problem solving and commercial awareness.

Previous definitions of employability have tended to stop here. But the report also suggests that people need the capability to exploit their assets. This includes:

2 *Marketing and deployment skills*. These include career management, job search skills, and mobility.
3 *Presentation*. Being able to get a particular job relies upon the ability to demonstrate assets. This includes the presentation of CVs etc., qualifications, interview techniques, and track record.
4 *The personal and labour market context*. Finally and crucially, the authors note, employability depends on the ability to actualize employability assets, which depends on external factors, including the individual's personal circumstances.

The report's authors conclude that 'while employers talk a lot about employability, relatively few go far beyond exhortation'.

corporations and those who work for them cannot resolve these issues by themselves. Third, a new social context is needed to legitimize and deal with the grief associated with the experiences of loss and betrayal in our working lives.

It is difficult to tell whether employability is more than a corporate convenience. Along with empowerment (the next concept), it may turn out to be something of a Pandora's box. Having opened the lid on the loyalty issue, most companies have yet fully to come to terms with the wider implications. In the coming years, with skills shortages predicted, they are likely to reap the whirlwind. Smart employees will master the new rules of the employment game and may hold employers to ransom at a later date. Having made it abundantly clear that they are prepared to dump employees when times are tough, organizations shouldn't be at all surprised if the most talented employees feel no sense of loyalty to them when times are good.

Key texts and further reading

Tamkin, P. and Hillage, J. (1999) 'Employability and Employers', Institute for Employment Studies, IES Report 361.

Makin, P.J., Cooper, C.L. and Cox, C.J. (1996) *Organizations and the Psychological Contract*, British Psychological Society, London.

Notes

1 Pascale, Richard (1996) 'The False Security of Employability', *Fast Company*, April.

2 Tamkin, P. and Hillage, J. (1999) 'Employability and Employers', Institute for Employment Studies, IES Report 361.

EMPOWERMENT

E mpowerment is one of the most overused (and misused) words to enter the business lexicon in recent years. As the word suggests, it is all about empowering workers – providing them with additional power. Logically, that means the power to make decisions and pursue the best interests of the organization.

In theory, empowerment is all about the removal of constraints which prevent an individual from doing his or her job as effectively as possible. The idea is to cascade power – especially discretionary decision-making power – down through the organization, so that the people performing tasks have greater control over the way they are performed. Worthy as that aspiration may be, often it fails to translate into practice.

'Empowerment describes a management style,' notes Harvard Business School's Quinn Mill. 'The term is very close in meaning to delegation, but if it is strictly defined, empowerment means the authority of subordinates to decide and act. It implies a large degree of discretion and independence for those who are empowered. Generally, empowerment takes place within a context of limitations upon the discretion of those empowered.'

The origins of the empowerment movement date back to the 1920s and the work of Mary Parker Follett, the forgotten prophet of modern management theory. Many of her observations are as relevant today as they were when she made them. Follett criticized hierarchical organizations; she detested the 'command and control' leadership style, favouring instead more 'integrated' democratic forms of management. She thought front-line employee knowledge should be incorporated into decision making.

About power, Follett observed, 'You can not coordinate purpose without developing purpose, it is part of the same process. Some people want to give the workmen a share in carrying out the purpose of the plant and do not see that that involves a share in creating the purpose of the plant.'[1]

She was equally prescient on the subject of coordination.[2] She observed: 'Collective responsibility is not something you get by adding up one by one all the responsibilities. Collective responsibility is not a matter of adding but interweaving, a matter of reciprocal modification brought about by the interweaving.'

In a still male-dominated field it is fitting, perhaps, that the work of Follett should find a modern day echo in the work of another woman, Rosabeth Moss Kanter. Kanter, editor of the *Harvard Business Review* from 1989 to 1992 and long-time professor at Harvard Business School, has championed empowerment in recent years.

Change Masters, the book that helped establish Kanter's reputation, also helped establish the concepts of empowerment and greater employee participation on the corporate agenda. These ideas were developed further in her next book, *When Giants Learn to Dance*, which foresaw the need for companies to transform themselves from lumbering behemoths into more nimble creations – which she described as 'post-entrepreneurial firms'. 'By empowering others, a leader does not decrease his power, instead he may increase it – especially if the whole organization performs better,' Kanter observed in 1997.[3]

But early signals of the empowerment revolution came from Japan – interestingly, Japanese industrialists discovered the work of Follett in the 1950s and credit her ideas, along with those of W. Edwards Deming on quality, as revitalizing their industrial base.

In 1979, at the time when Japanese companies and management techniques were wiping the floor with the competition, Konosuke Matsushita of Matsushita Corporation, gave a presentation to a group of American and European managers on a visit to Japan. Describing the commercial battle ahead, he quietly explained: 'We are going to win and the industrial West is going to lose. There's nothing you can do about it, because the reasons for your failure are within yourselves. Your firms are built on the Taylor model: even worse, so are your heads. With your bosses doing the thinking while the workers wield the screwdrivers, you're convinced deep down that this is the right way to run a business.

'For you, the essence of management is getting the ideas out of the heads of the bosses into the hands of labour. We are beyond the Taylor model. Business, we know, is now so complex and difficult, the survival of firms is hazardous in an environment that is increasingly unpredictable, competitive and fraught with danger, that their continued existence depends on the day-to-day mobilization of every ounce of intelligence.

'For us, the core of management is precisely this art of mobilizing and pulling together the intellectual resources of all employees in the service of the firm ... Only by drawing on the combined brainpower of

Ideas into action

Empowerment is a worthy idea. The trouble is that making it work, turning the popular phrase into reality, often becomes mired in organizational swampland. In a *European Management Journal* article[4] Martin Beirne of the University of Glasgow examines the lessons which can be profitably learned from the many failed attempts at turning empowerment into reality.

He distils down the usual advice on how to make empowerment work to create an atmosphere that supports empowerment and fosters mutual trust:

- 'engage' with people to give them a sense of belonging and freedom to develop their interests in work;
- reorient the organizational culture to integrate empowerment as a way of life; and
- demonstrate and maintain trust by coaching staff and giving them a living example to embrace.

Beirne then identifies the common stumbling blocks to achieving this. These are the hardy perennials which dog making anything happen in any organization – lack of managerial support; unwillingness to surrender power; and an enthusiasm for high decibel exhortation of managerial fads rather than a more considered approach.

Beirne's insights are based on research carried out in Scottish nursing management. From this, he provides 'four characteristics of reflective practice'. First, 'the experience of empowerment is often driven (and occasionally derailed) by factors outside the immediate control of project managers and practitioners'. Dividing lines are an important issue. Second, there is the issue of organizational politics. Machiavellians will out. Any power-related issue is liable to be influenced by and involve political issues. The third element is that of 'recognising a plurality of influences'. It is easy and tempting to regard empowerment as a them-and-us issue. Life is more complex than that. Understanding the dynamics of the situation requires understanding of functional, departmental and other differences and loyalties. The final issue is that of 'appreciating real fears and legitimate concerns'. Managers may talk of empowerment while riding roughshod over the concerns of employees.

The conclusions? Empowerment is far more complex and challenging than many management theorists would have us believe.

'Unfortunately, there are too many success stories which gloss over the complexity of the processes involved,' concludes Beirne. It is only by understanding – or seeking to understand – these processes that an organization is likely to make any progress towards empowerment at all.

A large number of empowerment initiatives in Western companies have not yielded the results expected. There are good reasons for this. For one thing, simply telling people they are empowered to make decisions does not mean they have the necessary support to do so. Decisions require resources (money, staff, etc.), authority and information. In many cases, companies that talked about empowerment failed to provide these.

But there is another problem. In organizations where operational decisions have previously been made by middle managers and supervisors, it is unrealistic to expect them to give up that power overnight, or for employees lower down to be ready to accept it.

In addition, before the empowerment movement could build up a good head of steam, in many companies it was overtaken by the downsizing bandwagon, which saw many companies stripping out layers of middle managers – the very people who were supposed to cascade decision making under empowerment. In many cases this resulted in mixed messages, compounded by deep-rooted and often justified paranoia in the ranks of middle management. Not surprisingly, many empowerment initiatives were simply stopped in their tracks by middle managers who had no desire to give up their power at a time when they already felt threatened by redundancy.

In other cases, the wholesale removal of middle management meant that the handover of responsibilities was too abrupt, and the transfer of skills required to make empowerment successful simply didn't happen. In the most extreme cases, the effect was to hollow out the middle of the organization to create a decision-making vacuum at the heart of the organization, with no one prepared to pick up difficult issues.

Many companies failed to think it through. This was especially evident in terms of the failure to put the necessary supporting mechanisms in place or the will of senior management to drive the cultural change required to support the new 'can do' approach. Few companies properly considered the implications for training, resourcing and rewarding their newly empowered workforces. Giving people additional responsibilities suggests they should also enjoy additional rewards, additional training to cope with their new responsibilities, and a working environment or culture which is supportive of the change.

Where empowerment has not taken root, one or more of these factors has been sadly lacking. In the UK, Dr Ian Cunningham, director of the Centre for the Study of Change, notes: 'With the flattening of hierarchies, empowerment has become a fashionable term. In practice, it is often just a synonym for delegation. Instead of granting genuine power to their staff, managers remain as likely as ever to make the important decisions and only pass on relatively unimportant tasks to others. Delegation starts off as part of a manager's job which he or she then delegates. Empowerment, however, involves removing constraints which prevent someone doing their job as effectively as possible.'

Those organizations which have made empowerment work have discovered that it requires a fundamental re-evaluation of the role of managers within the organization. In part, this is because their old decision-making powers are being dissipated to many more people, but also it is because the new culture – to support empowerment – requires a new way of managing people. That in turn requires a new set of management competencies and a new way of understanding what management is there for.

Belatedly in many cases, companies and commentators are now beginning to get to grips with what these changes really mean. So, for example, they are beginning to realize that the role of a manager in the future should be that of facilitator, coach and mentor – rather than decision maker, boss and policeman.

all its employees can a firm face up to the turbulence and constraints of today's environment.'

His point was that when a Japanese organization of 100,000 employees was in competition with a Western one of the same size, the Japanese firm would be bound to win because it utilized and empowered the brainpower of all 100,000 people whereas the Western company used only the brains of the 20,000 or so people called managers.

The message was clear – but it took several years and a great deal of painful learning before its implications dawned on Western companies. With typical gusto they seized on empowerment as the answer to all corporate woes. But what they didn't realize is that it is a lot easier said than done.

Key texts and further reading

Byham, William C. and Cox, Jeff (1988) *Zapp!: The Lightning of Empowerment*, Harmony Books, New York.

Blanchard, Kenneth *et al.* (1999) *The 3 Keys to Empowerment*, Berrett-Koehler, San Francisco.

Kanter, Rosabeth Moss (1983) *The Change Masters*, Simon & Schuster, New York.

Kanter, Rosabeth Moss (1989) *When Giants Learn to Dance*, Simon & Schuster, New York.

Notes

1 Pauling, Graham (ed) (1995) *Mary Parker Follett: Prophet of Management*, p. 178, Harvard Business School Press, Boston, MA.

2 The work of Follett, who emerged from the late 19th-century milieu of Boston and Cambridge, anticipated much of the modern management writing. Indeed, a number of management luminaries have noted that after reading Follett it is tempting to think there really is nothing new under the sun. Leadership guru Warren Bennis, for example, notes that he finds her work, which preceded his own early writings by at least 40 years, 'dispiritingly identical' to contemporary leadership theory.

3 Griffith, Victoria (1997) 'It's a People Thing', *Financial Times*, 24 July .

4 Beirne, Martin (1999) 'Managing to empower', *European Management Journal* , April.

FOUR Ps OF MARKETING

Among the central functions of business, marketing probably holds the distinction of being the one most bedevilled by fashionable acronyms. From the marketing audit to mega-marketing and marketing warfare, the majority emerge meteorically, only to disappear just as quickly into obscurity. Some, a small minority, have proved to be more robust.

In 1960, E. Jerome McCarthy introduced a new concept to the world of business theory. McCarthy took the marketing mix (defined by marketing's *eminence grise*, Philip Kotler, as 'the set of marketing tools that the firm uses to pursue its marketing objectives in the target market') and identified its critical ingredients as product, price, place and promotion. This became known as the four Ps of marketing. It is a formula that has stood the test of time, and is still recited by students and known by virtually everyone in business. (The renown of marketing's four Ps is such that purchasing sought to follow its example with its own four Os.)

Key texts and further reading

Kotler, Philip (1967) (9th edition, 1997) *Marketing Management: Analysis, Planning and Control*, Prentice Hall, Englewood Cliffs, NJ.

Kotler, Philip (1980) (7th edition, 1996) *Principles of Marketing*, Prentice Hall, Englewood Cliffs, NJ.

Kotler, Philip (1987) *Marketing – An Introduction*, Prentice Hall, Englewood Cliffs, NJ.

Levitt, Ted (1983) *The Marketing Imagination*, Free Press, New York.

McCarthy, E. Jerome and Irwin, Richard D. (1981) (9th edition) *Basic Marketing: A Managerial Approach*, Richard D. Irwin Inc., Homewood, IL.

Ideas into action

Despite its popularity and longevity, however, it would be wrong to view the idea of the four Ps as anything other than a catchy, and fairly accurate, *aide mémoire*. Knowing what the four Ps are is unrelated to the ability or willingness to do anything with them. Just as the seven S framework (*see* p. 193) is not going to transform a company's performance, the four Ps are unlikely to turn a company into a marketing superstar.

Even so, at the time of their inception, the four Ps encapsulated the essence of traditional marketing. A company which successfully focused its attention on all of the four Ps *could* develop a soundly based marketing strategy. A company which failed to do so – or which allowed its focus to shift – was unlikely to excel at marketing.

Examining the four categories, first there is the **product** (or the service) being offered. This appears straightforward enough – though Philip Kotler noted, 'The idea of a product seems intuitive; yet there is a real problem in knowing exactly what it embraces'. Kotler eventually settled for a definition of a product as 'a bundle of physical, services, and symbolic particulars expected to yield satisfaction or benefits to the buyer'. This has since been distilled down to, 'A product is something that is viewed as capable of satisfying a want'.

Next comes the self-explanatory issue of **pricing**. In recent years, this has become ever more complex with an array of pricing strategies covering everything from premium pricing to seasonal or even daily pricing.

The other two elements are more wide-ranging. **Place** embraces how and where the company makes the product accessible to potential customers. This includes, therefore, distribution and logistics – and, increasingly, includes cyberspace.

Finally, comes **promotion**. This hides a multitude of activities, all of which have enjoyed an explosion of growth over the last twenty or so years. These include communication, personal selling, advertising, direct marketing, sales promotion, and public relations.

The attraction of the four Ps is that they give four easily-remembered categories under which marketing activities can be considered. While, at a basic level, this may be useful, it is less useful in a complex modern organization – especially one that is in a service industry. The four Ps suggests that the categories can be viewed in isolation. In reality, there is a myriad of relationships between the various components of any marketing mix. To follow the four Ps structure religiously runs the risk of overlooking such relationships.

Over the years since the four Ps were first introduced, many thinkers have regularly offered alternative classifications. Indeed, there is an endless array of potential combinations. Albert Frey, in *Advertising*, advocates separation between the offering (made up of product, packaging, brand, price and service) and methods and tools (distribution channels, personal selling, advertising, sales promotion and publicity). In their book *Managerial Marketing*, William Lazer and Eugene Kelly suggest three mixes – the goods and service mix; the distribution mix; and the communications mix.

Others, including Philip Kotler, have correctly pointed out that the four Ps are essentially a seller's mix rather than a buyer's mix. They suggest that more attention be paid to a buyer's marketing mix – the four Cs of customer needs and wants, cost to the customer, convenience, and communication. Similarly, it has been suggested that the provision of customer service should be added to the list. (Philip Kotler counters this, arguing that customer service is an aspect of product strategy.) Yet another author suggests that people, physical evidence and processes should supplement the original four Ps. More recently, two academics have moved down the alphabet, suggesting the RS-model of content, context and infrastructure.

Emulation is a form of flattery. The four Ps were a useful summary of the dominant parts of the marketing mix in the 1960s when mass industrial marketing was the order of the day. However, the nature of business has changed. No longer is the emphasis on volumes, but on customer delight. No longer does a company blindly start with the product and then attempt to find a market, but the customer is the starting point.

The nature of marketing has also fundamentally changed. The divisions between the four Ps are increasingly blurred, sometimes non-existent. For example, the four Ps are of limited value if you are marketing and selling your products over the internet. Despite great technological leaps forward, product, price, place and promotion are still important. The trouble is that defining their exact meaning, role and potential is more and more difficult.

GAME THEORY

Game theory is based on the premise that no matter what the game, no matter what the circumstances, there is a strategy that will enable you to succeed. If you are formulating business strategy to increase market share, playing poker, negotiating salaries or bidding in an auction, rules are at work, however elusive and intangible they might be.

Game theory was conceived not in the classroom or in the board-room but in the casino. In the 1930s, when he was a student at Princeton and Harvard, John Von Neumann was an attentive spectator at poker games. Von Neumann was a mathematical genius rather than a gambler and the result was game theory, a unique mathematical insight into the possibilities and probabilities of human behaviour.

While Von Neumann went on to apply his genius to the develop-ment of the US's nuclear arsenal and the first computer, game theory developed its own Zen-like language of dilemmas and riddles. The most famous of these is the prisoner's dilemma.

Invented by Princeton University's Albert Tucker in 1950, the pris-oner's dilemma is an imaginary scenario. Two prisoners are accused of the same crime. During interrogation in different cells they are each told that if one confesses and the other does not, the confesser will be released while the other will serve a long prison sentence. If neither confesses, both will be dispatched to prison for a short sentence, and if both confess they will both receive an intermediate sentence.

Working through the possibilities, the prisoners conclude that the best decision is to confess. As both reach the same decision, they receive an intermediate sentence.

The prisoner's dilemma has a fundamental flaw: game theory is rational, reality is not. Companies which have expressed an interest in game theory tend to be from tightly regulated industries – such as power generation; ones in which there is limited competition or cartels (such as OPEC in the oil industry). With a limited number of players playing

Ideas into action

Game theory is more than rational rules for an irrational world. Behind its rationality lies a world of daunting irrationality and maddening paradox. It is best seen as a way of thinking about the future, a tool to get people to think. As a rationalist's guide to business paradoxes, game theory can be a useful business weapon. Instead of seeking out strategies driven by win/lose scenarios, companies begin to explore the merits of other strategies, which may be win/win, with mutual benefits for themselves, their customers, their suppliers and even their competitors.

This enables escape from the 'negative sum games' evident in many industries, where promotions and advertising are quickly countered by yet more promotion and advertising. In such scenarios, the costs of doing business increase, profits fall and market share tends to remain distressingly static. Game theory is dismissive of such short-term, knee-jerk reactions. If you are going to play the game you have to think ahead. You make your move in anticipation of what you have calculated the competition will do.

One potential growth area for game theory's as yet minimal usage lies in partnerships. Nash's initial work tackled non-cooperative games where competitors didn't communicate. Now, game theory has spread its tentacles to embrace the growing trend for partnerships, an area where the full range of uncertainties is evident. Game theory offers a means of rationally interpreting the possibilities of cooperation as managers grapple with the myriad intangibles produced by win/win relationships.

American academics Adam Brandenburger and Barry Nalebuff suggest the new onus should be on 'co-opetition,' an inelegant combination of competition and cooperation. They argue that 'looking for win/win strategies has several advantages. First, because the approach is relatively unexplored, there is greater potential for finding new opportunities. Second, because others are not being forced to give up ground, they may offer less resistance to win/win moves, making them easier to implement. Third, because win/win moves don't force other players to retaliate, the new game is more sustainable. And finally, imitation of a win/win move is beneficial not harmful.'

by accepted rules and behaving in a rational way, game theory can make sense of what the best competitive moves may be.

Broader interest in game theory was re-ignited in 1994, when the Nobel Prize for economics was awarded to three renowned thinkers – John Nash, John Harsanyi, and Reinhard Selten. Harsanyi has shown that even if players in a particular game are not well informed about each other, the game can still be analysed in the same way as other games. The precociously brilliant Nash (brought to life on the big screen by Russell Crowe in *A Beautiful Mind*) has carved the most notable academic furrow and is the creator of Nash's Equilibrium, an idea developed in his PhD thesis.

The Nash equilibrium is the point when no player can improve his or her position by changing strategy. Players in a game will change their strategies until they reach equilibrium. (In the prisoner's dilemma the Nash equilibrium is reached when both prisoners confess – they can no longer improve their situation by changing their strategy, as this would send them to prison for a longer period.)

In one classic example, an industry includes two competing companies. Each determines the price of its product. If both were to set high prices they would maximize their profits. Similarly, if both set their prices at lower levels they would remain profitable. The trouble comes when they choose different price levels. If one sets a high price and the other a low price, the company with the low price makes far more money. The optimal solution is for both to have high prices. The trouble is if one company has a high price, the other will undercut it. Eventually, both companies end up with low prices and lesser profits.

The key lesson from this and other scenarios explored by game theory is simply that the interactions of companies and other organizations are interdependent.

In fact, game theory encompasses some of the fundamental truths of decision making. If a company decides to make an investment it should consider how others – whether they be competitors, customers or suppliers – will react. Game theory acknowledges that real life is not conducted in a vacuum.

Instead, companies must visualize and anticipate the reactions and responses of their competitors. In the jargon, putting yourself in the shoes of your competitors, considering their future moves and their likely impact is labelled 'allocentrism'.

Key texts and further reading

Axelroad, Robert (1997) *The Complexity of Co-operation*, Princeton University Press.

Brandenburger, Adam and Nalebuff, Barry (1996) *Co-opetition*, Doubleday, New York.

Holland, John H. (1998) *Emergence: From Chaos to Order*, Addison-Wesley, Reading, UK.

Osbourne, Martin and Rubinstein, Ariel (1994) *A Course in Game Theory*, MIT Press, Boston, MA.

HOSHIN KANRI

oshin Kanri is a corporate-wide management approach that combines strategic management and operational management by linking the achievement of top management goals with daily management at an operational level. It is particularly associated with change management. *Hoshin Kanri* has its roots in two well-established management techniques: management by objectives (MBO) and total quality management (TQM). At its core lies the *hoshin*, which comprises a strategic objective, a statement on how to achieve that objective, and description of how implementation of the objective is to be monitored.

The etymological origin of the term *hoshin kanri* is instructive. *Hoshin* can be divided into two parts. Literally translated *ho* means direction and *shin* means needle. This gives direction needle or 'compass'. *Kanri* can also be divided into two parts; *kan* which means control and *ri* which means reason or logic. So we have reasoned control and management of the organization's direction. The metaphor of a number of ships using a similarly-aligned compass is one often used to describe *hoshin kanri*, as are phrases such as 'policy management' or 'policy deployment'.

The concept dates back to Japan in the 1960s when Japanese industry went through a sea-change during which it took management practices such as Management by Walking About and Statistical Quality Control and blended them together into what would become Total Quality Control. *Hoshin kanri* has come to the West largely through the practice of Western divisions of Japanese companies, through its adoption in a small number of forward thinking Western companies, and through the writings of Yoji Akao.

A number of innovative Western organizations have adopted the practice, the first probably being Hewlett-Packard where it is known as *hoshin*-planning. *Hoshin kanri* is less a management tool than an organizing framework. At H-P, for example, using *hoshins* alongside what H-P calls business fundamentals forms a relationship where the closeness of

Ideas into action

Research conducted into the application of *hoshin kanri* has identified a *hoshin* framework similar to the Plan, Do, Check, Act (PDCA) cycle introduced by W. Edwards Deming and used in TQM, except that it operates over the much longer timeframe of a year.[1] The *hoshin* cycle involves:

Focus – this corresponds with the Act phase. It is the stage during which strategic objectives are identified by the company and its management. An important aspect of this phase is the fact that only a few essential objectives are identified and focused upon, rather than a general formulation of strategy.

Alignment– corresponding with the Plan stage and is about alignment of the corporation's resources and priorities of individual business units towards achieving the identified objectives. In this phase, the vital objectives are iterated in the form of *hoshins*, or policies. The *hoshins* are agreed through a series of discussions or meetings between various managers. It is a cross-functional process. It is also consensual, with the final version of the *hoshins* arrived at through general agreement.

Integration – corresponding with the Do stage, this phase involves the integration of the *hoshins* into everyday management practice. The *hoshins* are woven into an implementation plan. In turn this forms part of the company's annual plan or integrated business plan.

Responsive – equivalent to the Check stage in the PDCA cycle, the responsive phase is where implementation of the *hoshins* is evaluated, monitored, and amended if necessary. Quality audits, either annually or on a more frequent basis, may assess the progress of *hoshin* implementation.

Feedback from the responsive phase will then be factored into the next annual cycle.

the *hoshin* plan to daily management provides a multi-perspective, distinctive way of doing business.

    Hoshin-planning was introduced into all Hewlett-Packard businesses in 1985, linking the company's TQM efforts and its well-known commitment to MBO. In the H-P approach, senior management in its *hoshins* specifies vital concerns that must be addressed organization-wide. Lower-level management then incorporates these into their own *hoshin* plans as *hoshin* objectives.

The success of Hewlett-Packard brought the concept to the attention of other major US corporations. Since Hewlett-Packard implemented its *hoshin*-planning, several major corporations have implemented their own systems, often under a different name. So what was *hoshin kanri* in Japan and *hoshin*-planning at Hewlett-Packard became 'policy management' at Florida Power and Light, 'managing for results' and 'policy deployment' in different parts of Xerox, 'goal deployment' at Exxon and the original *hoshin kanri* at Digital Equipment and in the Western divisions of Japanese companies. Other companies that deployed a similar concept included Rover cars in the UK, and IT companies such as Lucent Technologies and Texas Instruments.

Key texts and further reading

Akao, Y. (ed.) (1991) Hoshin Kanri: *Policy deployment for successful TQM*, (originally published as *Hoshin kanri katsuyo no jissai*, 1988), Productivity Press, Cambridge, MA.

Bechtell, M.L. (1996) *The Management Compass: Steering the corporation using* hoshin *planning, An American Management Association Management Briefing*, New York: AMA Membership Publications Division.

Note

1 Butterworth, Rosemary and Witcher, Barry, *The* Hoshin Kanri *Method* (A position paper) The Quality Journey, the second World Congress for Total Quality Management, June 1997, Sheffield Hallam University. *'The Use of* Hoshin Kanri *as a Planning Tool to Implement and Align Strategy in Operations'*, Economics and Social Research Council.

INTELLECTUAL CAPITAL

C apital used to be viewed in purely physical terms – factories, machinery, and money. Now, the quest is on for greater understanding of the most intangible, elusive, mobile and important assets of all: intellectual capital.

Intellectual capital can be crudely described as the collective brainpower of the organization. The switch from physical assets to intellectual assets – brawn to brain – as the source of wealth creation is already well underway in the developed economies. In *Intellectual Capital: The New Wealth of Organizations*, Thomas A. Stewart, a member of the board of editors of *Fortune* magazine, claims that the changes taking place are as significant as the Industrial Revolution.

'Knowledge has become the most important factor in economic life,' he says. 'It is the chief ingredient of what we buy and sell, the raw material with which we work. Intellectual capital – not natural resources, machinery, or even financial capital – has become the one indispensable asset of corporations.

'Intellectual capital,' Stewart says, 'is intellectual material – knowledge, information, intellectual property, experience – that can be put to use to create wealth. It is collective brainpower'.

In other words, it's intangible stuff – ideas, imagination, and know-how, and 'knowledge workers' – people such as software engineers, advertising executives and management consultants who can turn it on and off at the tap – are worth their weight in gold.

The bust-up at the former advertising agency Saatchi & Saatchi, which led to the departure of Maurice Saatchi and his coterie at the end of 1994, Stewart argues, wiped out a proportion of the company's intellectual capital. As a result, it lost key client accounts and the share price fell.

Furthermore, Stewart claims, the only group of American men to make gains in their real weekly earnings since 1979 are college graduates, who are now paid an average of 80% more than high school graduates. In the new economy, it pays to have an education.

The new 'knowledge economy', he says, also augurs the 'end of management as we know it'. 'The rise of the knowledge worker fundamentally alters the nature of work and the agenda of management. Managers are custodians; they protect and care for the assets of a corporation; when the assets are intellectual, the manager's job changes.' In essence, his argument is that the rise of knowledge workers means that the bosses no longer know more than the workers (if they ever really did). As a result, the logic of the management pyramid – a small number of people telling a large number of others what to do – is redundant.

Much of the traditional role of managers is based on what has become known as Taylorism – after Frederick Taylor, the industrial engineer who founded Scientific Management at the turn of the century. In his own way, Taylor who was famed for time and motion studies in factories, was a knowledge worker. He used his stopwatch to break down complex processes into simple tasks, thereby increasing efficiency.

Taylor saw the way that management organized labour as the limit of intellectual capital. In effect, he saw workers as nothing more than the components in a machine, which was operated by management. Today's knowledge workers, however, are much more than simply cogs and wheels. What has changed is that the value these workers add comes not from the machines they operate but from the application of what they know.

In other words, today's knowledge workers carry the tools of their trade with them between their ears. It is they and not their managers who are the experts and must decide how to best deploy their know-how. As a result, what they do has more in common with work carried out by people in the professions and must be assessed not by the tasks performed but by the results achieved.

'A lawyer is not evaluated on the number of words in her closing argument but on how well-chosen and effective they are; not on the number of footnotes in her brief but on whether it makes a winning argument', Stewart says.

The lawyer doesn't have a boss telling her how to do her job – 'she has a client, a customer, who expects her to plan and organize her own work'. But, he might add, is totally unqualified to tell her how to do it.

From this, he says, it follows that the professional model of organizational design should supersede the bureaucratic. So where does this leave managers? The answer, Stewart suggests, is that the only legitimate role for managers is around the task of leadership – although they don't yet have a proper understanding of what's involved.

He says, 'If "values" and "vision" and "empowerment" and "teamwork" and "facilitating" and "coaching" sometimes sound like so much mush-mouthed mish-mash – which they sometimes are – that's a reflection of the fact that managers are groping towards a language and a means for managing knowledge, knowledge work, and knowledge intensive companies.'

'Intelligence becomes an asset when some useful order is created out of free-floating brainpower', says Stewart. In other words, organizational intellect becomes intellectual capital only 'when it can be deployed to do something that could not be done if it remained scattered around like so many coins in a gutter'. Intellectual capital is useful knowledge that is packaged for others. In this way, a mailing list, a database, or a process can be turned into intellectual capital if someone inside the organization decides to 'describe, share and exploit what's unique and powerful about the way the company operates.'

Intellectual capital is usually divided into three categories:

1   human capital,
2   customer capital, and
3   structural capital.

Human capital is implicit knowledge; what's inside employees' heads. **Customer capital** involves recognizing the value of relationships that exist between the company and its customers. But **structural capital** is knowledge that is retained within the organization and can be passed on to new employees. According to Stewart, 'Structural capital is knowledge that doesn't go home at night.' It includes all sorts of elements including processes, systems and policies that represent the accumulation of the organization's experience over its lifetime.

Intellectual capital is irrevocably bound up with the notion of the knowledge worker and knowledge management (*see* p. 127). Their root, as with so many other ideas, lies in the work of Peter Drucker. His 1969 book, *The Age of Discontinuity,* introduced the term 'knowledge worker', to describe the highly trained, intelligent managerial professional who realizes his or her own worth and contribution to the organization. The knowledge worker was the antidote to the previous model, corporate man and woman.

Go further back, and you still encounter Drucker. The foundations of the idea can easily be seen in Drucker's description of management by objectives in his 1954 book, *The Practice of Management,* in which the worth, motivation and aspirations of the executive are integral to corporate success. The individual is not an unthinking functionary valued for an ability to do what is demanded, but an independent and committed force.

'The knowledge worker sees himself just as another *professional*, no different from the lawyer, the teacher, the preacher, the doctor or the government servant of yesterday,' wrote Drucker in *The Age of Discontinuity*. 'He has the same education. He has more income, he has probably greater opportunities as well. He may well realize that he depends on the organization for access to income and opportunity, and that without the investment the organization has made – and a high investment at that – there would be no job for him, but he also realizes, and rightly so, that the organization equally depends on him.'

Drucker recognized the new breed, but key to his contribution was the realization that knowledge is both power *and* ownership. Intellectual capital is power. If knowledge, rather than labour, is the new measure of economic society, then the fabric of capitalist society must change: 'The knowledge worker is both the true "capitalist" in the knowledge society and dependent on his job. Collectively the knowledge workers, the employed educated middle-class of today's society, own the means of production through pension funds, investment trusts, and so on.'

Drucker later developed his thinking, most notably in his 1992 book, *Managing for the Future*, in which he observes, 'From now on the key is knowledge. The world is becoming not labour intensive, not materials intensive, not energy intensive, but knowledge intensive.'

The information age places a premium on intellectual work. There is growing realization that recruiting, retaining and nurturing talented people is crucial to competitiveness. Intellectual capital is the height of corporate fashion – prompting, among other things, three books bearing the title *Intellectual Capital*.

The challenge is that talent or intellectual capital is a scarce and, therefore, highly prized resource (one, but by no means the only, explanation for booming executive pay).

The rise in interest is understandable and, perhaps, woefully late in the evolution of industrial life. 'Of course, knowledge has always mattered, but two things have changed,' argues Thomas Stewart. 'First, as a percentage of the value added to a product it has grown to be the most important thing. Costs used to be 80% on material and 20% on knowledge – now it is split 70:30 the other way. Second, it is increasingly possible to manage knowledge.'

Intellectual capital is, in many ways, simply concerned with fully utilizing the intellects of those employed by an organization. In the year 2000, it is calculated that the UK will have ten million people who could be termed knowledge workers and seven million manual workers. In the US, despite the downsizing epidemic, the numbers of managerial and professional workers has *increased* by 37% since the beginning of the 1980s.

Stewart's contribution to the debate is helpful. He displays a journalist's desire to debunk some of the claptrap being peddled as wisdom. That said, some of the arguments are flawed, and Stewart raises more questions than he answers. To be fair, though, that's something he is well aware of.

'Too many business people want someone to give them plug-and-play answers', he says. 'Too many business books indulge them. This isn't a cook book. I'm not competent to write one, and neither is anyone else: The whole field of intellectual capital is too new ...'

That just about says it all.

Ideas into action

Having identified intellectual capital (IC) as important, the next question is inevitable: how can it be measured? After all, what gets measured gets done. Intellectual capital is increasingly codified as part of corporate life. The Swedish insurance company Skandia has a 'director of intellectual capital' and others are following suit – with job titles at least. Skandia's Leif Edvinsson is one of the thought leaders in this field. Edvinsson has come to view IC as both what is in the heads of employees (human capital) and what is left in the organization when people go home at night (structural capital). The third category that is sometimes added to the IC equation is customer capital, which is an attempt to evaluate the relationships a company enjoys with its customers.

Human capital, in the Skandia model, is subdivided into customer focus, process focus, and renewal and development focus. For each of these, the different business units determine indicators. Edvinsson has developed a model for reporting on intellectual capital based around customers, processes, renewal and development, human factors, and finance. For example, one of Skandia's divisions measures process focus (defined as efficiency of administrative routines) by two indicators: (1) phone availability; and (2) the ratio of administrative costs to total funds managed. Another division uses two different indicators for the same category.

No one is suggesting such measures are entirely accurate, but the aim is to track whether IC is increasing or decreasing. As Edvinsson puts it, 'It is better to be roughly right, than precisely wrong.'

Key texts and further reading

Edvinsson, Leif and Malone, Michael (1997) *Intellectual Capital*, HarperBusiness, New York.

Klein, David A. (editor) (1997) *The Strategic Management of Intellectual Capital*, Butterworth-Heinemann, Oxford.

Roos, Johan (editor) (1998) *Intellectual Capital*, New York University Press, New York.

Stewart, Thomas A. (1997) *Intellectual Capital*, Doubleday, New York.

INTERIM MANAGEMENT

I n recent years, a number of high-profile cases in the US and Europe have drawn attention to the concept of interim management. Probably the best-known example is the appointment of Steve Jobs at Apple Computer. One of the original founders of Apple, Jobs, who had been advising the company for some time, was brought in in an attempt to get the business back on track after the early departure of CEO Gil Amelio. A formal announcement from the company in September 1997 said that Jobs had been appointed to the post of 'interim CEO.' (Jobs subsequently became full-time CEO.)

The move by Apple is just the best-known example of a growing trend to use interim managers for temporary positions or to fill in until a permanent appointment can be made. An article in the *New York Times* explained, 'They go into a company for a short period to fix problems for a daily rate, without all the bells and whistles that accompany so many pay packages. In essence, they like to make changes and move on, rather than manage a stable situation or jockey for position in the hierarchy of a large corporation.'[1]

It is hard to pinpoint exactly when the first interim manager emerged. But most commentators agree that the practice started in the Netherlands in the mid-to-late 1970s.[2] At that time, it was seen as a way to get around the strict Dutch labour laws, which meant that companies taking on full-time managers incurred substantial additional fixed costs. The opportunity to take on executives on a temporary basis was therefore seen as an ideal way to add additional executive resource without the negative effects.

Since then, the practice has spread to other countries. Interim management is seen as one solution to corporate crises and other managerial resourcing issues. It entails the hiring of highly qualified, highly experienced freelance executives and dropping them into a business dilemma, with a specific brief and a limited length of time to implement it.

Such appointments can actually reassure investors. In September 1996, for example, PepsiCo Inc. appointed Karl von der Heyden to be chief financial officer (CFO) and vice-chairman for a year. A former chief of RJR Nabisco, his main roles at Pepsi were to help chart strategy in the wake of a string of operational problems that had plagued the company and to find a 'world-class' CFO to succeed him. Wall Street clearly approved of the idea; when the announcement was made, Pepsi shares promptly jumped 50 cents to $29.50.

Today, the use of interim managers – also known variously as 'transition managers', 'flexi-executives', 'impact managers', 'portfolio executives', and 'Handymen' (after management guru Charles Handy, who was one of the first to advocate flexible working patterns) – is establishing itself as a key strategic resource for companies.

Irene Schoemakers, who wrote her doctoral thesis on the subject, provides a useful definition: 'Interim management is the temporary placement of highly-qualified managers with the specific task of ensuring continuity within an organization. It can also be put in place to augment the skills of an existing management team.'[3]

An alternative definition comes from the UK's Association of Temporary & Interim Executive Services (ATIES). According to ATIES, 'An interim manager is someone who is appointed to a temporary position within the management structure of an enterprise either as a functional manager or director, or to undertake a specific short-term project.'

In her recent book *Strike a New Career Deal*, Carole Pemberton explains the rise of interim management: 'An organization seeks help because there are major projects where it does not have sufficient in-house expertise, but where once the change has been introduced, the job can be managed internally. They (the top management team) know that they are getting an individual who has not only done the job before, but will probably have done it for a far larger enterprise'.

At the same time, the changing business environment in which companies operate has meant that the wider strategic significance of the interim management concept is also becoming increasingly apparent.

Some commentators have suggested that in the US, in particular, the increasing use of interims has coincided with other developments. In particular, they point to the use of more-flexible working practices and the widespread reliance on temporary, or contract staff, especially among start-up companies in California's Silicon Valley. As an article in the *Financial Times* put it, 'These companies often employed a core of essential staff on a permanent basis and made up the rest of their workforce with temporary contractors.'[4]

What is clear is that the interim concept is very much in tune with other employment trends. According to *Fortune* magazine,[5] for example, one in four Americans is now a member of the contingent workforce – people who are hired for specific purposes on a part-time basis. (The magazine

Ideas into action

In practice, interim management can be almost anything that an experienced manager is likely to have to confront. Scenarios where an interim manager might be considered could include any of the following:

- implementation of systems, particularly new or updated high-tech installations;
- helping companies to take advantage of expansion or new opportunities;
- an underperforming company, one in dire need of reorganization, preparing a subsidiary for sale; and
- the sudden or unexpected departure or illness of a senior executive.

There are a number of reasons for its rapid spread. In particular, the speed with which an interim manager can be put in place is a key factor. To get to the shortlist stage using a traditional executive search firm, or headhunter, for example, it normally takes between three and four months, but it can also take a lot longer. An interim can be put in place in a matter of days.

Talking to interim managers, most seem to agree that there are a number of distinct stages that are passed through during the course of an assignment. While no two assignments are ever the same, they say there are some common characteristics in the 'life cycle' of an assignment.

Typically, an assignment will go through the following cycle, starting with a preliminary stage prior to accepting or being selected for the position.

Preliminaries: Intelligence gathering

- Assignment briefing;
- interview with client; and
- administration/contract/fee negotiations etc.

Phase 1: Getting to know one another

- Induction into company, including background materials and introductions to team and direct reports; and

- drafting of business objectives and a preliminary plan of what the assignment will achieve.

Phase 2: Defining the mission

The interim makes an initial assessment of the situation on the ground – which may not be the same as in the brief. This usually takes from one to four weeks, and includes:

- an audit of staff, the business unit, or department, or the project, leading to a rapid assessment;
- this is then fed back to the board of directors; and is followed by
- a senior management buy-in. It is at this stage that they say 'yes'. If they can't agree, there has to be a parting of the ways.

Phase 3: Setting milestones

This is when the real planning begins. With a mandate from senior management (often the chief executive himself) the interim can get on with what needs to be done. In the third phase:

- the interim prepares a more detailed strategic plan with milestones for the next six months;
- establishes credibility and tries to win the trust of staff;
- champions are identified inside the management structure and brought on board;
- obstacles are identified and planned for – for example, infrastructure shortcomings, or lack of resources; and
- resistance, if necessary, is neutralized or removed.

Phase 4: Engagement

This is the middle part of the assignment. In this phase, the interim and the team start work on the implementation of the plan. Typically, it will include:

- some quick wins. These give the team a sense of achievement and help build morale (often there are opportunities which present themselves in the first couple of days and can be written into the plan later);
- getting the team members on board and motivating them;
- celebrating successes as each milestone is passed;
- mentoring direct reports, so that the interim's experience rubs off on younger managers who will carry on the work after the assignment is over;
- working towards a clear objective – typically a challenging target set by the interim; and
- regular progress reports to the senior management and the interim intermediary.

Phase 5: Exit

This is the final phase of the assignment. By now the milestones in the plan will have been achieved. But the interim must ensure that the company does not become dependent on him. Some projects come to a natural end, but with others the interim has to manage his own exit. This phase may include:

- recruiting a permanent replacement;
- grooming an internal replacement for the role;
- setting an end point – may be a date, an objective, or some other event or development. (This should also be the signal for the intermediary to begin the marketing for the next assignment); and
- evaluating the success of the assignment (often a report to the senior management team).

says that over the past two decades, *Fortune 500* industrial companies have eliminated one in every four permanent jobs they once provided.)

Others regard the emergence of interim management as the practical application of the writings of the management philosopher Charles Handy. But, whatever its provenance, there is little doubt that interim management is a timely addition to the corporate resourcing armoury. Interim managers are ideally matched to the changing business environment companies now face. They offer a potential solution to the greatest blight on corporate life in recent years – that of redundancies.

Key texts and further reading

Dearlove, Des and Clutterbuck, David (1999) *The Interim Manager*, Financial Times Management, London.

Golzen, Godfrey (1992) *Interim Management*, Kogan Page, London.

Notes

1 'More hired guns wear CEO hats', *New York Times*, 28 June 1998.
2 In his 1992 book *Interim Management*, Godfrey Golzen puts the actual year that interim management started as 1978.
3 Schoemakers, Irene (1989) *Executive Interim management: Het bedrijf en die managers in relatie tot de Engelse cultuur, economieen sociale factoren, Rijksuniversiteit te leiden.*
4 Donkin, Richard (1994) 'The permanent temp is a Handyman', *Financial Times*, 16 March.
5 Cited by Klein, Marcia (1998) 'Sheltered jobs giving way to contract work at all levels', *Sunday Times*.

JUST-IN-TIME (JIT) (*KANBAN*)

J ust-in-time is an approach to inventory management based on the efficient delivery of components to the production line at the time they are required. One of the management techniques associated with the Japanese economic miracle after World War II, it is one of a range of quality approaches introduced by, among others, the Toyota Motor Corporation and the Kawasaki Heavy Industries Group, and is an essential part of the lean production process (*see* Lean Production on p. 138).

As computer technology developed to handle greater amounts of production data, the Americans created materials requirements planning (MRP) to provide the parts for products as they were required for assembly. The Japanese, however, went one stage further with their *kanban* or just-in-time system, which was more exacting than MRP in terms of the timing of arrival of materials. The goal of *kanban* was zero inventory. The concept aimed for a system whereby components for final assembly should arrive just when they were needed, reducing the inventory carrying costs. Early production management emphasized ordering materials in economic lot sizes, but the new model utilized computer technology to emphasize timing rather than the amount of inventory.

Since the 1980s, international competition and lessons from Japanese practice have encouraged the adoption of just-in-time methods and quality management methods throughout the Western world. Technological advances too have had a major impact on inventory management.

New mechanical and automated equipment has made stock movement more efficient with better use of warehousing and major improvements in distribution and logistics management. In particular, IT-based stock control systems with bar coding are integrated with other systems to give better control over order assembly, stock availability and monitoring.

By creating a system which pulls in parts as and when they are needed, JIT dramatically reduces the amount of capital tied up in inventory laying idle, thereby increasing efficiency and reducing costs. Under

JIT, the company must manage the overall supply chain efficiently and effectively. One of the most important aspects of this approach is that it forces companies to look at the total supply chain. Reducing levels of stock in manufacturing is seen as both an internal and external matter involving relationships between workers at different stages in the production process and relationships with external suppliers.

JIT, however, is not an easy concept to apply. In the past, a number of Western companies attempted to introduce JIT in isolation from other total quality techniques, without understanding the wider implications, and without instigating the necessary changes in production management.

JIT system developments have to be seen against associated improvements in production and materials management systems. Japanese successes were not only based upon a different industrial culture, they were also (and possibly more importantly) based on an ability to integrate more effectively a range of production and control methods that were already available. The use of techniques in product and control involves their application in a complex system.

Historically, Western managers have tended to be less able than their Japanese counterparts to bring these different operational systems together so that they function seamlessly and co-operatively. The Japanese are particularly good at integrating technical production applications into a single working model. Thus the adoption of JIT systems tends to be associated with other strategies, tools and techniques – many learned or relearned from Japanese practice.

Ideas into action

With JIT, production demands and the management of supplies are linked strategically and operationally. There are three basic aspects to JIT:

1 Reduction/minimization of inventory in supply chains. This is based on lessons learnt from Japanese methods where substantial efficiencies are gained from frequent deliveries of small quantities to meet immediate demands. (This compares with methods of stock control such as the calculation of economic order quantities.)

2 The application of *kanban* – a 'pull' system of production/materials control. At Toyota, the production system traditionally used tickets/cards to control immediate material flows between a work-station and another downstream. The upstream station

(the server) receives ticket calls for small, fixed quantities from a downstream user (the client). When the supplies are sent, a production *kanban* is generated requesting the previous upstream server to make/supply a replacement quantity. In this way, users 'pull' off supplies as required, and direct shop-floor communication between client and supplier replaces instructions issued by a remote centre control point. Materials requirements, planning and other systems get rapid feedback on progress or delays.

3 An employee participation and involvement strategy involving the securing of commitment and changed work practices leading to improvements in production efficiency and elimination of waste. This contributes to a continuous-improvement process which further streamlines the JIT process.

Properly implemented, these three aspects create a seamless supply chain which is highly responsive to changes in customer orders. Planning (medium- and longer-term) is still needed to manage capacity along the supply chain, but *kanban* allows fine tuning. Fixed-quantity bins or containers or pallets are used to signal replenishment needs. Typically this involves the use of two bins, which are revolved. When the first bin is empty, a new full bin can be moved in within the usage time from the second bin. With well-designed floor layouts this system adds considerably to the efficiency of the operational environment.

With the integration of computer systems internally and externally with suppliers' systems, *kanban* data and instructions can flow between the linked systems. If the production system itself is flexible, with quick set-up times for product changes, then the data flowing in the JIT system and the ability of servers to respond are critical.

However, JIT is not possible without:

- reliable delivery;
- short distances between client and server;
- consistent quality so that server performance and throughput is unaffected (the Kawasaki Production System, for example, places great attention on testing components before they arrive at the production line, thus improving efficiency by ensuring untested parts are not stockpiled and do not enter the production process); and
- stable, predictable production schedules; and the ability to respond quickly to small fluctuations in demand.

The human aspects of quality management are sometimes over-looked. Quality management systems that emphasize a 'right first time' philosophy also promote the 'empowerment' of employees *via* team development, quality circles and training. In particular, plant mainte-nance improvements to reduce down time and secure better reliability of machinery are integral to the successful application of JIT. This is coupled with improved 'housekeeping', to maintain clean, tidy, orderly facilities. Typically, this is part of a 'team or cells' discipline with staff making a vital contribution to the overall efficiency of the approach.

In recent years, many firms have implemented ISO 9000 systems to define quality standards, processes and control systems with documen-tation of action taken to ensure quality. Introduction of such systems involves close examination of existing production, operational and sup-port processes (including inventory standards and flows). Standards and systems are improved as a consequence. (The process of securing ISO 9000 accreditation is a learning and problem-solving process.)

Close examination before documentation enables changes to be made and foolproofing to be built in. Documentation itself, and the controls it reflects, involves a cost but it should also mean that problems, and action to tackle them, become visible. Customer orientation has encouraged product and service design improvements. These themselves may help to regularize material flows. Parts and materials can be stand-ardized using modular designs and fewer parts.

JIT is an important operational system for manufacturing and sup-plying companies to adopt and implement. Technically, procedurally and managerially it requires:

- attention to data, information and communication;
- assessment of requirements programmes to change the structure of production, materials handling, manufacturing processes and distribution facilities;
- improved methods of controlling unit supply costs; and
- a reappraisal of the buyer–supplier partnership and the possibility of strategic collaboration.

If change is piecemeal and management attention wanes, then JIT is unlikely to produce the desired improvements. An integrated perspec-tive is needed with coherent strategic direction to secure improvements in productivity/effectiveness at each operational level so that the whole supply chain has a competitive edge. JIT is only as good as the weakest link in the production chain.

Key texts and further reading

Ohno, Taiichi (1988) *Toyota Production System*, Productivity Press, New York.

Womack, James P. and Jones, Daniel. T. (1996) *Lean Thinking: Banish Waste and Create Wealth in Your Corporation*, Simon & Schuster, New York.

Womack, James P. and Jones, Daniel. T. (1991) *The Machine That Changed the World: The Story of Lean Production*, Simon & Schuster, New York.

KAIZEN (QUALITY CIRCLES)

A s much a social system as an industrial process, *kaizen* is at the heart of the quality philosophy, and involves the use of quality circles – or small teams of workers – to analyse and make suggestions for improving their own work tasks. In his book *Kaizen*, translated into English in the early 1980s, Masaaki Imai describes the continuous improvement concepts that underpin the quality approach.

The American quality pioneer W. Edwards Deming is credited with introducing the continuous improvement philosophy into Japan (*see* Total Quality p. 233). Deming's work inspired small, problem-solving teams of workers, supervisors and experts (later called quality circles) with the aim of improving the efficiency and quality of work. The idea was developed by Japanese companies, notably Toyota, and quality circles were instrumental in the Japanese economic miracle. While many Western concepts are based on the notion of a step-change improvement, *kaizen* is precisely the opposite. The word literally means 'gradual progress', or 'incremental change'. Through continuous gradual improvements, *kaizen* aims to achieve continual evolutionary rather than revolutionary change – hence the term continuous improvement.

Kaizen-consciousness is based on a group of shared values rooted in the Japanese culture. These include self-realization, recognition of diverse abilities, and mutual trust. These values lead to a strong belief that individual workers are the experts at their jobs and therefore know better than anyone else how to analyse and improve their work. This is the basis for a system which encourages groups of workers to propose, test and implement suggestions for improvements. Integral to this is an understanding that managers will consider and, where possible, support their efforts to improve the work processes.

The whole notion of *kaizen* is based on the Japanese philosophy of continuous incremental improvements. The pendulum may now be swinging back towards the Western style of thinking and the notion of a 'leap forward'. Interestingly, the pace of change means that many of the high-tech companies that have emerged in recent years take a much

Ideas into action

Quality circles are not a panacea for quality improvement but, given the right top management commitment, employee motivation and resourcing, they can support continuous quality improvement at shop-floor level. Quality circles involve quality improvement teams (typically of between three and nine workers) that meet regularly to discuss quality-related work problems so that they may examine them and generate solutions. The circle is empowered to promote and bring the quality improvements through to fruition.

The team members challenge assumptions and existing methods, examine data and explore possibilities. They need to be able to call in expertise and ask for training, the quality circle needs a budget so that members can be responsible for tests and possible pilots. They need a skilled team leader who works as a facilitator of team efforts, not as a dominator.

The circle needs to have a very good approach to analysing the context of the problem and its situation, defining just exactly what the problem is, the relationship between its component parts, and, especially, how it originated. Emphasis is placed on verifying that the causes are correctly diagnosed, otherwise solutions may be developed that fail to address the real problem. Problem definition requires quantitative measurement and often a consensus of qualitative judgement.

Specific techniques that may be used by quality circle participants include:

- process flow charts;
- *ishikawa* (or fishbone) diagrams;
- brainstorming;
- cause and effect analysis;
- reverse engineering; and
- Pareto analysis.

Team members require training and support to apply these to the context and the issue they are experiencing. Management has to believe in the quality team process, listen to proposals and enable feasible solutions to be progressed through pilot stages and into full operation. Open-mindedness and a desire to avoid blocking are essential.

more revolutionary approach to innovation, favouring 'discontinuous change' over 'incremental improvement'. According to MIT's Nicholas Negroponte, 'incrementalism is innovation's worst enemy'.

Key texts and further reading

Imai, Masaaki (1989) *Kaizen: The Key to Japan's Competitive Success*, McGraw-Hill, New York.

Imai, Masaaki (1997) *Gemben Kaizen: A Commonsense Low-Cost Approach to Management*, McGraw-Hill, New York.

KNOWLEDGE MANAGEMENT

K|nowledge management (KM) is one of the most influential new concepts in business today. A logical follow-on from the concept of intellectual capital, knowledge management is based on the idea that companies should make better use of their existing knowledge – everything from licences and patents to internal processes and information about customers. The concept has been steadily gaining ground since the early 1990s.

In a now-famous statement attributed to Lew Platt, the former Hewlett-Packard CEO said, 'If H-P knew what it knows, we'd be three times as profitable'. This sums up the challenge facing firms who want to create value from the knowledge that exists, in fragmented forms, inside their organizations. The logic is that in an accelerated business world, a company's knowledge base is really its only sustainable competitive advantage. This precious resource must be protected, cultivated, and shared among employees. More and more firms want to preserve their competencies and create corporate expertise, using employees' intelligence and know-how to strategic advantage. They see the key to success as making an asset out of what their workforce knows. Knowledge management helps groups gain insights from their own experience. It recognizes that a firm's competencies – not buildings, logos, or strategy statements – are its identity and the source of its competitive advantage.

In their efforts to corral know-how and expertise, some companies have even created the new post of chief knowledge officer (CKO). Those attempting to capture and exploit their hitherto hidden know-how include Unilever, BP, Xerox, General Electric and Motorola. Behind their efforts is the idea that they are sitting on a treasure trove of knowledge that could improve their business operations if only it could be captured and made available to everyone in the organization. Often, one department knows the answer to another department's problems.

'To make knowledge work productive is the great management task of this century, just as to make manual work productive was the great management task of the last century,' Peter Drucker observed.

The emergence of knowledge management at the threshold of the twenty-first century may be seen as a natural evolution from the development of quality management in the 1980s and business process re-engineering in the 1990s.

Quality management placed great emphasis on measurement, change and cross-functional teaming. Re-engineering emphasized the role of technology in streamlining business processes. With these lessons firmly embedded in management culture, businesses are turning their attention to growth. In pursuit of customer value, operational excellence and product innovation, organizations must now become ever more effective in managing the drivers of growth. These drivers are:

* productivity improvements among knowledge workers; and
* harnessing the organization's collective knowledge.

More and more people are becoming aware that knowledge is their most valuable organizational resource. But how can they determine the conditions that foster its generation, capture and re-use? By eliminating duplication and learning from best practice, companies believe that better use of existing knowledge could give them a competitive advantage.

Managing something as ethereal as know-how, however, is problematic.

The aim is that competitive advantage be gained from know-how that can be catalogued and made available to everyone. This has the added benefit that when employees walk out of the door, their knowledge doesn't walk with them.

What research has been done in this area, however, suggests that many knowledge management initiatives have failed to make a significant contribution to corporate effectiveness. In part, the problem seems to lie with the corporate mindset, and more specifically with over-zealous IT departments. Technology has its uses, of course, but it is diverting attention from the human dimension of knowledge creation. In particular, there seems to be some confusion about what constitutes knowledge and what is merely data.

In many companies, technology is being invoked as the solution to the knowledge-management issue. At present, much of the focus is on designing IT systems to capture the information that is swilling about inside organizations, rather than on how that information can be transformed into something useful that could be described as knowledge. Many knowledge management initiatives have involved the creation of large-scale repositories of information in databases or intranet sites. To

Ideas into action

A good example of effective knowledge management involves part of Rank Xerox, the 80% owned subsidiary of Xerox. According to Thomas A. Stewart, the story's origins trace to Xerox's almost religious belief in benchmarking (*see* p. 22) and sharing best practice. 'Like a lot of companies, Xerox usually applied benchmarking to the cost side of the ledger,' Stewart notes.[1] 'But in late 1993, managers at Rank Xerox's headquarters in Marlow, England, had the idea of applying it to the revenue side. The project was given to a team called Team C.'

Team C consisted of a couple of dozen people drawn from the sales, service and administrative staffs based in Marlow and in operating divisions across Europe, the Middle East and Africa. Team C's initiator was Lyndon Haddon, a Rank Xerox director. A programme was initiated to gather all sorts of sales data, making country-by-country comparisons. Within a few weeks it had identified eight cases in which one country dramatically outperformed the others. From the data, for example, it emerged that France somehow sold five times more colour copiers than its sister divisions, and that Switzerland's sales of digital copiers were ten times greater than those of the other countries.

After further analysis, Team C put together a book for each country's sales and service managers which showed how they benchmarked against the others, and how the top performers' systems worked. The team selected cases so that no country was the benchmark in more than one case. This meant that most got to teach as well as learn. Country managers were then told to pick three or four best practices to implement. In most cases, country managers visited the benchmark territory and were able to imitate its processes in a matter of weeks.

The results were impressive. By copying France's best practice in selling colour copiers, for example, Switzerland increased sales by 328%, Holland by 300% and Norway by 152%. In the first year the company calculates the knowledge-sharing exercise added $65 million to sales revenue.

some extent, this misses the point by simply collecting data without the understanding of its significance or usefulness.

There is a major flaw in this approach. Knowledge is not simply an agglomeration of information; it is the ability of the individual or the company to act meaningfully on the basis of that information. Information is not knowledge until it has been processed by the human mind.

Technology may be the conduit, but the rubber hits the tarmac at the point where the human brain and the technology meet.

In this way, a mailing list, a database, or a process can be turned into intellectual capital if someone inside the organization decides to 'describe, share and exploit' what's unique and powerful about the way the company operates.

But that is harder said than done. Research by Booz·Allen & Hamilton consultants Charles Lucier and Janet Torsilieri found that most knowledge management (or equivalent) programmes have limited results. Indeed they estimate that 'about one-sixth of these programmes achieve very significant impact within the first two years, half achieve small but important benefits, and the remaining third – the failures – have little business impact.'

Modern technology makes transmitting information easy, but companies have to create the right environment and incentives to persuade individuals to share what they know. The trouble is that 'knowledge', as the old adage tells us, 'is power'. One of the greatest barriers to effective knowledge management lies in the basic insecurity and fear that prevails in many companies.

The real issue for companies is: how do you persuade individuals to hand over their know-how when it is the source of their power – and the only guarantee of their continuing employment? Until companies address this, for most of them, knowledge management will remain a pipedream.

Key texts and further reading

Edvinsson, Leif and Malone, Michael (1997) *Intellectual Capital,* HarperBusiness, New York.

Klein, David A. (editor) (1997) *The Strategic Management of Intellectual Capital,* Butterworth-Heinemann, Oxford.

Roos, Johan (editor) (1998) *Intellectual Capital,* New York University Press, New York.

Stewart, Thomas A. (1997) *Intellectual Capital,* Doubleday, New York.

Horibe, Frances (1999) *Managing Knowledge Workers,* John Wiley & Sons, Toronto.

Note

1   Stewart, Thomas A. (1996) *Fortune,* October.

LEADERSHIP

People have been debating the nature of leadership for as long as records have been kept – certainly as far back as Homer. Today, the topic continues to fascinate and enthral us, but the way we understand the role is changing. Where once we looked to military and political leaders for inspiration and insight, today, increasingly, it is business leaders who occupy our attention and provide our role models.

The new interest is reflected in a plethora of business books and articles on the subject. Most writings on good management and what it takes to get to the top focus on leadership. No wonder, then, that it is regarded as one of the most important areas of personal development. This is reflected in the growing interest in leadership courses.

Just what makes an effective leader, however, is elusive. 'A leader is a dealer in hope,' Napoleon once observed. 'Managers do things right. Leaders do the right thing,' Warren Bennis, the American academic and leadership expert, added almost two centuries later.

There must be almost as many theories on leadership as there are leaders. Certainly too many to cover here in all their glorious detail. A potted history follows. Back a few centuries, Niccolo Machiavelli (1469– 1527) advocated a combination of cunning and intimidation as a way to more effective leadership. A Florentine diplomat and scholar of human nature, Machiavelli's main contribution to management theory consists of a volume on managing a principality, *The Prince*. An early entry in the 'how-to' book genre, it was written for the Medici rulers of Florence. In return, he hoped for career advancement. Machiavelli was an early advocate of the *Power and Influence* theory of leadership. At the heart of Machiavelli's theory was the idea that 'the ends justify the means'. Leaders can, and indeed should, be ruthless in their actions in order to achieve their objectives – which primarily consist of remaining in power. His philosophy, if not his practices, became unfashionable a while ago.

Great Man theories were popular in the nineteenth century and the early twentieth century, and were based on the notion of the born leader with innate talents that could not be taught. *Trait Theory*, an alternative approach and one still in vogue, tries to identify the key traits of effective leaders. *Behaviourist Theory* prefers to see leadership in terms of what leaders do rather than their characteristics, identifying the different roles they fulfil.

Much recent work has concentrated on trying to understand why some leaders are more effective than others by looking at their environment and context. *Situational Theory* views leadership as specific to the situation, for example, rather than the personality of the leader. It is based on the idea that different situations require different styles of leader. From this comes *Contingency Theory*, in which situational variables are taken into account to select the most appropriate leadership style in a given set of circumstances.

Leadership models have come and gone but, until quite recently, in one important regard our ideas about leaders remained constant. The image of the all-powerful leader at the top of the hierarchy persisted right up until recent times. Today that is changing. As the traditional command and control structures of companies give way to flatter delayered ones, so the old notions are giving way to new ideas about what leadership is. If anything, in today's non-hierarchical organizations, leadership is more important than ever. Where once attention focused on the individual who occupied the role, today, the emphasis is switching away from what many commentators now regard as the 'myth of the heroic leader'.

Some favour a more holistic approach, moving the focus away from the leader altogether to examine what makes others prepared to follow. In 1988, an important article in the *Harvard Business Review*, 'In Praise of Followers', began to shift attention away from the machismo of leadership to the less glamorous side of the same equation, the role of 'followership'. This moved the leadership debate towards *Transactional Theory*. This focuses on the mutual benefits to leader and followers from their relationship. Followers accept the leader's authority if they believe that person offers real benefits.

What the advocates of followership recognized was that to become an effective leader most people first have to learn how to be good followers. With a very few exceptions, this is as true of the corporate world as it is of military and political leaders. Aristotle noted, 'He who has never learned to obey cannot be a good commander'.

More than ever today, business executives have to operate as both leaders and followers in the daily round of their job. Leadership writers began to take more interest in the 'psychological contract' between leader and followers. In other words, they began to ask what makes people prepared to follow one leader and unwilling to follow another. *Attribution*

Theory looks behind the relationship between leader and followers to see why they are prepared to follow.

Transformational Theory is the other side of the leadership coin. Transactional theory views leadership as a bargain between followers and leader, and is based on the notion of self-motivation. It focuses on the commitment of the leader rather than the willing compliance of the followers. The transformational leader is self-selected.

These are some of the ideas that are now changing both the way we think about leadership and the style of leaders. This is in tune with other social and organizational developments including the move to more participative management and the rise of industrial democracy. Today, it is widely accepted that there must be leaders at every level of an organization.

Other new ideas are also gaining ground. For example, the notion of 'emotional intelligence', covered elsewhere in this book, is only now beginning to be widely understood. For the leaders of the future, it is likely to be as important as a high IQ. This may explain why someone like Richard Branson, who twice failed his elementary maths exam, makes a better leader than someone with a degree from Harvard Business School. Branson's emotional intelligence – his 'people radar' – is much more keenly developed.

Most important of all, the role of leaders in developing the next generation has too often been neglected. If we are to grow as a society this must be the priority for the future. As Sir Adrian Cadbury, former head of Cadbury Schweppes, observed, 'Good leaders grow people, bad leaders stunt them; good leaders serve their followers, bad leaders enslave them.'

Key texts and further reading

Adair, John (1988) *Effective Leadership*, Pan, London.

Adair, John (1989) *The Action Centred Leader*, Industrial Society, UK.

Bennis, Warren (1989) *On Becoming a Leader*, Addison-Wesley, Reading, MA.

Bennis, Warren (1989) *Why Leaders Can't Lead*, Jossey-Bass, San Francisco.

Kouzes, Jim and Posner, Barry (1995) *The Leadership Challenge*, Jossey-Bass, San Francisco.

Kouzes, Jim and Posner, Barry (1995) *Credibility: How Leaders Gain and Lose It*, Jossey-Bass, San Francisco.

Kotter, John (1999) *John Kotter on What Leaders Really Do*, Harvard Business School Press, Boston, MA.

Ideas into action

Action-centred leadership

Fashionable in the 1970s and 1980s, action-centred leadership (ACL) was invented by the British leadership expert John Adair (born 1934). For practising managers, it remains one of the most useful frameworks. Adair was a senior lecturer at the Royal Military Academy, Sandhurst, where he developed a model of leadership based on three overlapping areas of task, team and individual, represented by three interlocking circles.

Unimpressed by what he had been taught as a young officer cadet, he began to question the way leadership was being taught in the military. 'The kind of instruction I was given, as a second lieutenant in my National Service days (training to be one), was a list of 32 essential qualities as a leader,' he later observed. 'It occurred to me that I would have become a much better platoon commander at the age of 20 if I'd had better leadership development and training. It was on that simple principle that I began to persuade the army to review their approach to leadership.'

To replace the qualities or traits approach, Adair developed a functional approach to leadership (behavioural theory), drawing on (amongst others) Fayol's classic theories and Maslow on motivation. Adair saw a clear difference between 'managing' and 'leading'. He said that 50% of performance within teams comes from self (agreeing with McGregor's Theory Y) but the other 50% comes from the quality of leadership. Leaders should be good at inspiring others: this depends on their own motivation and their ability to communicate and share that enthusiasm and commitment with the rest of the team.

Adair identified the key leadership functions as planning, initiating, controlling, supporting, informing and evaluating, and he used these functions as a framework. But his model is best known for its three overlapping areas of leadership responsibility. The leader, he said, had a responsibility to help a group to achieve its task, to build it as a team, and to develop and motivate the individual members. (Britain's armed forces still base their leadership training on Adair's approach.) In the business context, action-centred leadership was all about transforming managers from administrators into leaders. The concept established Adair as an internationally respected authority on the subject. Adair's conception of three overlapping areas of task, team and

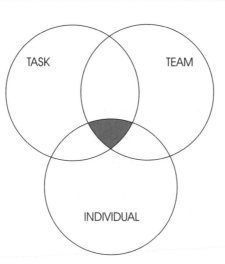

Action-centred leadership

individual was condensed into a Venn diagram of three interlocked circles. The logo was printed on laminated cards and handed to countless supervisors and managers long before flipcharts and overhead projectors were adopted.

According to Adair's model, the role of the leader is akin to that of a juggler trying to keep three circles representing task, team and individual in the air at the same time as making sure they don't fall out of harmony with each other. If the team circle becomes too dominant, the team will degenerate into a committee. Concentrate too much on the task, and the leader ends up as a dictator. Allow the individual circle to fall away from the others, and anarchy beckons.

When he left the army, Adair worked extensively in industry. His business career included a ten-year stint at ICI, where he helped develop the company's 'Manager-Leader' concept. Among British managers, he observed, leadership was often lacking. This led him to conclude that there were important differences between the traditional role of the manager and that of a leader. Traditional managers, he noted, kept the organization or company running. Their function was to control and administer. The role of business leaders, on the other hand, was to give direction, particularly in times of change. Their job was to inspire or encourage, to build teamwork or to set an example.

He applied the model he had developed at Sandhurst, taking the best of the military approach to the business world. In Adair's view, leadership was tempered through action – being placed in situations where leaders could experience leadership for themselves. At Sandhurst, he had learned the importance of combining theory with practice, and back in civilian life he sought to apply the same lessons.

His functional approach to leadership was widely applied in civilian organizations, thanks largely to the evangelical efforts of the Industrial Society, a training organization which took it as the basis for a management course called Action-Centred Leadership. Central to the approach was a belief that the skills of leadership were practical and could be learned by almost anyone.

The success of action-centred leadership reflected the growing interest in training at the time. In the 1950s and 1960s, there was little to help aspiring executives gain the leadership skills they needed. By the 1970s, a number of approaches were emerging to fill this need. Early management gurus from America sold books by the thousand, and from Japan came rumours of new non-hierarchical ways of working. In Britain, Adair reworked War Office and Sandhurst techniques for consumption in civilian life.

The context in Britain was especially fertile for ideas imported from the military. The 1970s was the era of industrial unrest. The term 'the British disease' denoted what many saw as the poor management and industrial relations record of British industry. The military provided a codified method of telling people what to do, in a class-riven workplace environment that mirrored the divide between officers and men. From the military came the precursors of the Outward Bound movement, and leadership training has been associated with fording rivers and scaling mountains ever since. But the hunger for military techniques also represented an attempt to try to bring order to the chaos.

In another curious precursor to modern training techniques, the 1949 war film *Twelve O'Clock High*, directed by Henry King, was shown to business managers to teach them the importance of accountability, long before the arrival of training videos. The Oscar-nominated film, which was already being used in military training establishments, features a beleaguered American bomber crew based in England, whose commanding officer is removed because he's thought to be too closely involved with his men. Military trainers would stop the film at the point when the commander is dismissed, and question their students about the leader's flaws and whether it was right to dismiss him. As the film unfolds, they would review the leadership approach and flaws of the new commander – played by Gregory Peck.

For years, managers attending the Industrial Society's action-centred leadership courses would find themselves watching *Twelve O'Clock High* and then discussing its application to their own workplaces. It may seem somewhat outdated today, but Adair's teaching was revolutionary at the time. He and other early leadership writers filled a vacuum in the business world. The military may no longer be a fashionable business model, but Adair's work anticipated the shift that many companies are currently trying to achieve in management development.

The belief that leaders tend to be made, not born, is now widely accepted in the business world, as is the need for leadership as well as administrative skills among managers.

'Management is a dead duck now,' Adair has observed. 'To compete and grow in global market places companies must concentrate on being creative and innovative, and to achieve this they will need people-centred leaders, not old-style macho managers. But too many managers will see themselves as controllers, allocators or accountants.'

LEAN PRODUCTION

L ean production is a catch-all term to describe a combination of techniques used to help companies attain low cost status (e.g. just-in-time and TQM). The lean production system was pioneered by Toyota and involves three main points: redesigning each process step so that it is part of a continuous flow; setting up multi-functional teams; and continually striving for improvement, both in terms of quality and of cost reduction.

Although it is a relatively new term, the genesis of lean production goes back much further. Its origins lie in Japan in the years after World War II, and specifically with the development of the Toyota Motor Company. In the beginning – in 1918 – the company was called the Toyoda Spinning & Weaving Co. In the 1930s the development of automatic looms convinced the company that its future lay elsewhere. Kiichiro Toyoda, the founder's son, had studied engineering, and visited the US and Europe. He decided the future lay in car making and changed the company's name to Toyota in 1936. In the aftermath of World War II, Toyoda announced his company's intention to 'catch up with America in three years. Otherwise, the automobile industry of Japan will not survive.' (Toyoda remained as company president until 1950 and the company was run by a member of the Toyoda family until 1995.) Within twelve years, the company began its assault on the US automobile industry.

Ideas into action

The name of one company is synonymous with lean production – Toyota. Through the diligent application of total quality management techniques, Toyota progressed to what became labelled lean production, or the Toyota Production System. (The architect of this is usually acknowledged as being Taichi Ohno, who wrote a short book on the Toyota approach and later became a consultant.) From Toyota's point of view, there was nothing revolutionary in lean production. In fact, lean production was an integral part of Toyota's commitment to quality and its roots can be traced back to the 1950s and the ideas of W. Edwards Deming.

Lean production was based on three simple principles. The first was that of just-in-time production. There is no point in producing cars, or anything else, in blind anticipation of someone buying them. Waste (*muda*) is bad. Production has to be closely tied to the market's requirements. Second, responsibility for quality rests with everyone and any quality defects need to be rectified as soon as they are identified. The third, more elusive, concept was the 'value stream'. Instead of seeing the company as a series of unrelated products and processes, it should be seen as a continuous and uniform whole, a stream including suppliers as well as customers.

Toyota's production philosophy reached its high point in 1990 with the launch of the Lexus. The Lexus was initially greeted as a triumph for Japanese imitation. Media pundits laughed at the company's effrontery – 'If Toyota could have slapped a Mercedes star on the front of the Lexus, it would have fooled most of the people most of the time.'

With the Lexus, Toyota moved the goalposts. It out-engineered Mercedes and BMW. Toyota is keen to tell you that the Lexus took seven years; $2 billion; 1400 engineers; 2300 technicians; 450 prototypes; and generated 200 patents. Its standard fittings include a satellite navigation system and much more. Typically, no detail was overlooked. Toyota made great play of the fact that the car was tested in Japan on mile after mile of carefully built highways which exactly imitated roads in the US, Germany or the UK. Toyota even put in the right road signs.

While the product stood up to scrutiny, where the Lexus really stole a march on its rivals was through the Lexus ownership experience. Even when things went wrong, the service was good. (In a sense, customer service can be seen as an extension of the lean production philosophy of JIT beyond manufacturing.) An early problem led to a product recall. Lexus had dealers call up people personally and immediately. Instead of having a negative effect, this strengthened the channel. Lexus screwed things up like everyone else, but then they sorted the problem out in a friendly, human way. With the Lexus, Toyota proved that its capacity to stay ahead of the pack remains undiminished.

How the company achieved its remarkable aim is the story of lean production. Visitors to the Toyota headquarters building in Japan can still find three portraits. One is of the company's founder; the next of the company's current president; and the final one is a portrait of the American quality guru, W. Edwards Deming. Deming was the inspiration and the original source of the techniques that gave rise to the lean production concept.

The first Toyota car was the Model AA. (As something of an insurance policy, the company also continued in its old business – looms were still produced until the early 1950s.) In the 1950s Toyota established offices in Taiwan and Saudi Arabia. It began making forklift trucks (and is now the world number one in that market) and entered the American market (1958) and later the UK market (1965).

Its initial foray into the US proved unsuccessful. Its Crown model was designed for the Japanese market and was ill-suited to American freeways. A willingness to adapt and sheer tenacity meant that despite its initial disappointment, in the 1960s the company managed to establish itself in the US market. In 1968 the success of the Corolla enabled it to make a great leap forwards – by 1975 it had replaced Volkswagen as the US's number one auto importer. Along the way, the company acquired an unrivalled reputation for build quality and reliability. In 1984, Toyota entered into a joint venture with General Motors to build Toyotas in California. (The joint venture also makes the GM Prizm.) This joint venture led to a rise in Western interest in the company and its methods.

More successes followed. The Toyota Camry was the best-selling car in the US in 1997. Toyota is now the third biggest car maker in the world (behind GM and Ford). It produces 4.5 million vehicles a year. In Japan it has nearly 40% of the market. Its pre tax profits in the financial year ending March 2002 were 1.11 trillion yen, making it the first non-financial firm to post profits in excess of 1 trillion yen ($7.5bn)

Behind all this lurks the presence of Deming and Walter Shewhart, whose work on statistical control process (SCP) was instrumental to many of the new production techniques, and the practical application of their ideas. Toyota's decision to follow Deming's quality philosophy was one of the most influential of the twentieth century. While Western companies produced gas-guzzling cars with costly, large and unhappy workforces in the 1970s, Toyota was forging ahead with implementation of Deming's ideas. In the early eighties, Western companies finally woke up and began to implement Deming's quality gospel. By then it was too late. Toyota had moved on. (In fact, it didn't mind telling Western companies all about total quality management for this very reason.)

Key texts and further reading

Monden, Yasuhiro (1988) *Toyota Production System*, Institute of Industrial Engineers.

Ohno, Taichi (1988) *Toyota Production System*, Productivity Press, Portland, OR.

Womack, James and Jones, Daniel T. (1996) *Lean Thinking*, Simon & Schuster, New York.

Womack, James, Jones, Daniel T. and Roos, Daniel (1990) *The Machine That Changed The World*, Rawson Associates/Macmillan.

THE LEARNING ORGANIZATION

T he work of Peter Senge at MIT's Sloan School of Business has been influential in convincing companies that the ability to learn is a key success factor for organizations. Senge has undoubtedly done much to develop and popularize the concept of the learning organization. However, the term was first used by Harvard Business School's Chris Argyris (born 1923) to mean a firm that learns as it goes along, adjusting its way of doing business very responsively.

Closely involved in and greatly influenced by the human relations school of the late 1950s, Argyris has examined learning processes, both in individual and corporate terms, in depth. 'Most people define learning too narrowly as mere *problem solving*, so they focus on identifying and correcting errors in the external environment. Solving problems is important, but if learning is to persist managers and employees must also look inward. They need to reflect critically on their own behaviour,' he says.[1] Problems with learning, as Argyris has revealed, are not restricted to a particular social or professional group. Indeed, it is the very people we expect to be good at learning – teachers, consultants and other 'professionals' – who often prove the most inadequate at actually doing so.

Argyris's most influential work was carried out with Donald Schön (most importantly in their 1974 book, *Theory in Practice,* and their 1978 book, *Organizational Learning*). Argyris and Schön originated two basic organizational models. Model 1 was based on the premise that we seek to manipulate and form the world in accordance with our individual aspirations and wishes. In Model 1, managers concentrate on establishing individual goals. They keep to themselves and don't voice concerns or disagreements. The onus is on creating a conspiracy of silence in which everyone dutifully keeps his or her head down.

Defence is the primary activity in a Model 1 organization, though occasionally the best means of defence is attack. Model 1 managers are prepared to inflict change on others, but resist any attempt to change their own thinking and working practices. These organizations are characterized by what Argyris and Schön labelled 'single-loop learning' ('when the detection and correction of organizational error permits the organization to carry on its present policies and achieve its current objectives').

In contrast, Model 2 organizations emphasize 'double-loop learning' which Argyris and Schön described as 'when organizational error is detected and corrected in ways that involve the modification of underlying norms, policies, and objectives'. In Model 2 organizations, managers act on information. They debate issues, they respond to change, and they are prepared to change. They learn from others. A virtuous circle emerges of learning and understanding. 'Most organizations do quite well in single-loop learning but have great difficulties in double-loop learning,' concluded Argyris and Schön.

In addition, Argyris and Schön proposed a final form of learning which offered even greater challenges. This was 'deutero-learning', 'inquiring into the learning system by which an organization detects and corrects its errors'.

While defensiveness has remained endemic, corporate fashions have moved Argyris's way. 'Any company that aspires to succeed in the tougher business environment of the 1990s must first resolve a basic dilemma: success in the marketplace increasingly depends on learning, yet most people don't know how to learn. What's more, those members of the organization that many assume to be the best at learning are, in fact, not very good at it,' he noted in a 1991 *Harvard Business Review* article.[2]

The entire concept of learning was brought back on to the agenda with the publication and success of the 1990 book, *The Fifth Discipline*. Written by MIT's Peter Senge, it was released to immediate acclaim. 'Forget your old, tired ideas about leadership,' *Fortune* magazine advised its readers, 'The most successful corporation of the 1990s will be something called a learning organization.'

The Fifth Discipline brought the learning organization concept to a mass audience. It was the result of extensive research by Senge and his team at the Centre for Organizational Learning at MIT's Sloan School of management. In it, Senge argued that learning from the past is vital for success in the future. 'In the simplest sense, a learning organization is a group of people who are continually enhancing their capability to create their future,' he said. 'The traditional meaning of the word *learning* is much deeper than just *taking information in*. It is about changing individuals so that they produce results they care about, accomplish things that are important to them.'

The organizations that thrive, Senge claimed, would be those that discovered how to tap their people's commitment and capacity to learn at every level in the company. This involved encouraging managers and other employees to experiment with new ideas and feed back the results to the wider organization.

Ideas into action

In *The Fifth Discipline*, Peter Senge claimed that successful companies of the future would be learning organizations. What would distinguish these learning organizations from the traditional 'controlling organizations' would be mastery of certain key disciplines. Senge identified five new 'competent technologies' which provide the vital dimensions in building organizations that can truly learn. These are:

- *Systems thinking*. Senge champions systems thinking, recognizing that things are interconnected. He introduced the idea of systems archetypes, to help managers identify unhelpful repetitive patterns and problems. He also explicitly recognized that organizations are complex – and messy – systems.
- *Personal mastery*. Learning is not a passive process. Senge grounds this idea in the familiar competencies and skills associated with management, but also includes spiritual growth – opening oneself up to a progressively deeper reality – and living life from a creative rather than a reactive viewpoint. It is only by exercising their will to learn that individuals can master the complex processes involved. This discipline involves two underlying movements – continually learning how to see current reality more clearly – and the ensuing gap between vision and reality produces the creative tension from which learning arises.
- *Mental models*. Noting that many of the best ideas never get put into practice, Senge asserts that this is not the result of weak intentions but because the new ideas are in conflict with deeply held internal images of how the world works. The organization's current view of the world and assumptions about reality get in the way. These 'mental models' limit organizations to familiar ways of working. Senge alerts managers to the power of patterns of thinking at the organizational level and the importance of non-defensive inquiry into the nature of these patterns.
- *Shared vision*. Here Senge stresses the importance of co-creation and argues that shared vision can only be built on personal vision. At its simplest level, he says, shared vision is the answer to the question: 'What do we want to create?' It may be inspired by an idea, but once it becomes compelling enough to acquire the support of more than one person, it moves beyond an abstraction. He claims that shared vision is present when the task that follows

from the vision is no longer seen by the team members as separate from the self. 'A shared vision is a vision that many people are truly committed to, because it reflects their own personal vision.' 'Shared vision is vital for learning organizations because it provides the focus and energy for learning.'

- *Team learning.* This requires alignment of goals but also a clear understanding of two practices: dialogue and discussion. The former is characterized by its exploratory nature, the latter by the opposite process of narrowing down the field to the best alternative for the decisions that need to be made. The two are complementary, but the benefits of combining them only come from having previously separated them. Most teams lack the ability to distinguish between the two and to move consciously between them.

The book looked at how firms and other organizations can develop adaptive capabilities in a world of increasing complexity and rapid change. Senge argues that vision, purpose, alignment and systems thinking are essential for organizations. He gave managers tools and conceptual archetypes to help them understand the structures and dynamics underlying their organizations' problems. 'As the world becomes more interconnected and business becomes more complex and dynamic, work must become more *learningful*,' wrote Senge.

For the traditional company, the shift to becoming a learning organization poses huge challenges. In the learning organization managers are researchers and designers rather than controllers and overseers. Senge argues that managers should encourage employees to be open to new ideas, communicate frankly with each other, understand thoroughly how their companies operate, form a collective vision, and work together to achieve their goals.

'The world we live in presents unprecedented challenges for which our institutions are ill prepared,' says Senge.[3] Whatever the official line, it is the underlying culture of the organization which sets the tone. Senior managers can talk about learning organizations until they are blue in the face, for all the good it will do if those behaviours are not supported by the culture.

In particular, managers are unlikely to shoulder additional responsibilities voluntarily if the message from the organization's culture is that the most likely outcome of putting their heads above the parapet is having them shot off.

One of the clearest indications of the decision-making culture of an organization is how tolerant it is of mistakes. To a large extent this will

determine how willing managers are to take risks. It is also an important factor in whether the organization has the ability to learn. Soichiro
Honda, the founder of Honda Motor Corporation, once said, 'Many
people dream of success. To me success can only be achieved through
repeated failure and introspection. In fact, success represents the 1% of
your work which results only from the 99% that is called failure.'

Yet despite current thinking, which suggests that experimentation is
vital for companies to remain vigorous, in many corporate cultures there
is a very low tolerance of mistakes, and individuals' career prospects can
be severely damaged if a creative decision goes wrong. Creating learning
organizations in practice has proved difficult, not least because companies
are set in their ways.

'I know people who've lost their jobs supporting these theories,'
Senge later noted. 'Yet they go on. One man told me that by adopting
the learning organization model, he'd made what he called "job-limiting
choices". What he meant was that he could have climbed the corporate
ladder faster by rejecting my theories and toeing the company line. But
what would that have brought him? A higher pension fund and more
stock, maybe. That's not what matters.'

Key texts and further reading

Argyris, C. and Schön, D. (1978) *Organizational Learning*, Addison-
  Wesley, Reading, MA.
Argyris, C. (1993) *On Organizational Learning*, Blackwell, Cam-
  bridge.
Senge, Peter M. (1990) *The Fifth Discipline*, Doubleday, New York.
Senge, Peter M. *et al.* (1994) *The Fifth Discipline Fieldbook*, Nicholas
  Brealey, London.
Senge, Peter M. *et al.* (1999) *The Dance of Change*, Nicholas Brealey,
  London.

Notes

1   Argyris, Chris (1991) 'Teaching smart people how to learn', *Harvard
    Business Review*, May–June.
2   Ibid.
3   Senge, Peter (1997) 'A growing wave of interest and openness',
    Applewood internet site.

THE MANAGERIAL GRID

T he managerial grid was invented by Dr Robert R. Blake and Dr Jane Mouton. It seeks to identify an individual's management style. In it, Blake and Mouton set out to capture human interactions and management orientation in numbers and graphs. Their work led to the now famous grid system – first published in 1964 – marketed through their company Scientific Methods.

Crude as it is, the grid helps people who are not conversant in psychology to see themselves and those they work with more clearly, to understand their interactions, and identify the sources of resistance and conflicts. The grid arose out of Blake's experience working as a consultant with Esso (Exxon), where he observed the effects of different managers' personalities in a traditional corporate environment. Organizations and the people within them, he realized, were ill-equipped to understand, let alone deal with, the spectrum of human personalities and the different styles of management they gave rise to.

'The desperate need was for a comprehensive formulation of leadership styles,' Blake later explained. The managerial grid was a way of characterizing managers in terms of their orientation toward employees (people skills) and toward production (task skills). This became a three-dimensional model with the addition of motivation as a third axis. What Blake and Mouton did, essentially, was to build on the two dimensional models developed by earlier theorists such as Douglas McGregor. McGregor had a bipolar design that ran between x and y. This, Blake and Mouton felt, was an inadequate formulation of all of the variations. It didn't satisfy their concept of what they were seeing every day at Exxon.

With the managerial grid, concern for production is represented on a 1 to 9 scale on the x axis (the horizontal axis). Concern for people is represented on a 1 to 9 scale on the y axis (the vertical axis). So a score of 1 on the x axis and 9 on the y axis would be designated by the coordinates 1,9 and indicates someone with a low concern for task completion and a high concern for people. The managerial grid argues strongly for

Ideas into action

With the managerial grid, concern for production is represented on a 1 to 9 scale on the x axis (horizontal axis). Concern for people is represented on a 1 to 9 scale on the y axis (vertical axis). So a score of 1 on the x axis and 9 on the y axis would be designated by the coordinates 1,9, and indicates someone with a low concern for task completion and a high concern for people. Using this system, Blake and Mouton identified five key manager styles:

- *1,1 – do nothing manager.* The manager exerts a minimum of effort to get the work done with very little concern for people or production.
- *1,9 – country club manager.* The manager gives considerable attention to the needs of people, but minimum concern for task accomplishment (production). This style is often found in small firms that have cornered the market, and in public sector organizations where work outputs and goals or outcomes are hard to measure.
- *9,1 – production pusher.* The manager achieves efficiency in operations by creating systems which ensure minimal human interference.
- *5,5 – organization person.* The manager maintains adequate organizational performance (production) and adequate morale (concern for people). Mediocrity is perpetuated, but the wheels keep turning. Many public and private sector managers either consciously or unconsciously pursue this management style.
- *9,9 – team builder.* The manager is able to elicit high productivity from a committed group of subordinates. Goals of the organization (production) are achieved and people are successfully integrated, with morale being high.

The grid system provides a framework for exploring what happens when, say, a 9,1+ needs something from a 1,1–. It offers a lens through which people can see themselves and their organizations more clearly. Like many other management concepts, the managerial grid has also spawned a consulting business. Most managers, Blake argues, are not self-aware enough to be able to place themselves on the grid.

'You need help to accurately place yourself on the Grid. It's not something that you could take a test on. We know that if we could have produced a test, over the years we could have made a killing. But we have never produced a test that would give you valid result. I don't know of any other method to do it accurately besides attending one of our seminars. To the best of my knowledge we are the only ones who have devoted ourselves with rigour and discipline over many years to the conditions that induce change.

'We deal with this self deception in the Grid seminar. Before you attend the seminar you read the book, and you place yourself on the Grid. At the end of the week-long seminar, when you've had a tremendous amount of feedback and the critiques of other colleagues who have done the same thing, you rate yourself again. We have found that in the pre-work, the original self-ranking, some 80% of people accord themselves a 9,9 rating. By the end of the seminar, that 80% is down to 20%. So there is a 60% self-deception factor. It's just not realistic to try to induce change against that magnitude of self-deception. That, in my view, is where much of the change effort totally breaks down.'

a 9,9 management style. The team-builder approach in most cases, it is argued, will result in superior performance.

Motivation is the third dimension, running from negative (motivated by fear) to positive (motivated by desire). This is indicated by a + or – sign. By focusing on the three measurable dimensions that have the greatest effect on the ways people work – their concern for productivity, their concern for people, and their motivation – Blake and Mouton sought to fine-tune their classification of managerial personality and style.

According to Blake, 'The third dimension is critical: it's motivation. It's a bipolar scale, running from a minus motivation (below the grid) through neutral to a plus motivation (above the grid). The negative motivations are driven by fear, the positive ones by desire. The 9,1 corner, for instance, is down to the lower right – very high on concern for production, little or no concern for people. At that corner, 9,1+ illustrates the desire for control and mastery. At the same corner, 9,1– represents a fear of failure. These two work together. If I need control I rely to the most limited degree possible on you, because you're liable to screw up and the failure will reflect on me.'

What the third dimension does is clarify the emotional driver underlying the grid style. So, for example, 1,9+ describes a 'people-pleaser' who cares little for production, and operates wholly from a desire to be loved. On the other hand, 9,1– describes a whip-cracker who cares little about people, and operates in fear of something going wrong.

More sophisticated analysis using the grid also takes account of the reaction of subordinates. Blake and Mouton identified additional management styles that combine various grid positions. The 'paternalist' style combines the whip-cracking (1,9) and the people-pleasing (9,1) depending on the response of the subordinate. A subordinate that cooperates, for example, is rewarded with a 'people-pleasing' relationship; one that doesn't is subjected to the whip. The 'opportunist' manager on the other hand, is a chameleon, taking on whatever grid style seems appropriate for the interaction of the moment, never revealing his or her own true feelings.

Mouton died in 1987, but Blake, along with various co-authors, has explored the grid and its uses in a steady stream of work. Blake's publications on this concept and other matters, for example, runs to 45 books, 115 chapters in anthologies, 214 articles and half a dozen monographs stretching back to 1945. Probably the most useful book for executives who want to explore the usefulness of the grid idea is his *Leadership Dilemmas – Grid Solutions,* written in 1991 with Anne Adams McCanse.

Blake is now chairman emeritus of Scientific Methods, in Austin, Texas. The managerial grid publications, including the fourth edition, have sold in excess of two million copies and are available in twenty languages. The original managerial grid publication was re-released to celebrate its 30th anniversary in May, 1994.

Key texts and further reading

Blake, Robert S. with McCanse, Anne Adams (1990) *Change by Design,* Addison-Wesley, Reading, MA.

Blake, Robert S. with McCanse, Anne Adams (1991) *Leadership Dilemmas – Grid Solutions,* Gulf Publishing, Houston, TX.

Blake, Robert S. with McKee, Rachel (1993) 'The Leadership of Corporate Change', *Journal of Leadership Studies,* November.

Blake, Robert S. with McKee, Rachel (1994) *Solution Selling: The Grid Science Approach,* Gulf Publishing, Houston, TX.

Blake, Robert S. (1995) 'Memories of HRD' *Journal of the American Society for Training and Development,* March.

MASLOW'S HIERARCHY OF NEEDS

O ne of the best-known theories explaining the actions of people is that of Dr Abraham Maslow. In his book *Motivation and Personality* published in 1954, Maslow hypothesized that people are motivated by a hierarchy of needs. When low-level needs are satisfied, individuals are no longer motivated by them. As each level of needs is met, individuals progress to higher-level motivators.

Before Maslow, the psychological world was awash in behaviourism and psychoanalysis. Before Maslow the focus was on dysfunctional personalities, but he moved away from this narrow view to examine the operation of healthy personalities and successful individuals, popularizing psychological humanism. In so doing, he made a major contribution both to psychology and to business. Maslow's hierarchy of needs has been used to underpin a variety of people-management techniques, especially approaches to motivation.

Maslow examined the lives of successful people such as Abraham Lincoln instead of concentrating only on people with problems. Although he studiously avoided the use of the word 'spiritual', Maslow seemed to suggest that aside from people with emotional limitations and problems, there were times when man was at his best. He introduced psychology to the abstract, though nevertheless important, concepts of truth, goodness, beauty, unity, transcendence, aliveness, uniqueness, perfection, justice, order and simplicity. These values he called 'B-values'.

Maslow asserted that people are not merely controlled by mechanical forces (the stimuli and reinforcement forces of behaviourism) or unconscious instinctive impulses as asserted by psychoanalysis, but should be understood in terms of human potential. He believed that humans strive to reach the highest levels of their capabilities. People seek the frontiers of creativity, and strive to reach the highest levels of consciousness and wisdom. People at this level and below were labelled by other psychologists as 'fully functioning' or possessing a 'healthy personality'. Maslow called the people who were at the top 'self-actualizing' persons.

Ideas into action

There are five basic levels in Maslow's hierarchy of needs:

1 *Physiological needs.* These needs are biological and consist of the needs for oxygen, food, water, and a relatively constant body temperature. These needs are the strongest because if deprived of them a person would die.

2 *Safety needs.* Except in times of emergency or periods of disorganization in the social structure (such as widespread rioting) adults do not experience their security needs. Children, however, often display signs of insecurity and their need to be safe.

3 *Love, affection and belongingness needs.* People have needs to escape feelings of loneliness and alienation and give (and receive) love, affection and the sense of belonging.

4 *Esteem needs.* People need a stable, firmly based, high level of self-respect, and respect from others in order to feel satisfied, self-confident and valuable. If these needs are not met, a person feels inferior, weak, helpless and worthless.

5 *Self-actualization needs.* Maslow describes self-actualization as an ongoing process. Self-actualizing people are, with one single exception, involved in a cause outside their own skin. They are devoted, and work at something, some calling or vocation.

This, Maslow said, explained why a musician must make music, an artist must paint, and a poet must write. If these needs are not met, the person feels restlessness, on edge, tense, and lacking something. Lower needs may also produce a restless feeling, but the cause is easier to identify. If a person is hungry, unsafe, not loved or accepted, or lacking self-esteem, the cause is apparent. But it is not always clear what a person wants when there is a need for self-actualization.

Maslow believed that the only reason that people would not move through the needs to self-actualization is because of the hindrances placed in their way by society – including their employer. Work can be a hindrance, or can promote personal growth. Maslow indicated that an improved educational process could take some of the steps listed below to promote personal growth:

- teach people to be authentic, to be aware of their inner selves and to hear their inner-feeling voices;

- teach people to transcend their own cultural conditioning and to become world citizens;
- help people to discover their vocation in life, their calling, fate or destiny. This is especially focused upon finding the right career and the right mate;
- teach people that life is precious, that there is joy to be experienced in life, and if people are open to seeing the good and joyous in all kinds of situations, it makes life worth living.

Maslow created a hierarchical theory of needs. The animal or physical needs were placed at the bottom, and the human needs at the top. This hierarchic theory is often represented as a pyramid, with the base occupied by people who are not focused on values because they are concerned with the more primal needs of physical survival. Each level of the pyramid is dependent on the previous level. For example, a person does not feel the second need until the demands of the first have been satisfied.

Key texts and further reading

Maslow, A.H. (1954) *Motivation and Personality*, Harper & Row, New York.

Maslow, A.H. (1971) *The Farther Reaches of Human Nature*, Viking, New York.

Maslow, A.H. (1968) *Toward a Psychology of Being*, D. Van Nostrand Company, New York.

Maslow, A.H. (1998) *Maslow on Management*, John Wiley & Sons, New York.

MATRIX MODEL

An organizational structure adopted by many multinational companies, the matrix model is an attempt to deal with the complexities of managing large organizations across different national markets. The concept was developed by the electronics company Philips after World War II, and represents a compromise between centralization and decentralization. Matrix management seeks to clarify responsibilities and reporting lines in large companies with operations in more than one national market. It is an attempt to impose order on what might otherwise be a chaotic mess.

Under a simple matrix management system, a marketing manager in, say, Germany reports ultimately to a boss in that country, but also to the head of the marketing function back in the company's home country. The two reporting lines (more complicated matrix structures have multiple reporting lines) are the two sides to the matrix, which has a geographical and a functional axis.

As a theoretical model, the matrix is a neat solution to the complexity of large companies. However, in reality, power cannot be evenly balanced and conflicts inevitably arise. When you add in additional complexity such as cross-functional reporting lines in project teams or start-up operations, a manager can find himself or herself trying to please several different bosses at the same time.

The real question with a matrix structure is where does the power lie? Is it with the national manager, or is it with the function head back at HQ? Attempts to resolve this sort of problem have been largely a case of fudging the decision-making structure to suit the circumstances. Many multinationals continue to operate as matrix management structures simply because they haven't come up with a better model. The structure grew out of the increasing complexity faced by large companies.

In the beginning, management was concerned with command and control. Organizations were neat, hierarchical and linear with simple chains of command. Worker A reported to manager B who reported to senior manager C who reported to board member D who reported to the managing director or CEO. Corporate life was relatively simple, understandable and clear-cut.

As companies became bigger in size, they began to organize themselves differently. In the 1920s, the American company Dupont championed the idea of what became known as federal decentralization. This gave the headquarters responsibility for core central functions such as finance and marketing. Business units were granted greater autonomy and responsibility for their own performance. This approach was championed by Alfred P. Sloan at General Motors – and later emulated by the likes of General Electric and Shell.

Federal decentralization brought professional rigour to management. However, its fundamental flaws were that one central function tended to emerge as the dominant one (in the case of General Motors, finance became the behemoth); it did little to share value, information and knowledge between units; and it helped to create an entire layer of headquarters-based middle managers whose value-adding role was increasingly difficult to determine.

The inevitable rebuff to decentralization is centralization, taking power back to the corporate centre. The trouble is that this involves a degree of dictatorship and commitment which few senior managers can carry through for any length of time. Perhaps the greatest example is that of Harold Geneen, who managed ITT with obsessional vigour during the 1960s. He centralized information in his own formidable brain. Geneen got results, but the company unravelled on his departure.

Matrix management is a middle way. It is a hybrid of decentralization and centralization. A matrix organization is organized in such a way that each unit has at least two bosses. Instead of being based around a linear chain of command, the matrix is multi-dimensional – depending on how many dimensions are deemed to be useful or practically possible. An organization may include:

- regional managers;
- functional managers;
- country or continental managers; and
- business sector managers.

Thus, a manager in a Venezuelan business unit of a multinational widget maker may be answerable – at different times – to the manager of the business unit, the country manager for Venezuela, the South American manager, the marketing chief, and the widget industry supremo.

And herein lies the problem. The mythical matrix boss is seven-headed. Matrix management is complex, ambiguous and confusing.

Ideas into action

Asea Brown Boveri (ABB) the Swiss-Swedish industrial giant is one of the most notable exponents of matrix management in recent times.

ABB came about from the merger of the Swedish company Asea, then led by the redoubtable Percy Barnevik, and the Swiss company, Brown Boveri. The merger was announced on 10 August 1987. The corporate world was stunned by its suddenness. The *Wall Street Journal* said that it was a merger 'born of necessity, not of love'. This overlooked the uncanny fit between the two companies. It was truly a marriage made in corporate heaven. Brown Boveri was international, Asea was not. Asea excelled at management, Brown Boveri did not. Technology, markets and cultures fitted together. Of course, whether this was luck or strategic insight is a matter of continuing discussion.

Barnevik became the CEO of the resulting ABB and revolutionized its organization and performance until he was succeeded by Goran Lindahl in 1997.

Under Barnevik, the company erected a complex matrix system with a group of 250 handpicked 'global' executives (including 136 country managers and 50 business area managers) leading 210,000 employees in 1300 companies divided into 5000 profit centres located in almost 150 countries and in four product segments and one financial services segment.

The ABB system displayed the full complexity of matrix management. Business segments – run by a senior manager – were divided into business areas which were treated as worldwide businesses. On the other axis of the matrix, ABB was organized by regions (the Americas, Asia, Europe) or groupings of countries.

The key to making this labyrinth actually work was Barnevik's passionate belief in communication. Matrix management was a means of ensuring that information and resources found their optimum place. This could only be achieved through incessant communication between managers – the kind of communication which matrix management necessitates.

Then, quite simply, Barnevik made it work. 'The challenge set by Barnevik was to create – out of a group of 1300 companies employing 210,000 people in 150 countries – a streamlined, entrepreneurial organization with as few management layers as possible,' write Kevin Barham and Claudia Heimer in their book examining the company,

ABB: The Dancing Giant.[1] To enable this to happen, Barnevik introduced a complex matrix structure – what Lindahl has called 'decentralization under central conditions'. The company is run by an executive committee, with the organization below divided by business areas, company and profit centres, and country organizations. The aim is to reap the advantages of being a large organization while also having the advantages of smallness.

Natural or not, the truth is that ABB's structure is complex, paradoxical and ambiguous. As a corporate role model ABB is a complete non-starter. ('I do not believe that you can mechanically copy what another company has done,' advised Barnevik.) As a sophisticated means of managing this particular organization it has proved highly effective. What holds this 'globally connected' company together is:

- deep-rooted local presence;
- global vision;
- cross-border understanding;
- global values and principles for managing creative tension;
- global connection at the top; and
- global ethics.

In addition, it required a CEO with the rare dynamism and intelligence of Barnevik to implement the structure.

While matrix management clearly worked for ABB, it was also heavily reliant on the dynamic brilliance of Percy Barnevik. He effectively made sense of the manifest ambiguity and confusion caused by the system. He made it work. It is significant that his successor, Goran Lindahl, has partly dismantled the matrix structure. Indeed, since Barnevik's departure the company's progress has faltered and undergone various restructurings to make it more customer focused.

ABB undoubtedly exhibits the potential of matrix management. It can be made to work. At its heart, however, lies an element of ambiguity and uncertainty which managers remain uncomfortable with. Managers tend to suggest that ambiguity and uncertainty are all very well when companies are undergoing major change, but not as constants of working life. The trouble is that management theorists and researchers are virtually all agreed that ambiguity and uncertainty are the new facts of corporate life. Matrix management – in one form or another – may be the most appropriate means of making organizational sense of these disturbing realities.

Little wonder that it has generally had a bad – and somewhat bemused – press. In *In Search of Excellence,* Tom Peters and Robert Waterman were dismissive of matrix organization as 'a logistical mess', arguing that 'it automatically dilutes priorities' and that structure should be kept as simple as possible. The hackneyed criticism is that a matrix organization is 'an organization in which nobody can make any decision on his or her own, but anybody on his own can stop a decision being made'.

There is little doubt that these criticisms are generally justified. Matrix management is hugely complex and perhaps unnecessarily so. But, as with most aspects of organizational life, it is not necessarily that simple. The matrix organization is, in fact, a more realistic delineation and description of responsibilities and hierarchies. In any healthy organization, different units must share information, resources and experiences. There are a great many overlapping areas of expertise and activity. Federal decentralization sought to deny them, actively working against such corporate teamwork.

The matrix organization is basically built around a network of responsibilities. It fosters broader perspectives. Managers don't view things within the narrow perspectives of their unit, their function or their fiefdom. Instead, they have to view things from a variety of perspectives – local, corporate, national, international, global, functional.

It is notable that the companies which have made matrix management work successfully are large European multinationals. Philips developed the concept after 1945, but found that national management structures came to dominate – something it spotted and changed. Royal Dutch Shell also used matrix management.

Key texts and further reading

Barham, K. and Heimer, C. (1998) *ABB: The Dancing Giant,* FT/ Pitman, London.

Campbell, A. Goold, M. and Alexander, M. (1994) *Corporate-Level Strategy,* John Wiley, New York.

Sloan, Alfred P. (1963) *My Years with General Motors,* Doubleday, New York.

Note

1   Barham, Kevin and Heimer, Claudia (1998) *ABB: The Dancing Giant,* FT/Pitman, London.

MENTORING

When Odysseus, king of Ithaca, left for the Trojan War around 800 BC, he was faced with a problem: who would look after the royal household and groom his son, Telemachus, for the throne in his absence? Odysseus turned to Mentor, his trusted companion, and instructed him to assume the role of father figure, adviser, counsellor, tutor, and role model to Telemachus while he was away. Greek mythology also tells us that the goddess Athena would speak to Telemachus in the guise of Mentor. Jump from the writings of Homer to the present day, when the word 'mentor' has become part of our language, signifying a wise and trusted counsellor, a sagacious adviser, a tutor.

Modern definitions of the term include that of Linda Phillips-Jones, one of the leading experts on mentoring, who describes mentors as 'skilled people who go out of their way to help you clarify your personal goals and take steps toward reaching them'. In her book *Mentors and Protégés*, she describes some characteristics of mentors and the mentoring relationship:

- mentors are usually older than their protégés;
- mentors frequently – but not always – initiate the relationship;
- mentor–protégé relationships do not need to be particularly close;
- it is possible to have more than one mentor at a time;
- there are patterns and cycles in mentor–protégé relationships;
- mentoring should benefit both partners equally.

In an organizational setting, mentoring may cover the following areas: appropriate dress, conflict resolution, communication, company protocol and culture, ethical practice, leadership, networking, office politics, presentation, project management, time management, and work–life balance.

The mentor's role varies according a variety of factors, including the quality of the relationship between mentor and mentee, the level of

Ideas into action

In the various literature on mentoring, a number of specific roles associated with mentors have been identified:

- **Acceptor** as acceptor, the mentor provides unconditional support and encouragement for the mentee. With unreserved support, mentees will not be afraid to fail and will be encouraged to take risks and push themselves beyond their normal boundaries. Good mentors are fans of their mentees. They visualize how, through their efforts, their mentees will be improved to fulfil their full potential. In return the mentor receives affirmation of his or her own qualities through the respect and trust and admiration of the mentee.
- **Counsellor** the mentor can help the mentee with their personal problems. Ethical issues, such as the balance between maintaining personal integrity and values and career advancement, or the struggle to maintain a work–life balance, can be discussed. If the mentor can empathize with the mentee, personal internal conflict can be worked through and resolved. If left unaddressed, this internal conflict can cause withdrawal, can interfere with career satisfaction and can adversely affect both the quality of work and the quality of life.
- **Coach** the role of coach is one of the most important that a mentor can play. As coach, the mentor may provide crucial information about an organization's mission, vision, and goals. Mentors can suggest appropriate strategies for completing tasks as well as providing critical feedback. Without a mentor to coach him or her, a new recruit will be at a distinct disadvantage, lacking critical information and insight about the organization.
- **Challenger** by pushing the mentee through the assignment of difficult and challenging tasks, the mentor prepares the mentee for promotion and greater responsibility. Mentees must be prepared to work outside their comfort zone; the mentor can help break the barrier.
- **Friend** the mentor as a friend may provide a different generational perspective to that which the mentee usually enjoys. Such mentors will also teach the mentee to be more comfortable when in the company of senior figures. Mentors may be re-energized by the friendship of someone younger than themselves, and gain a renewed sense of vitality that enhances their lives.

- **Listener** another essential and important role of the mentor is that of listener. Non-judgmental listening is a rare skill. Listening may sound easy, but try out some of your friends and acquaintances and see how well they listen, and whether they judge or are critical.
- **Promoter** as promoter, the mentor exposes the mentee to influential people and situations that may benefit the mentee.
- **Inquisitor** the mentor as inquisitor adopts the methods of some of the great mentors of all time such as Buddha, Confucius, and Moses. Like the great philosopher Socrates they teach by asking questions. The Greek philosophers called this technique Socratic dialogue. It involves the mentor leading the mentee on a path to wisdom, through effective and provocative questioning. When *Fortune 500* CEOs were asked what made their mentors so effective, the most common answer was 'they asked great questions'.
- **Protector** as protector, the mentor prevents the mentee from taking unnecessary risks. In certain circumstances, the mentor may shield the mentee from blame, or from taking credit. Mentors must be careful not to overprotect their charges and thereby inhibit their professional and personal growth.
- **Role model** the mentor as a role model influences the mentee through the values, behaviour, and attitudes he or she imparts. These traits are adopted by the mentees as they mould their own identities.
- **Sponsor** the mentor as sponsor acts as an advocate for the mentee both within and outside the organization. With only a single mentor acting as sponsor, the fortunes of the mentee are very closely linked to those of the mentor. If the mentor leaves the organization, or falls from grace, then the career of the mentee is likely to suffer. It is better, and safer, for the mentee to obtain more than one sponsor if possible.

The perfect mentor, someone who can assume all of the roles above, probably does not exist. Rather than pursuing a fruitless quest to find the perfect mentor, it is better for a potential mentee to assess which type will be most valuable to them, then look for a mentor who embodies those qualities. It also pays to learn how to become a perfect mentee, so that mentors will more willing to participate. A mentee should realistically assess whether he or she is an attractive proposition to a mentor. For example, mentees should consider whether they are ambitious, willing to confide in others, willing to learn.

skills and knowledge of both parties, the time available, and organizational culture.

With an experienced mentor and relatively inexperienced mentee, the mentor may take on the role of tutor, counsellor, encourager, life-coach. If both parties are located close to one another they may, over time, develop a strong friendship.

For a more experienced mentee, the mentor's role may be closer to sponsor and facilitator. The mentor may provide a sounding board; someone to discuss and explore ideas and experiences with.

Mentoring can be an extremely effective way of assimilating a new employee into an organization, but that depends on the quality and dedication of the mentor. Mentors do not necessarily have to come from within the organization. There are many human-resource consultancies that offer mentoring and coaching services. In these cases, the mentor may be providing his services to many executives at the same time.

Key texts and further reading

David Clutterbuck (1999) *Mentoring Executives and Directors,* Butterworth-Heinemann, Oxford.

Linda Phillips-Jones (1982) *Mentors and Protégés,* Arbor House, New York.

OUTSOURCING

O utsourcing involves an organization passing the provision of a service or the execution of a task previously undertaken in-house to a third party to perform on its behalf.[1] The American entrepreneur Ross Perot, among others, has been credited with starting the modern outsourcing industry back in the 1960s. But the idea behind it is as old as business itself.

Basically, it is a response to the question: 'Which areas of activity are central to our business, and which can best be performed by external suppliers?'

It arises from the recognition that no company can excel at everything. Activities involving competencies that are not central to what the business does may be best left then to those who specialize in them. An outsourcing agreement, in essence, usually allows the provider company (the outsourcer) to supply a customer with services or process that the customer is currently supplying internally.

What has made outsourcing a hot topic is its application to information technology. Mary Lacity and Leslie Willcocks, two academics at Oxford University, link this to a decision taken by Eastman Kodak in 1989.[2] At that time, Eastman Kodak turned over the bulk of its IT operations to three outsourcing partners. In so doing, say Lacity and Willcocks, it ignited the fashion for outsourcing. Other *Fortune 500* companies followed suit and signed long-term contracts worth hundreds of millions of dollars with IT outsourcing partners. Among them were Continental Airlines, Continental Bank, Enron, First City, General Dynamics, McDonnel Douglas, and Xerox. In the UK, similar outsourcing deals followed involving companies such as British Petroleum, British Aerospace and British Home Stores, and central government departments including the Inland Revenue and the Department of Social Security.

The trend has gathered pace ever since. By 1994, some 51% of UK organizations were outsourcing some part of their IT needs. In the public sector, this trend was encouraged by the government's compulsory competitive tendering initiatives and privatization policies. Worldwide, it has been calculated that \$33 billion worth of information management was outsourced by major corporations in 1996 alone.

Outsourcing, however, is another simple concept that is hard to apply in practice. Striking the right balance between who gets the projected benefits – in particular, how cost savings are divided between the company and the vendor of the outsourced IT services – requires careful consideration (all too often the bulk of the savings go in profits to the vendor or supplier of the outsourced services, as, for example, do the intellectual property rights from developing new technology).

In recent years, the understanding of which functions can be sensibly removed from the core business and sourced from outside has begun to change. Outsourcing is no longer being applied just to IT. In the past, for example, many administrative activities were seen as part and parcel of running the business. As a result, it simply didn't occur to companies to outsource areas such as pay-roll, delivery of finished goods, and secretarial services. That has now changed as it has become fashionable for companies to focus on their core activities – those which provide competitive advantage.

In recent years, however, companies and commentators have begun to question the benefits of outsourcing. Over a three-year period, for example, Lacity and Willcocks, carried out extensive research into a number of IT sourcing decisions in 40 US and UK companies.[3] Of 61 IT

Ideas into action

Mary Lacity and Leslie Willcocks[4] identify seven important variables which can affect the outcome of the outsourcing decision. These are:

1 scope;
2 decision makers (senior managers/IT managers);
3 evaluation process;
4 scale of operations;
5 contract length;
6 contract type; and
7 contract date.

Important dimensions include:

- *Providing adequate protection if something goes wrong.* The risk of outsourcing is that the company is the one which suffers if employees from the supplier/vendor make a mistake. Adequate contractual protection is vital to protect the interests of the organization if, for example, the outsourced computer system fails. In some cases, inadequate safeguards can even put lives at risk, as the example of the London Ambulance Service illustrates.

- *Managing redundancies.* What happens to employees whose jobs are replaced by the outsourcing arrangement? Typically, part of the cost savings from outsourcing result from reduced head count. This introduces an emotional dimension to the decision. The cost of redundancies should be carefully factored into the calculations to allow for a humane solution. Failure to do so can also result in additional costs – including legal fees.
- *Loss of capacity.* The inevitable result of outsourcing is a reduction in the in-house capability of the host organization to carry out the outsourced activity. This can have important implications for the future if the decision is reversed or if the outsourced activity becomes core to the business further down the road. It can also result in the company missing out on important developments or strategic options later.
- *Agreeing service levels that meet the organization's immediate and projected needs.* Whatever performance measures are used, service levels need to take account of likely improvements required to remain competitive. Customers' expectations are continually rising. With insufficient flexibility built into contracts, renegotiating service levels to keep pace with market demands can be extremely expensive. For example, 48-hour delivery may be acceptable to customers now, but if a competitor offers same-day delivery the company will have to upgrade its own service offering.

The decision to outsource IT needs involves an additional requirement:

- *Agreeing the implications of moving to new technology if required.* (It will be required at some point, after all.) Failure to reach agreement on this can be very expensive.

With IT, there is now a clear trend towards shorter outsourcing contracts.

outsourcing decisions, they suggest, 34 (56%) were successful, 14 (23%) were unsuccessful, and in 13 cases (21%) it was too early to tell. (For the purposes of evaluating the impact of these decisions, the key success indicator was defined in terms of 'achieving anticipated cost savings'.)

In a 1998 article, David Bryce and Michael Useem, two academics from the University of Pennsylvania's Wharton School, one of America's most influential business schools, examined the outsourcing experience and evaluated its consequences.[5]

Bryce and Useem examine four areas in which outsourcing is generally expected or hoped to add value. These include stock price. The authors consider if there is evidence to show that outsourcing has an affect on stock price. Nothing proven, but likely to be positive, they conclude. Other areas of potential value creation are, it seems, bogged down by the lack of direct research. Most notably, evidence of effects on operating costs remain limited. Service and strategic advantages are also disputed or inconclusive.

Even so, Bryce and Useem conclude that while outsourcing is not the cure to all known corporate ills, it is an extremely useful and value-creating business tool. 'Outsourcing will never be a silver bullet nor a turnaround engine, but the evidence to date indicates that it is one of contemporary management's more promising new tools.' What is perhaps most astonishing is that so little research has been done in this area of such massive corporate activity.

Key texts and further reading

Reilly, P. and Tamkin, P. (1996) *Outsourcing: A Flexible Option for the Future?* Institute for Employment Studies, Brighton, UK.

Lacity, Mary and Willcocks, Leslie (1996) 'Best Practice in Information Technology Sourcing', *Oxford Executive Research Briefings*, Templeton College, Oxford University.

Bragg, Steven M. (1998) *Outsourcing*, John Wiley & Sons, New York.

Notes

1   Reilly, P. and Tamkin, P. (1996) *Outsoucing: A Flexible Option for the Future?* Institute for Employment Studies, Brighton, UK.

2   Lacity, Mary and Willcocks, Leslie (1996) 'Best Practice in Information Technology Sourcing', *Oxford Executive Research Briefings*, Templeton College, Oxford University.

3   Ibid.
4   Ibid.
5   Bryce, David and Useem, Michael (1998) 'The impact of corporate outsourcing on company value', *European Management Journal,* vol. 16, No. 6, December.

PORTER'S FIVE COMPETITIVE FORCES

Harvard Business School's Michael Porter remains one of the world's most influential business thinkers. When it appeared in 1979, his article in the *Harvard Business Review*, 'How Competitive Forces Shape Strategy', changed the way companies thought about strategy forever. The article has been rated the tenth most influential *HBR* article of all time.

In his 1980 book *Competitive Strategy: Techniques for Analysing Industries and Competitors*, Porter developed the model still regarded as essential reading for strategy makers and MBA students the world over. His timing was impeccable. Publication of his model coincided with a wholesale rethink of Western business principles. In the 1970s, corporate America had watched in horror as Japanese companies stole market share in industry after industry. Initially, US companies put Japanese competitiveness down to cheap labour, but by the end of the decade it was dawning on them that something more fundamental was occurring. Porter encouraged a complete re-evaluation of the nature of competitiveness.

While completing his PhD at Harvard, Porter was influenced by the economist Richard Caves, who became his mentor. He joined the Harvard faculty at the age of 26, becoming one of the youngest tenured professors in the school's history. He subsequently left the Harvard economics department to join the faculty of Harvard Business School. In so doing, Porter was one of the first serious academics to recognize the wider applications of his discipline to the business community. At HBS, Porter's great achievement was to produce well-researched models of competitiveness at a corporate, industry-wide and national level. He took an industrial economics framework called the structure-conduct performance paradigm (SCP) and translated it into the context of business strategy. In so doing, he adapted and popularized a model which might otherwise have remained buried in the academic literature.

From this emerged the five forces framework developed in his 1980 book. 'In any industry, whether it is domestic or international or produces a product or a service, the rules of competition are embodied in five competitive forces,' he wrote.

These five forces, he asserted, shape the competitive landscape. Initially, they were passively interpreted as the facts of competitive life – the current rules of engagement. But by laying them bare, Porter provided a framework for companies to understand and challenge the competitive markets in which they operate. For strategy makers, the five forces represented levers upon which any strategy must act on if it is to have an impact on a company's competitive position.

'The collective strength of these five competitive forces determines the ability of firms in an industry to earn, on average, rates of return on investment in excess of the cost of capital. The strength of the five forces varies from industry to industry, and can change as an industry evolves,' Porter observed.

A late addition to his book was the concept of generic strategies. He argued that there were three 'generic strategies', 'viable approaches to dealing with ... competitive forces'. Strategy, in Porter's eyes, was a matter of *how* to compete. The first of Porter's generic strategies was ***differentiation***, competing on the basis of value added to customers (quality, service, differentiation) so that customers will pay a premium to cover higher costs. The second was ***cost-based leadership***, offering products or services at the lowest cost. Under this strategy, quality and service are not unimportant, but cost reduction provides differentiation. The third generic strategy identified by Porter was ***focus***. It asserted that companies with a clear strategy outperform those whose strategy is unclear or those who attempt to achieve both differentiation and cost leadership.

'Sometimes the firm can successfully pursue more than one approach as its primary target, though this is rarely possible,' he said. 'Effectively implementing any of these generic strategies usually requires total commitment, and organizational arrangements are diluted if there's more than one primary target.'

If a company failed to follow any of the three generic strategies it was liable to encounter problems. 'The firm failing to develop its strategy in at least one of the three directions – a firm that is *stuck in the middle* – is in an extremely poor strategic situation,' Porter wrote. 'The firm lacks the market share, capital investment, and resolve to play the low-cost game, the industry-wide differentiation necessary to obviate the need for a low-cost position, or the focus to create differentiation or low cost in a more limited sphere. The firm stuck in the middle is almost guaranteed low profitability. It either loses the high-volume customers who demand low prices or must bid away its profits to get this business away from

Ideas into action

Porter's five competitive forces are:

1 *The entry of new competitors* new competition necessitates some sort of competitive response which will inevitably require resources, thus reducing profits;

2 *The threat of substitutes* the presence of viable alternatives to your product or service in the marketplace will mean that the prices you can charge will be limited;

3 *The bargaining power of buyers* if customers have bargaining power they will use it. This will reduce profit margins and, as a result, affect profitability;

4 *The bargaining power of suppliers* given power over you, suppliers will increase their prices and adversely affect your profitability; and

5 *Rivalry among existing competitors* competition leads to the need to invest in marketing, R&D or price reductions, which will reduce your profits.[1]

The five forces analysis has since been updated by Porter acolytes and a sixth force has been suggested. This is *complementors*, the dependencies that you develop in a business on companies whose products work in conjunction with yours, so that they have synergy. In modern business, this is an increasingly significant force. The example often cited is the synergistic link between Microsoft and Intel.

low-cost firms. Yet it also loses high-margin businesses – the cream – to the firms who are focused on high-margin targets or have achieved differentiation overall. The firm stuck in the middle also probably suffers from a blurred corporate culture and a conflicting set of organizational arrangements and motivation system.'

When *Competitive Strategy* was published, in 1980, Porter's generic strategies offered a rational and straightforward method of companies extricating themselves from strategic confusion. It was, however, short-lived. Less than a decade later, companies were having to compete on all fronts. They had to be differentiated, through improved service or speedier development, and be cost leaders, cheaper than their competitors.

'Porter's translation did not resolve, and could not resolve, the fundamental weakness of the SCP approach. Why did some companies manage the five forces better than others?' notes John Kay, former head of Oxford's Said Business School.[1]

Key texts and further reading

Porter, Michael (1979) 'How Competitive Forces Shape Strategy', *Harvard Business Review*.
Porter, Michael (1980) *Competitive Strategy*, Free Press, New York.
Porter, Michael (1985) *Competitive Advantage*, Free Press, New York.
Porter, Michael (1990) The *Competitive Advantage of Nations*, Macmillan, London.

Note

1   Kay, John (1997) 'Why gurus should cross the bridge into business', *Financial Times*, November 17.

THE PSYCHOLOGICAL CONTRACT

D uring the more stable times of the 1950s and 1960s, the careers enjoyed by corporate executives were built on an implicit understanding and mutual trust. They were influenced by their parents' hardships in the 1930s to value job security, and by their parents' military service in World War II to be obedient to those above. The term 'organization man' or 'corporate man' was invented for this generation (corporate woman was virtually non-existent at this time).

Implicit to such careers was the understanding that loyalty and solid performance brought job security. This was mutually beneficial. The executive gained a respectable income and a high degree of security. The company gained loyal, hard-working executives. This unspoken pact became known as the psychological contract. The originator of the phrase was the social psychologist Ed Schein of MIT. Schein's interest in the employee/employer relationship developed during the late 1950s. Schein noted the similarities between the brainwashing of POWs which he had witnessed during the Korean War and the corporate indoctrination carried out by the likes of GE and IBM. The ability of strong values to influence groups of people is a strand which has continued throughout Schein's work.

As Schein's link with brainwashing suggests, there was more to the psychological contract than a cosy, mutually beneficial deal. It raised a number of issues.

First, the psychological contract was built around loyalty. 'The most important single contribution required of an executive, certainly

Ideas into action

Recent years have seen radical changes to the psychological contract between employers and employees. The rash of downsizing in the

1980s and 1990s marked the end of the psychological contract which had existed for decades. Expectations have now changed on both sides. Employers no longer wish to make commitments – even implicit ones – to long-term employment. The emphasis is on flexibility. On the other side, employees are keen to develop their skills and take charge of their own careers. Employability (*see* page 87) is the height of corporate fashion.

As a result, the new psychological contract is more likely to be built on developing skills than blind loyalty. The logic is that if a company invests in an individual's development, the employee will become more loyal. The trouble is that the employee also becomes more employable by other companies.

In effect the balance has shifted. The original and long-standing psychological contract created an artificial balance based on inefficient behaviour. Its emphasis was on loyalty and reliability rather than performance. Performance was assumed. Downsizing and the decimation of middle management moved the pendulum towards corporations. Managerial job security was overturned. Now, it is employees who potentially hold the balance of power. In the age of flexible employment, downsizing and career management, loyalty is increasingly elusive as managers flit from job to job, company to company.

The old psychological contract, with its inherent safety and clarity, is now being re-evaluated as a corporate nirvana. We never had it so good. The trouble is that the concept of jobs for life was largely a mirage. Companies may have been prepared to stick with the same managers throughout their careers, but often the companies themselves didn't last. (Whether this was due to the inertia of management is open to debate.) Research repeatedly shows that companies don't last very long. One survey of corporate life expectancy in Japan and Europe came up with 12.5 years as the average life expectancy of all firms. London Business School's Arie de Geus estimates that the average life expectancy of a multinational corporation is 40 to 50 years. One-third of 1970s *Fortune 500* had disappeared by 1983.

The new reality of corporate life means that the traditional psychological contract is unlikely to return. But there will always be a psychological contract between employer and employee. In any employment deal, each side carries expectations, aspirations and an understanding – which may be right or wrong – of the expectations and aspirations of the other side. The new challenge is for both sides to make the psychological contract an explicit arrangement.

the most universal qualification, is loyalty [allowing] domination by the organization personality,' noted Chester Barnard in *The Functions of the Executive* (1938). The word 'domination' suggests which way Barnard saw the balance of power falling. While loyalty is a positive quality, it can easily become blind. What if the corporate strategy is wrong, or the company is engaged in unlawful or immoral acts? Also, there is the question of loyal to what? Thirty years ago, corporate values were assumed rather than explored.

The second issue raised by the psychological contract was that of perspectives. With careers neatly mapped out, executives were not encouraged to look over the corporate parapets to seek out broader viewpoints. The corporation became a self-contained and self-perpetuating world supported by a complex array of checks, systems, and hierarchies. The company was right. Customers, who existed in the ethereal world outside the organization, were often regarded as peripheral. In the fifties, sixties and seventies, executives didn't lose their jobs for delivering poor quality or indifferent service. Indeed, in some organizations, executives only lost their jobs by defrauding their employer or insulting the boss. 'Jobs for life' was the refrain and, to a large extent for executives, the reality.

Clearly, such an environment was hardly conducive to the fostering of dynamic risk-takers. The psychological contract rewarded the steady foot-soldier, the safe pair of hands. It was hardly surprising, therefore, that when she came to examine corporate life for the first time in her 1977 book, *Men and Women of the Corporation,* Rosabeth Moss Kanter found that the central characteristic expected of a manager was 'dependability'.

The reality was that the psychological contract placed a premium on loyalty rather than ability and allowed a great many poor performers to seek out corporate havens. It was also significant that the psychological contract was regarded as the preserve of management. Lower down the hierarchy, people were hired and fired with abandon.

Key texts and further reading

Makin, P.J., Cooper, C.L. and Cox, C.J. (1996) *Organizations and the Psychological Contract*, British Psychological Society, London.

Schein, E.H. (1997) *Organizational Culture and Leadership,* Jossey-Bass, San Francisco, CA.

Schein, E.H. (1980) (3rd edition) *Organizational Psychology*, Prentice Hall, Englewood Cliffs, NJ.

RE-ENGINEERING

R e-engineering (or business process re-engineering – BPR – as it is also known) was brought to the fore by James Champy, co-founder of the consultancy company CSC Index, and Michael Hammer, an electrical engineer and former computer science professor at MIT. The roots of the idea lay in the research carried out by MIT from 1984 to 1989 on 'Management in the 1990s'.

Champy and Hammer's book, *Reengineering the Corporation*, was a bestseller which produced a plethora of re-engineering programmes; the creation of many consulting companies; and a deluge of books promoting alternative approaches to re-engineering. (Thanks to the popularity of re-engineering, CSC also became one of the largest consulting firms in the world.)

The basic idea behind re-engineering is that organizations need to identify their key processes and make them as lean and efficient as possible. Peripheral processes (and, therefore, peripheral people) need to be discarded. 'Don't automate; obliterate,' Hammer proclaimed. Champy and Hammer defined re-engineering as 'the fundamental rethinking and radical redesign of business processes to achieve dramatic improvements in critical measures of performance such as cost, quality, service and speed'.

As can be seen, the beauty of re-engineering was that it embraced many of the fashionable business ideas of recent years and nudged them forward into a tidy philosophy. There were elements of total quality management, just-in-time manufacturing, customer service, time-based competition and lean manufacturing in the re-engineering concept. Big name corporations jumped on the bandwagon and Champy and Hammer's book was endorsed, somewhat surprisingly, by no less a figure than Peter Drucker.

In *Reengineering the Corporation*, Hammer and Champy set out what they described as a 'manifesto for business revolution'. Far from revolutionary, however, some commentators have observed that re-engineering was simply a logical next step following on from scientific management

Ideas into action

To Champy and Hammer, re-engineering was more than dealing with mere processes. They eschewed the phrase 'business process re-engineering', regarding it as too limiting. In their view the scope and scale of re-engineering went far beyond simply altering and refining processes. True re-engineering was all-embracing, a recipe for a corporate revolution.

To start the revolution, it was suggested that companies equip themselves with a blank piece of paper and map out their processes. This was undoubtedly a useful exercise. It encouraged companies to consider exactly what were their core activities and what processes were in place, and needed to be in place, to deliver them efficiently. It also encouraged companies to move beyond strict functional demarcations to more free-flowing corporate forms governed by key processes rather than fiefdoms.

Inevitably, the optimum processes involved more effective utilization of resources. Functional organizations (as opposed to process-based ones) tend to contain elements of self-serving protectionism. Different functions do not necessarily share knowledge or work to the same objectives as other functions. Clearly this is, at best, inefficient. As a result, some stages in processes were eliminated completely. Others were streamlined or made more effective through use of information technology. Having come up with a neatly engineered map of how their business should operate, companies could then attempt to translate the paper theory into concrete reality.

The concept was simple. While its relative simplicity made it alluring, actually turning re-engineering into reality has proved immensely more difficult than its proponents suggested. The revolution has largely been a damp squib.

The first problem was that the blank piece of paper ignored the years, often decades, of cultural evolution which led to an organization doing something in a certain way. Such preconceptions and often justifiable habits were not easily discarded. Functional fiefdoms may be inefficient, but they are difficult to break down.

The second problem was that re-engineering appeared inhumane. In some cases, people were treated appallingly in the name of re-engineering. Re-engineering, as the name suggests, owed more to visions of the corporation as a machine than a human, or humane, system. The human side of re-engineering has proved its greatest stumbling block.

To re-engineering purists, people were objects who handle processes. De-personalization was the route to efficiency. (Here, the echoes of Taylor's management by dictatorship are most obvious.)

Re-engineering became a synonym for redundancy and downsizing. For this the gurus and consultants could not be entirely blamed. Often, companies which claimed to be re-engineering – and there were plenty – were simply engaging in cost-cutting under the convenient guise of the fashionable theory. Downsizing appeared more publicly palatable if it was presented as implementing a leading edge concept.

The third obstacle was that corporations are not natural or even willing revolutionaries. Instead of casting the re-engineering net widely, they tended to re-engineer the most readily accessible process and then leave it at that. Related to this, and the subject of Champy's sequel *Reengineering Management*, re-engineering usually failed to impinge on management. Not surprisingly, managers were all too willing to impose the rigours of a process-based view of the business on others, but often unwilling to inflict them upon themselves. 'Senior managers have been re-engineering business processes with a passion, tearing down corporate structures that no longer can support the organization. Yet the practice of management has largely escaped demolition. If their jobs and styles are left largely intact, managers will eventually undermine the very structure of their rebuilt enterprises,' Champy noted in 1994 at the height of re-engineering's popularity. In response, he suggested re-engineering management should tackle three key areas: managerial roles, managerial styles and managerial systems. In retrospect, the mistake of re-engineering was not to tackle re-engineering management first.

(Taylorism), industrial engineering, and business process improvement (TQM). What re-engineering had going for it, though, was that it fitted the needs of companies looking for a reason to continue the attack on bureaucracy and complacency, and with them the traditional hierarchical decision-making structures.

In essence, the message of BPR was that organizations needed to identify their key processes and 're-engineer' them to make them as efficient as possible. To some extent, then, BPR was the sword to cut the Gordian knot of bureaucracy that had become institutionalized in many companies

Key texts and further reading

Champy, James and Hammer, Michael (1993) *Reengineering the Corporation*, HarperBusiness, New York.

Champy, James (1995) *Reengineering Management*, HarperBusiness, New York.

Hammer, Michael and Stanton, Steven (1995) *The Reengineering Revolution*, HarperCollins, New York.

RELATIONSHIP MARKETING

Relationship marketing refers to the benefits that ongoing relationships with key customers can bring to an organization. The idea behind it goes back to the earliest trading times, but the term entered the vocabulary of management during the 1980s. At that time, management writers observed it at work within the high-tech business community of California's Silicon Valley.

Among them was Regis McKenna, the Silicon Valley marketing guru and chairman of the management and marketing consulting firm the McKenna Group. McKenna worked with a number of entrepreneurial start-ups during their formation years, including Apple, Compaq, Lotus, Microsoft, and Silicon Graphics.

In 1985, McKenna wrote the first book devoted to the marketing of high-technology companies – *The Regis Touch*. The book explained McKenna's marketing theories and strategies. In it, he examined the marketing of high-technology companies. 'Many of the small highly-innovative Silicon Valley companies didn't market new products to the larger computer companies on an individual basis in the traditional way,' he observed. Instead they sought to establish strategic relationships with them, and this allowed the smaller company to work almost as part of the customer's organization.

In a very fast-moving industry, the closeness of these relationships was critical to the ability of the smaller firms to develop solutions that met the needs of their customers. It became apparent that their success often depended on personal relationships which had developed into close friendships. Rather than attend to the marketing of products or projects through traditional means, these smaller companies worked extra hard at maintaining ongoing relationships.

His second book, released in February 1989, was called *Who's Afraid of Big Blue?* It discussed how small, entrepreneurial companies were challenging IBM and winning. This book predicted the difficulties IBM was about to face in the next decade. *Relationship Marketing*, his third book, focused on the interactive relationships vital to market acceptance in the 'age of the customer', and drew wider attention to the concept of relationship marketing. New interest in relationship marketing led to greater awareness among companies in a variety of other industries.

Relationship marketing is now being applied to online commerce, and appears to hold the key to profitable e-commerce. In 1997, Regis published *Real Time: Preparing For The Age of the Never Satisfied Customer.*

Ideas into action

The logic of relationship marketing is simple; rather than communicate intermittently with key customers, it makes more sense to develop a relationship of mutual trust so that the dialogue is continuous. Everyone in business has been told that success is all about attracting and retaining customers. Such words of wisdom are soon forgotten. Once companies have attracted customers they often overlook the second half of the equation. They forget what they regard as the humdrum side of business – ensuring that the customer remains a customer.

Failing to concentrate on retaining as well as attracting customers costs businesses huge amounts of money annually. It has been estimated that the average company loses between 10 and 30% of its customers every year. In constantly changing markets this is not surprising – what is surprising is the fact that few companies have any idea how many customers they have lost.

Organizations are now beginning to wake up to these lost opportunities and calculate the financial implications. Cutting down the number of customers a company loses can make a radical difference in its performance. Research in the US found that a 5% decrease in the number of defecting customers led to profit increases of between 25% and 85%.

Rank Xerox takes the question of retaining customers so seriously that it forms a key part of the company's bonus scheme. In the US, Domino's Pizzas estimates that a regular customer is worth more than $5,000 over ten years. A customer who receives a poor quality product or service on a first visit and as a result never returns is losing the company thousands of dollars in potential revenue (more if you consider how many people such dissatisfied customers are liable to tell about their bad experience).

The route to customer retention is relationship marketing; nurturing relationships with customers which create loyalty. Relationship-building programmes now cover a multitude of activities from customer magazines to vouchers and gifts. Basically, they aim to persuade a person to use a preferred vendor in order to take advantage of the benefits on offer, whether a trip to Acapulco or a price-reduction voucher for a calorie-controlled canned drink. Sceptics will say that there is nothing new in this. Indeed, businesses have been giving their long-standing customers discounts and inducements since time immemorial. What is now different is the highly organized way in which companies are attempting to build relationships and customer loyalty.

The technique often depends on getting close to, and forming personal relationships with, key individuals. The idea is that if you are constantly aware of what your customers or partners require and keep them informed of developments within your own organization, then the customer/supplier link becomes almost a seamless web. In relationship marketing, the details of the products and services become subservient to the trust which has been established. Why, after all, would a customer go elsewhere if you constantly monitor and adjust what you are doing to meet his needs now and in the future? The advantage of such an arrangement is that problems can be averted before they become a crisis. The only reason for losing the customer is if the relationship breaks down.

The real strength of relationship marketing is its ability to tap into the power of human interaction. It is one thing to read a proposal from a potential supplier, it is quite another to discuss it on the golf course with someone you have known for years whom you trust and respect.

Technology is likely to have a marked effect on relationship marketing. On the one hand, the emergence of the internet as a global market place means that customers are likely to become increasingly promiscuous, able to flirt with suppliers all over the world. At the same time, technology also means that relationship-marketing programmes are becoming ever more sophisticated. When it comes to creating loyal customers, the database is king. Databases mean that companies can target audiences more effectively. Technology also means that one programme tends to blend into another. In fact, putting the simple idea into practice has become increasingly complex. Customers are now more highly demanding and fickle than ever before. They are organized and use their lobbying power more effectively. Expectations are high, but companies are quickly realizing that customers with a conscience create new markets.

Companies are now developing relationship programmes which are directly related to the conscience of their customers. There is a plethora of products which pledge to donate money to help save the rainforests or support medical research, if you buy them. Such loyalty-building creates a situation in which all sides appear to win.

Relationship marketing is likely to become ever more ambitious. The potential for mutually beneficial link-ups is never ending. A credit card from General Motors would have been unthinkable a few years ago. Now, it is the tip of an expanding iceberg. Some supermarkets already give customers a 'smart card' which means the company knows the contents of each customer's weekly shopping basket.

Amid the enthusiasm, the issue of which programmes are effective – if any – has tended to be forgotten as managers have joined yet another in a long line of bandwagons. Research by Australia-based academics Grahame Dowling and Mark Uncles does not provide good news for organizations which have invested heavily in loyalty programmes (or for consulting companies which have hyped customer loyalty). Writing in the *Sloan Management Review* (Summer 1997), Dowling and Uncles argue that there is little evidence to suggest that programmes change the structure of markets. Instead, they tend to involve increased expenditure with little added brand loyalty. Indeed, loyalty appears depressingly thin on the ground – research has shown that a mere 10% of buyers are 100% loyal to a particular brand. Customers appear cynically opportunistic and are 'loyal' to a variety of products at differing times.

Given this fickleness, nurturing customer loyalty is an ambitious task. Dowling and Uncles suggest that success requires that a programme must 'leverage the value of the product to the customer'. To do so, it must include a 'perception of value'. It must offer something tangible and worthwhile, which can be attained in the near future. An instant cash prize is preferable to a distant prize of something of limited value or use.

As well as offering genuine benefits, a customer loyalty programme must be planned to enhance the value proposition of the product or service, to be fully costed, to maximize the buyer's motivation to buy again, and to consider market conditions. The trouble is, as Dowling and Uncles point out, it may not even be worth that much effort. Loyal customers are as fickle as any others and you cannot assume that they cost less to service, are less price sensitive, or that they recommend products to others.

The battle of the future lies in utilizing customer information more effectively than the competition and in building relationships with customers that generate value. The bottom line is simple: while 30% of customers are price-sensitive, 70% are more sensitive to value.

To take advantage of this, companies need to ensure that they take the lead in building up knowledge about their customers. If they are fully informed and take advantage of that knowledge, they are less prone to be beaten to the punch by new entrants. Companies must also focus on 'sources of new value for the industry, not just redistributing or even destroying value'. Imaginative use of differentiated pricing and better-targeted offerings can create new value. Those who make do with old value will find it withering in their arms.

Key texts and further reading

McKenna, Regis (1992) *Relationship Marketing*, Perseus Press, CA.

McKenna, Regis (1997) *Real Time: Preparing For The Age of the Never Satisfied Customer*, Harvard Business School Press, Boston, MA.

Christopher, Martin, Payne, Adrian and Ballantyne, D. (1991) *Relationship Marketing*, Butterworth-Heinemann, Oxford.

Cram, Tony (1995) *The Power of Relationship Marketing*, FT/Pitman, London.

Payne, Adrian (1993) *The Essence of Services Marketing*, Prentice Hall, New Jersey.

Reichheld, Frederick (1996) *The Loyalty Effect*, Harvard Business School Press, Boston, MA.

SCENARIO PLANNING

S cenario planning involves testing business strategies against a series of alternative futures. The technique was invented in the 1940s by Herman Kahn, the famous futurist from the Rand Corporation and the Hudson Institute. The term scenario – meaning a detailed outline for the plot of a future film – was borrowed from Hollywood by Kahn's friend, the screenwriter and novelist Leo Rosten.

Kahn was best known for his scenarios about nuclear war – and his trademark phrase 'thinking the unthinkable'. Other early pioneers of scenario thinking also tended to look at the macro-level – the future of mankind, for example, or the economy of an entire region.

'These stories about the future aimed at helping people break past their mental blocks and consider the "unthinkable" futures, which would take them by surprise if they weren't prepared,' explains management commentator Art Kleiner in *The Age of Heretics*. 'The point was not to make accurate predictions (although like all futurists he [Kahn] gleefully loved being right), but to come up with a mythic story that brings the point home.'

Although only now coming into wider use, scenario planning has been practiced in one form or another in the business world since the early 1960s. It was first used by a far-sighted team of planners at the oil company Royal Dutch Shell. They began to build on Kahn's work, developing their own version of the scenario approach as a possible answer to two questions: 'how do we look up to 20 to 30 years ahead?' and 'how can we get people to discuss the "unthinkable" together?' Using the technique, they foresaw the energy crises of 1973 and 1979, the growth of energy conservation, the evolution of the global environmental movement, and even the break-up of the Soviet Union, years before these events happened. What Shell realized, however, was that managers need a translation of these grand scenarios into something more recognizable. To have practical use in business, the story needs to be focused on a particular audience or issue. Learning to focus scenarios on a specific business purpose was part of the company's contribution to the practice.

In the 1990s, a string of books, including *The Art of the Long View* by futurist Peter Schwartz, *The Living Company* written by former Shell manager Arie de Geus, and the *Age of Heretics* by Art Kleiner, who interviewed Shell managers, has drawn attention to scenario planning, placing it firmly on the management agenda. It is no coincidence, of course, that the technique is coming to the fore now, at a time when so many seemingly unassailable companies have been wrong-footed by changes in their trading environments.

Timely as it is, even Shell has been guilty of taking its eye off the ball recently in allowing environmental pressure groups to dictate the pace of change. Other companies have much to learn if the technique is to offer a useful tool. As de Geus notes in his book *The Living Company*, today scenario planning 'remains surrounded by vagueness and an air of mystery. People are unsure whether it is a process for reaching better decisions; a way to know the future better; or a combination of both.'

In fact, many of those who use the technique say it is a way to facilitate lateral thinking in an organization. Although sometimes confused with disaster planning or contingency planning – which deal with how a company should respond when things go wrong – scenario planning is a way to identify both threats and opportunities that flow from decisions.

Despite the changing nature of the modern business world, an important aspect of scenario planning is the recognition that there is an element of predictability about the future. The art is to find out how much of the ambiguity is due to ignorance and limited perspective and how much is due to inherent uncertainty.

According to Clem Sunter, head of scenario planning at Anglo American Corporation and another leading authority on the technique, 'Scenarios are to organizations what radar is to a pilot. They help us look for the first signs of changes that can profoundly affect how we work, and make us think about our responses.'

Key texts and further reading

Schwartz, Peter (1991) *The Art of the Long View*, Wiley, Doubleday, New York.

Van der Heijden, Kees (1996) *Scenarios: The Art of Strategic Conversations*, Wiley, Chichester, UK.

de Geus, Arie (1997) *The Living Company*, Harvard Business School Press, Boston, MA.

Ringland, Gill (1998) *Scenario Planning*, Wiley, Chichester, UK.

Ideas into action

Scenarists talk about 'wind tunnelling' strategies and policies. In effect, each scenario – or story about the future – represents a different set of conditions in the wind tunnel. A policy – or strategy decision – is the prototype aircraft that must be tested in the wind tunnel to see how it performs under varying conditions. A strategy may stand up well in one scenario, the argument goes, but the wings could drop off in another.

Professor Kees van der Heijden of Strathclyde University in Scotland was head of scenario planning at Shell in the 1980s. His team was responsible for developing scenarios that, among other things, looked at the impact of environmental issues on Shell's business. 'Traditional planning is based on identifying trends and extrapolating into the future,' he says. 'But no matter how good the analysis, it is always a projection of the past. Yet we know the future is uncertain, and that there is more than one possible future that a company may have to operate in.'

As with traditional planning, the starting point with scenario planning is to try to identify what is predictable and what is not. But the scenario planner tries to get behind the trends or patterns to understand the 'driving forces'. These make up what is called the 'causal texture' which gives a common structure for scenarios. It is possible then to develop a number of stories within that structure representing different conditions or futures.

This is a radical departure for most companies. Businesses have traditionally preferred a 'one solution' view of strategy, taking a bet on one future and planning accordingly. Most large companies have little experience of entertaining several equally plausible futures. But once they accept that it is impossible to predict the future, the need for 'multi-future thinking' becomes apparent.

Scenario planning is all about living with ambiguity. It can be applied at many different levels.

'Operational decisions should be wind tunnelled in the same way as top-level strategy,' says Professor van der Heijden. 'It could relate to recruitment, reward levels, or skills training, but what you try to do is see how a decision will perform under different scenarios.'

One of the most powerful demonstrations of how scenario planning can make a difference was in South Africa. In the mid-1980s, Clem Sunter, head of scenario planning at Anglo American Corporation, was asked by the De Klerk government to put together some scenarios for what would happen following Nelson Mandela's release. Sunter visited Mandela in prison and talked to key members of De Klerk's cabinet.

Based on those discussions, Sunter and other members of his team gave numerous lectures to the public, outlining scenarios for South Africa to the year 2000. The country, they said, could all too easily revert to civil war, with tragic consequences. But at the same time they challenged South Africans to 'think the unthinkable'. What if all South Africans sat down at a negotiating table to work out a new constitution peacefully instead of having a civil war? What if sanctions were lifted and trade resumed with the rest of the world?

Sunter says, 'By presenting a positive future for South Africa as a possibility when all around were so utterly negative about the country's prospects, we helped change the direction of the national debate.'

SCIENTIFIC MANAGEMENT

The concept of scientific management will forever be associated with the name of the industrial engineer and inventor Frederick Winslow Taylor. *Principles of Scientific Management,*[1] the book he published in 1911, made Taylor one of the most influential figures of the twentieth century.

Taylor's 'science' (which he described as 'seventy-five percent science and twenty-five percent common sense') came from the minute examination of individual workers' tasks. Having identified every single movement and action involved in performing a task, Taylor believed he could determine the optimum time required to complete it. Armed with this information, a manager could decide whether a worker was doing the job well.

Famous for his time and motion studies at the Midvale Steel Works, where he was chief engineer, Taylor used his stopwatch to break down complex processes into simple tasks thereby increasing efficiency. A visionary in his own right, Taylor anticipated the rise of reductionism, which had a great influence on twentieth century thinking. (Reductionism is based on the belief that if a problem can be reduced to its smallest component, and that component understood, then it is possible to comprehend the whole. Scientists believed for a time that if they could understand how the smallest particle in the universe worked, then they would unlock all its other secrets.)

The origins of scientific management lay in his observations of his fellow workers. He noticed that they engaged in what was then called 'soldiering'. Instead of working as hard and as fast as they could, they deliberately slowed down. They had no incentive to go faster or to be more productive. It was in their interest, Taylor said, to keep 'their employers ignorant of how fast work can be done'. 'Nineteen out of twenty workmen throughout the civilized world firmly believe that it is for their best interests to go slow instead of to go fast. They firmly believe that it is for their interest to give as little work in return for the money that they get as is practical,' Taylor later wrote in *The Principles of Scientific Management*.

Ideas into action

A famous example of Taylorism involved a theoretical pig iron handler called Schmidt. Taylor calculated that Schmidt, working in the most efficient manner, could load 47 tons a day rather than the more usual 12½ tons. Such precise calculations of productivity, he believed, meant that workers would know exactly what was expected of them and that managers knew exactly how much should be produced. It also meant that more accurate piecework rates could be set with more reliable bonuses and penalties.

The introduction of Taylor's ideas at the Watertown Arsenal reduced the labour cost of making certain moulds for the pommel of a pack-saddle from $1.17 to 54 cents. The labour cost of building a six-inch gun carriage fell from $10,229 to $6950. The logic was simple. Measurement increased production as everyone knew what he had to do. Increased production was achieved with lower costs and this led to bigger profits. The gap between the increases in production and those in pay was increased profit. Typically, Schmidt increased production by 400% while receiving 60% more pay.

Taylor's ideas were picked up by Henry Ford, who used them as the basis for his model for mass production. Ford had created a manufacturing process in which cars mounted on cradles were pushed from one work-station to the next, while workers swarmed around them assembling components. To fill demand for the Model T, Ford had to scrap this system. In 1913, he redefined the work to stop the swarming. 'The man who puts in a bolt does not put on the nut; the man who puts on the nut does not tighten it,' said Ford.[2] Partially assembled cars were also roped together so they could be pulled past the workers at a predictable speed. In a single year, production doubled to nearly 200,000 while the number of workers fell from 14,336 to 12,880. The forerunner of the modern assembly line was born.

Outdated though Taylorism may seem today, it was one of the first serious attempts to create a science of management. As Lyndall Urwick, the British champion of scientific management, noted in 1956: 'At the time Taylor began his work, business management as a discrete and identifiable activity had attracted little attention. It was usually regarded as incidental to, and flowing from, knowledge-or-acquaintance-with, a particular branch of manufacturing, the technical know-how of making sausages or steel or shirts.'

Taylor, then, helped put management on the map, and his work has had a profound impact throughout the world, leaving a lasting legacy.

Although he is now largely disregarded, Taylor's fingerprints can be seen on much of the management literature produced in the twentieth century, and his ideas actually underpin a great deal of management thinking. His emphasis on measurement, for example, foreshadowed the emergence of the total quality management movement, which still dominates many industries.

A 1997 *Fortune* article noted, 'Taylor's influence is omnipresent: It's his ideas that determine how many burgers McDonald's expects its flippers to flip or how many callers the phone company expects its operators to assist.'

Peter Drucker has cited Taylor's thinking as 'the most lasting contribution America has made to Western thought since *The Federalist Papers*'. Taylor's influence, he suggests, was greater even than Henry Ford. The assembly line was simply a logical extension of scientific management.

The workers had one notable advantage: their superiors had no idea how long the job should take. No one had thought to examine the nature of people's work. Irritated by such brazen inefficiency, Taylor set to work. Armed with a stopwatch, he examined in intimate detail exactly what happened and how long it took. Taylor surmised that minute examination of a task would enable the observer to establish the best means of carrying out the job. A single, preferred, efficient means of completing the task could then be established and insisted on in the future.

However, Taylor saw the way that management organized labour as the limit of decision making within an organization. In effect, he saw workers as nothing more than the components in a machine, which was operated by management.

Today, happily, workers are seen as much more than simply cogs and wheels. What has changed in recent years is that the value that so-called knowledge workers in particular add comes not from the machines they operate but from the application of what they know.

Key text and further reading

Taylor, F.W. (1911) *The Principles of Scientific Management*, Harper & Row, New York.

Frederick Taylor

Frederick Winslow Taylor was born in Germantown, Pennsylvania, on 20 March 1856 into an affluent Philadelphia family. Taylor's father was a lawyer from an old Pennsylvania Quaker family; his mother, Emily Winslow, from an old New England Puritan family. (Her father was a New Bedford whaler.) Emily was a prominent anti-slavery agitator and a campaigner for women's rights.

Educated in France and Germany, he travelled throughout Europe before eventually returning to the Phillips Exeter Academy. (Taylor retained strong European connections throughout his life. He spent vacations in Brittany and shortly before his death saluted the French and Belgian attempts at repelling the German forces in World War I.)

Despite his well-heeled background, Taylor began his working life at the bottom of the engineering ladder. He initially worked as an apprentice at the William Sellers Company in Philadelphia. In 1878, he went to work at the Midvale Steel Company, near Philadelphia. At Midvale, Taylor began as a clerk, though he soon moved back down the company's ranks to become a labourer. Taylor's role appeared to change almost monthly. In six years at Midvale he was keeper of tool cribs, assistant foreman, foreman, master mechanic, director of research, and finally chief engineer of the entire plant. While working, he also reactivated his academic career. (He had been destined for Harvard before poor eyesight reputedly intervened.) Taylor spent three years (1880 to 1883) studying engineering at evening classes at the Stevens Institute. He stayed at Midvale until 1889, and it was his observations there that formed the basis for his theories of what became known as scientific management.

He later worked at a variety of places, most notably the Bethlehem Steel Company. At Bethlehem he attempted wide-ranging changes. Not all of these were either successful or popular and Taylor was eventually fired in 1901. Ten years later, he published *The Principles of Scientific Management*.

Notes

1   The title *Scientific Management* was decided on by a small group of engineers and thinkers who met in 1910 in New York. They

included the lawyer Louis Brandeis and Henry Gantt. Among the alternative titles considered were: *Shop Management; Efficiency; Functional Management;* and *The Taylor System.*

2   Stewart, Thomas A., Taylor, Alex, Petre, Peter and Schlender, Brent (1999) 'The Businessman of the Century', *Fortune,* 22 November 1999.

SEVEN S FRAMEWORK

T he seven S framework is no more than a simple distillation of the key elements that make up an organization's personality. Developed around 1980 by two business school academics and a group of consultants at McKinsey and Company, it provides a useful checklist for thinking about what makes a business tick. It advocates examination in seven basic areas, all beginning with S: strategy; structure; systems; style; skills; staff; and shared values.

Two factors make the seven S framework stand out from the countless concepts developed every year in consulting firms and business schools. First, it provides a surprisingly robust and useful tool. And second, a number of those involved went on to become famous business writers and commentators. The story of the seven S framework is linked to two of the most influential business books of the past 30 years.

In the summer of 1978, McKinsey consultant Robert Waterman asked two academics, Richard Pascale from Stanford and Anthony Athos from Harvard, to help him out. Waterman and his McKinsey colleague Tom Peters were trying to make sense of some research they had done on the characteristics of successful companies, and which would eventually form the basis of the best-selling book *In Search of Excellence*. They were struggling to establish the crucial links.

It was agreed that the four would spend five days in a small room discovering what they knew and didn't know about organizations. The idea was straightforward, though Athos and Pascale had reservations about the human dynamics. Concerned that the hyperactive Peters would hijack the proceedings, Athos suggested that an agenda for the five days was essential.[1] He recalled an approach used by one of his colleagues, Cyrus (Chuck) Gibson, which would provide a useful framework for the discussions. Gibson had a scheme – strategy, structure and systems – which he had developed for Harvard's Programme for Management Development which Gibson and Athos ran. Athos suggested they use this as the framework for their discussions, starting with strategy on Monday, then moving on to structure on Tuesday, and systems on Wednesday. To this he added his own themes of 'guiding concepts', which he renamed 'super-ordinate goals', and 'shared values'. Pascale suggested 'style', and between them the two academics arrived with five of what eventually became the seven Ss.

The idea of creating an accessible model was not new. Peters and Waterman later acknowledged their debt to Harold Leavitt's 'Diamond' model, which boiled the facts of managerial life down to task, structure, people, information, control and environment. Leavitt's model is not a million miles away from what became the seven S model. But Athos and Pascale persuaded Peters and Waterman to use the alliterative labelling, arguing that its advantages outweighed its lack of sophistication. Peters suggested adding 'skill' to the framework. So, armed with six words beginning with S, Peters and Waterman acquainted interested parties in McKinsey with their developing model.

A few weeks later, they introduced the six Ss at an internal meeting. In preparing for the meeting, Peters and Waterman, still aided by Athos and Pascale, laboured over how to make their message more accessible and understandable. Not content with six variables, Peters and Pascale suggested another was needed, one that had to do with timing and implementation. Athos and Pascale proposed calling it 'sequencing'.

This version of the magnificent seven proved short-lived. Julien Phillips, an associate in McKinsey's San Francisco office, then joined the team. He argued that sequencing should be replaced by staff. The other four quickly agreed. Peters had suggested 'people' should be included and, in his teaching at Harvard, Athos was using the awkward and decidedly unalliterative 'aggregates of people'. Peters also weighed in with the possibility of adding 'power' somewhere. This didn't happen. So, the group was left with seven: systems, strategy, structure, style, skills, shared values and staff.

The quartet agreed on seven Ss. These were then passed on to McKinsey's graphics department, which created an image of a molecule. The seven S model was born. It was neatly alliterative, accessible, understandable and with its logo (later named 'the happy atom') highly marketable. The decision was then made to take the model to the real world. Managers seemed to like it. The seven S model was a business theory to fit all occasions, encapsulated on a single page.

The seven S model first saw the light of day in published form in June 1980. Waterman, Peters and Phillips put together an article: 'Structure is not organization'. This was published in *Business Horizons*, the journal of Indiana University's Graduate School of Business. The article was tentative, almost apologetic – 'As yet the seven S framework is admittedly no more than a rough conceptual tool for helping managers to understand the complexity of effective organization change – and to design change programmes that are rich in concept and humble in expectations. The Framework's virtues – realism and relative simplicity – are likely to have a good deal more appeal to practising managers than the academic researchers.'

Meanwhile, Pascale and Athos were working on what was to become *The Art of Japanese Management,* published in 1981. They decided to use the seven S model in the book. This introduced it to a mass audience. For Athos and Pascale, the seven Ss provided a useful framework to analyse the differences between Western and Japanese companies. In particular, it highlighted the greater emphasis that Japanese companies afforded to the softer elements of style, shared values, skills and staff, at a time when Western companies were obsessed with the hard Ss of structure, systems and strategy.

'The framework is nothing more than seven important categories that managers pay attention to,' Pascale later observed. 'There is nothing sacred about the number seven. There could be six or eight Ss. The value of a framework such as the Seven Ss is that it imposes an interesting discipline on the researcher.'

Peters and Waterman also featured the framework in *In Search of Excellence* when it was published a year later (despite the fact that Tom Peters initially thought the seven S framework 'corny').

Simple it may have been, but the seven S framework set the business research agenda for the next twenty years. Most of the business books that have followed, intentionally or unintentionally, start from the seven S framework.

Perhaps its enduring legacy is that it provided a useful way to classify the components that made up an organization. As a result, the seven S framework offered a common platform for academics, consultants and practitioners to discuss organizational characteristics. As a starting point for further examination it was invaluable.

Today, when Japanese companies have fallen off their pedestal and the cult of 'excellence' started by Peters and Waterman seems finally to have run its course, it's easy to forget how influential the ideas behind them were. For the first time, the seven S framework enabled meaningful comparisons to be made between companies from completely different sectors, national cultures and histories. As a way to cover the basics, it remains a useful concept.

The seven S framework was a product of its time. In his 1990 book *Managing on the Edge*, Richard Pascale, one of its originators, sought to demolish the very movement that it helped give rise to. Once again, his book captures the mood of the decade. He rails against the simplicity of Peters and Waterman's *In Search of Excellence*. 'Simply identifying attributes of success is like identifying attributes of people in excellent health during the age of the bubonic plague,' he says. 'Passions and obsession frequently degenerate into simplistic formulae e.g. acronyms such as KISS (keep it simple stupid).'

Pascale had moved on. Orderly answers are no longer appropriate. Instead the new emphasis should be on asking questions. Companies must become 'engines of enquiry'. Like the Boston matrix, the seven S framework belongs to an era that is gone. The simple truths it uncovered are no longer considered worthy of our attention. But as a milestone in the evolution of management theory, it still has much to tell us.

Key texts and further reading

Pascale, Richard and Athos, Anthony (1981) *The Art of Japanese Management,* Penguin, London.

Peters, Thomas J. and Waterman, Robert H. (1982) *In Search of Excellence,* Harper & Row, New York.

Crainer, Stuart (1997) *Corporate Man to Corporate Skunk: A biography of Tom Peters,* Capstone, Oxford.

Note

1   Crainer, Stuart (1997) *Corporate Man to Corporate Skunk: A biography of Tom Peters*, Capstone, Oxford.

Ideas into action

The attraction of the seven Ss is that they are memorable and simple. The framework is a model of how organizations achieve success. Inevitably a model which simplifies something as complex as organizational behaviour is open to abuse, misinterpretation and criticism. The seven S framework has suffered more than its fair share. (Contrast this with the generally positive response still reserved for Michael Porter's five forces model of competitiveness, which simplifies something equally as complex but does so in a far more analytical and academic way.)

The matter of how practically useful the seven S framework actually is continues to be discussed – in business school classrooms at least. The truth is that no one ever ran a business with a framework. The seven Ss are a helpful summation of the major issues which bedevil managerial life. But they are only practically useful as a memory jogger, a structure around which to build, or as a filter to determine key issues. They are not, never could be, and were never intended to be, set in stone.

THE SHAMROCK ORGANIZATION

I n recent years the organizational structure most appropriate for the future has been widely discussed and has given rise to a number of new models. British management thinker Charles Handy has been one of the most considered participants in this debate. He anticipated that certain forms of organization would become dominant. These were the type of organization most readily associated with service industries.

First, and most famous, was Handy's shamrock organization. The shamrock organization[1] describes a type of organizational structure with three parts, or leaves – 'a form of organization based around a core of essential executives and workers supported by outside contractors and part-time help'. The consequence of such an organizational form was that organizations in the future are likely to resemble the way consultancy firms, advertising agencies and professional partnerships are currently structured.

This model, or some variation of it, is often used to explain the move to outsourcing non-core functions. In Handy's analogy, the first leaf of the shamrock represents the core staff of the organization. These people are likely to be highly trained professionals who make up the senior management. The second leaf consists of the contractual fringe – either individuals or other organizations – and may include people who once worked for the organization but now provide it with services. These individuals operate within the broad framework set down by the core but have a high level of discretionary decision-making power to complete projects or deliver contacts. The third leaf includes the flexible labour force. More than simply hired hands, in Handy's model these workers have to be sufficiently close to the organization to feel a sense of commitment, which ensures that their work – although part-time or intermittent – is carried out to a high standard.

The second emergent structure identified by Handy was the federal organization – not, he pointed out, another word for decentralization. He provided a blueprint for federal organizations in which the central function coordinates, influences, advises and suggests. It does not dictate terms or short-term decisions. The centre is, however, concerned with long-term strategy. It is 'at the middle of things and is not a polite word for the top or even for head office'.

The third type of organization Handy anticipated is what he called 'the Triple I' – information, intelligence and ideas. In such organizations the demands on personnel management are large. Handy explained, 'The wise organization already knows that their smart people are not to be easily defined as workers or as managers but as individuals, as specialists, as professionals or executives, or as leaders (the older terms of manager and worker are dropping out of use), and that they and it need also to be obsessed with the pursuit of learning if they are going to keep up with the pace of change.'

More recently, Handy has suggested that successful organizations of the future will be what he calls 'membership communities'. His logic is that in order to hold people to an organization that can no longer promise them a job for life, companies have to offer some other form of continuity and sense of belonging. To do this, he suggests, companies have to imbue members with certain rights.

What Handy is advocating is, in fact, some notion of the federal organization, built on the principle of subsidiarity. This places a large degree of trust in its core professionals and other knowledge workers. As he told Joel Kurtzman in an interview for *Strategy & Business*:[2]

'You must leave as much power as low as possible in the organization as that's where the knowledge and experience are. It seems to me that subsidiarity is at the heart of professionalism. Think for a moment about the doctor in the emergency room of a hospital. The doctor is in charge even though she may be straight out of medical school and her specialty training. The doctor is in total charge in that place at that time because she has the knowledge and the skills. As a consequence all the decisions are hers to make.

'This is how I conceive of the members of the corporation … Decisions have to be made where the knowledge is. So I believe professionals have rights within the organization. I believe they need rights to do their jobs.'

Under Handy's membership community model, the centre is kept small and its primary purpose is to be 'in charge of the future'. Only if the organization is severely threatened does decision-making power revert to the centre. This allows the company to react quickly in a crisis. The rest of the time, decision making is highly decentralized.

In this sense, it is similar to the United States of America, where authority over foreign policy and other issues affecting national security reside in Washington, but the individual states retain much of the power over local decisions.

Ideas into action

As with all visionaries, Handy's view of the future does not remain stationary, but continues to evolve. His 1996 book *The Hungry Spirit* again challenged the *status quo*. 'I detect a growing disillusionment with the market system. An insecurity that drives organizations and managers to over-compensate by over-working and over-earning,' he wrote.

Building on the shamrock model and his other earlier work, this marks a new concern with the essential humanity of businesspeople. 'We can't go on managing people as we have. The focus of careers is "how rich can I get". That's very sad. Great groups are not motivated by money but a sense of what they can achieve. A bit of Darwinian jungle is good; it keeps an organization on its toes. But too much kills it. We have created a mercenary society. Getting richer and richer, and bigger and bigger has become a substitute for not believing in what we are doing.'[3]

The Hungry Spirit draws on the changes he documented in earlier work including the *Age of Unreason* and its sequel *The Empty Raincoat*. As ever, the writing has an elegant simplicity, a crispness of delivery that others of the genre can only aspire to. Many of the ideas were not new, but Handy has always had a knack of picking up on what's floating around in the ether and making it accessible to people who can use it.

The Hungry Spirit involved a shift of perspective. Handy was painting on a bigger canvas. There was a struggle to put it all together; to make sense of a chaotic world and to provide a sustainable framework for the future. He was reaching for a new business lexicon, urging others to discard the dehumanizing and mechanistic language of business – typified by words such as 'engineering' and 'resource management' – for one based on people and relationships.

'Life-time employment is not realistic,' he says, 'but what's happened in recent years has encouraged people to behave like mercenaries. Employability is just another word for look after yourself, mate. You have to offer people some guarantees if you want their commitment. Otherwise you will get an awful lot of short-term thinking. To some extent, it's a reversal of what I used to say. Instead of pushing people out to portfolio careers, companies now have to find a way of locking their best people in.'

At the heart of his new model is the idea of citizenship. To retain their key people, he suggests, organizations should make them citizens. As citizens, they would enjoy certain rights and obligations, which would be enshrined in a written constitution for the organization

– and a bill of rights. 'I prefer to think of rights and expectations,' says Handy. 'Companies already have an expectation that people will do their damnedest to advance the cause, but at the moment the company refuses to make any commitment of its own to them.'

But not everyone would be given full citizen status, only those on whom the organization relies for its future success and survival: those who make up its core, about a third by Handy's calculations. They would include senior managers, some specialists, the future senior managers, and some people with special responsibilities such as heads of overseas operations.

'People would have to earn citizenship. Like getting a green card, they would have to prove they can do jobs that no one else can. As citizens they would not be guaranteed a job for life but would have the security of a fixed-term contract for ten years or so.'

For examples of how such a system might work, Handy points to professional partnerships, where managers must earn their spurs and demonstrate commitment to the firm before being made partners. In the US, universities bestow tenure only on those they fear losing. The British army, he says, offers another working model.

'It is an organization with terrific commitment, both ways. The army needs a few wise old heads with experience, but it doesn't need that many. So it starts out by offering a recruit a seven-year contract. It also says, "We'll train you so that you'll be more valuable when you leave". After seven years the army can offer another contract for ten years or so, but it doesn't offer that contract to everyone.'

Such an arrangement, he believes, would be a first step towards a system which motivated people through a sense of belonging and an alignment of personal and professional aspirations rather than fear and greed. 'I think companies have to wake up to the idea that making more money for shareholders is not the point. I think people are hungry for a better world, hungry for some sense of meaning in their work. I don't think I'm a prophet in the wilderness. I'm trying to give a voice to the silent majority. I think if they had a voice they'd say life could be better, and it could be richer. Some people will say I'm naive, but it's the belief that others feel it too that makes me optimistic.'

At times of great threat to the survival of the USA, however, power flows to the executive arm, so that the president has complete authority over the armed forces as commander-in-chief. The same, Handy suggests, should happen with the new-style company.

Key texts and further reading

Handy, Charles (1989) *The Age of Unreason*, Century Business Books, London.
Handy, Charles (1997) *The Hungry Spirit*, Random House, London.
Kurtzman, Joel (1995–6) 'An interview with Charles Handy,' *Strategy & Business*, Issues 1–3.

Notes

1   Handy, Charles (1989) *The Age of Unreason*, Century Business Books, London.
2   Kurtzman, Joel (1995–6) 'An interview with Charles Handy', *Strategy & Business*, Issues 1-3, .
3   Author interview.

SHAREHOLDER VALUE

S hareholder value arrived with the sort of trumpeting which usually accompanies a big idea. Yet it really didn't say anything new. Shareholder value simply contends that a company should aim to maximize its value to shareholders. Indeed, this should be the *raison d'être* of the company. The concept gave rise to that of value-based management, which suggested that generating profits was not enough, and that share price performance in particular should be viewed as a key indicator of corporate competence.

This exposes two very different views about the role of companies. It suggests that shareholders are the only ones that count. This overlooks the responsibility to employees and the wider community. (Many would argue that simply serving shareholders is not, and never can be, the be-all and end-all of a company's purpose, and that the crystallization of shareholder value as an explicit concept is simply the last hurrah of an outdated notion of business.)

But to large organizations, this perspective can be attractive for a number of reasons. First, it articulates the reasons for a company's existence with commendable clarity. There is none of the vagueness of making *reasonable* profits and pleasing all the company's stakeholders. It sounds both laudable and achievable – and shareholders are duty bound to like the idea. Second (with some adjustments), it fits in with the entire idea of the stakeholder corporation. Shareholders are stakeholders and their numbers are increasingly likely to include other stakeholders such as employees. Clearly, adding value to the investments of shareholders can have widespread benefits inside and outside an organization. Of course, cynics are fond of pointing out that the fact that many senior executives hold large swathes of shares as part of their remuneration packages adds little to the attractiveness of maximizing shareholder value.

In one important respect, emphasizing shareholder value may serve an important purpose. Its advocates claim that it encourages a longer-term view of corporate performance. Instead of desperately seeking to boost quarterly results, executives can channel their energies into creat-

Ideas into action

Shareholder value remains a popular concept, especially with share-holders. The trouble is that actually calculating shareholder value or, indeed, the value of anything, is a hazardous exercise. Keen to cash in on the fashion for shareholder value, consulting firms have produced a bewildering variety of products which promise to explain – and meas-ure – all. The alternatives include economic value added; cash flow return on investment; and value-based management. These revolve around a variety of measures and approaches.

It is at this point that the going becomes complex. Approaches differ. Alfred Rappaport concentrates on measuring what he labels 'value drivers' – these include sales-growth rates, operating profit mar-gins and the cost of capital. Others champion the case for measuring total shareholder return (TSR) which calculates the rate of return from the original purchase; the dividend stream received by the investor; and its sale at the end of the holding period. Still others argue that the three most important things companies need to measure are customer satisfaction, employee satisfaction and cash flow.

Eventually, through one measure or another, a company will be able to assess its value-related performance. Then comes the next step, which is equally challenging: what rate of value growth is achievable and desirable? Average performance in the FTSE 100 over three years requires a TSR of about 6 to 8% (plus the inflation rate), while top quartile performance requires an additional 5 to 8%.

While sceptics suggest that shareholder value is simply another consulting invention, its popularity among companies like Lloyds-TSB Group and top US conglomerates suggests that it is a robust tool, at least to monitor performance. And, for global businesses, perhaps the greatest advantage of shareholder value is that it provides universally consistent corporate results rather than ones produced to the dictates of local accounting rules.

ing long-term value growth for shareholders. Institutional shareholders like the long view and this element was vital in the development of the concept. During the 1980s, companies lived in fear of the attentions of corporate predators who identified lack of shareholder value as a con-vincing case for a takeover. As arguments for takeover go, this is the one most likely to succeed with shareholders. (The next question must be whether shareholder value is then the best way to run a business. This is a more weighty matter.)

Critics of the concept also voice doubts about whether long-term perspectives are encouraged. After all, they argue, downsizing was popular among shareholders who, perversely, often saw the value of their investments go up when a company announced it was downsizing.

While such arguments are difficult to prove either way, what can be said is that value-based management seeks to bridge the gap between the aims of executives and employees and those of shareholders. In the past, companies tended to measure success solely in terms of profits. If profits increased year on year, executives felt they were doing a good job. If, at the same time, the share price under-performed, they offered reassurance to institutional investors, but little else. In contrast, value-based management is as interested in cash and capital invested as it is in calculations about profitability. 'Cash is a fact, profit is an opinion,' argues one of the creators of the concept, Alfred Rappaport of Northwestern University's Kellogg School of Management. Indeed, in many ways, shareholder value transports the small business phobia of cash flow to larger corporations.

Indeed, value-based management goes against some of the first principles of corporate life. Most obviously it calls into question the accounting model of measuring corporate performance. Erwin Scholtz of Ashridge Management College is among those who pour a measure of scorn on the traditional accounting model whose currency is profits rather than cash. Scholtz suggests that the accounting model is:

- *incomplete* (as it does not account for the full cost of capital);
- *complex* (it uses multiple performance measures);
- *inconsistent* (producing conflicting signals);
- *incorrect* (as accounting conventions may distort true economic performance); and
- *ineffective* (as it is often disconnected from the management systems and operational drivers of the business).

Key texts and further reading

Black, Andrew, Wright, Philip, Bachman, John E., Davies, John, Maskall, Mike and Wright, Phillip (1998) *In Search of Shareholder Value: Managing the drivers of performance*, Financial Times Management, London.

Knight, James A. (1997) *Value Based Management: Developing a systematic approach to creating shareholder value,* McGraw-Hill, New York.

Rappaport, Alfred (1997) (revised edition) *Creating Shareholder Value: A guide for managers and investors,* Free Press, New York.

Stewart, G. Bennett (1991) *The Quest for Value: the Eva™ Management Guide,* HarperBusiness, New York.

STRATEGIC INFLECTION POINT

S trategic inflection point is a term associated with Andy Grove, chairman of the microprocessor company Intel. Strategic inflection points, Grove says, occur when a company's competitive position goes through a transition. It is the point at which the organization must alter the path it is on – adapting itself to the new situation – or risk going into decline. It is concerned with how companies recognize and adapt to 'paradigm changes'.

'During a strategic inflection point, the way a business operates, the very structure and concept of the business, undergoes a change,' Grove writes. 'But the irony is that at that point itself nothing much happens. That subtle point is like the eye of a hurricane. There is no wind at the eye of the hurricane, but when it moves the wind hits you again.

'That is what happens in the middle of the transformation from one business model to another. The irony is that, even though these are the most cataclysmic changes that a business can undertake, more often than not those changes are missed.'

Grove was so enamoured of the term that *Strategic Inflection Points* was the original title of his 1996 book – until the publishers rejected it in favour of the more memorable *Only the Paranoid Survive*. What adds to the credibility of the concept is that it comes from one of the leading business practitioners of recent years. Andy Grove is one of the best-known figures in the computer industry. He helped found Intel in 1968, along with Gordon Moore and Robert Noyce, and guided the company to much of its current success as Intel's president, chief executive officer, and chairman.

Grove was born in 1936 in Hungary, and received a PhD from the University of California at Berkeley in 1963. After graduating, he joined the Fairchild Semiconductor Corp. before co-founding Intel. In 1997, *Time* magazine named Grove as its Man of the Year. In 1998, he stepped down as CEO of Intel, but continues as chairman of the board. Grove also teaches at the Stanford University Graduate School of Business.

Ideas into action

The trouble with traditional strategic planning approaches is that they tend to extrapolate the past to create a view of the future. As a result they often preserve, rather than challenge, industry assumptions. Traditional planning processes tend to analyse external factors individually, therefore missing the power that is unleashed when trends converge. The theory of strategic inflection points recognizes this phenomenon and gives it a name.

Some strategic theory, notably around core competencies, suggest that companies extrapolate today's capabilities and market conditions into the future, rather than establishing where a company wants to be in the future and then identifying what must happen to get there. Grove recommends that senior managers watch out for warning signs. 'If suddenly things don't work the same way they always used to, you may be on the cusp of a strategic inflection point,' he notes. 'Here's how to recognize the signs: First, there is a troubling sense that something is different. Things happen to your business that didn't before. Your business no longer responds to your actions. Customers' attitudes toward you are different. Competitors you wrote off or hardly knew existed are stealing business from you. You find yourself befuddled by what's going on. You increasingly hear the telling phrase: "Something has changed!"'

What can companies do in response? Grove suggests that CEOs must be prepared to experiment, and let chaos reign for a while (he calls this second phase 'strategic dissonance.') This can involve changing marketing or product focus that seems way-out, and then monitoring responses. This phase is about deciding how the business should respond. This sort of 'chaotic catharsis', he suggests, helps clear the mind of the old restraints put in place by old assumptions. From it, a clear picture should emerge about how to deal with the inflection point. The CEO then has to end the experimentation – to 'rein in chaos' – and set the new strategic direction. Once the new course is clear, swift action is vital.

'Looking back over my own career, I have never made a tough change that I haven't wished I had made a year or so earlier,' Grove observes. 'So build in your bias for delay, and force yourself to commit to a course of action as soon as you grasp what needs to be done.'

In the real world, the need to spot paradigm changes is most acute for high-tech companies such as Intel. Indeed, it was IBM's original failure to spot the switch from mainframe to personal computers that allowed Intel and Microsoft to create their dominant market positions. Both companies have inculcated their cultures with the lesson. Grove underscores his message by examining his own record of success and failure, including how he navigated the events of the flawed Pentium chip, which threatened Intel's reputation in 1994, and how he has dealt with the explosions in growth of the internet.

Grove explicitly recognizes that the pace of change in the modern business world is such that entire markets and industries can change almost overnight. This places an increasing burden on strategy makers to try to anticipate what's just around the next corner and position their company to take maximum advantage. For companies that enjoy dominant positions, such as Intel, the name of the game is scanning the horizon to spot paradigm shifts that could undermine their market leadership.

Where once companies focused on incremental change, improving products and services a little bit all the time, the emphasis is increasingly on discontinuous change. The new game is all about jumping from one paradigm to the next. It is about who can get to the future first.

It involves the ability to discard current assumptions to shape the future of the industry – before someone else does. Grove calls this '10x change', and it can either undermine a business model or create tremendous new growth opportunities. Companies that do this recognize that traditional strategic planning approaches are insufficient for identifying and capitalizing on such change. The hard part is correctly anticipating where a market will go and how to get there first. Yet some companies seem able to do it year after year.

'Strategic anticipation is about facing the future, which for most industries is likely to be a future characterized by discontinuous change,' Rob Duboff, a director in the Boston office of Mercer Management Consulting, has noted. 'These are the changes that take place in discrete bursts, rather than evolving slowly and steadily – changes that force customers and companies to give up long and widely-held assumptions.'

Key text and further reading

Grove, A. (1996) *Only the Paranoid Survive*, Doubleday, New York.

STRATEGIC MANAGEMENT

Although he has been referred to as the 'father' of strategy, to say that Igor Ansoff invented the concept would be an overstatement. What can be said is that in 1965 he published the first book specifically devoted to strategy. It was called *Corporate Strategy*. For the first time, it viewed the role of strategic decision making by senior management as a distinct activity.

Ansoff was born in Vladivostok in December 1918, a year after the Russian Revolution. As his father was American and his mother Russian, Ansoff was entitled to American citizenship but his parents opted to live, for a time, in Moscow. In 1936, the Ansoff family moved to New York. The 17-year-old Igor arrived convinced that America's capitalistic system was corrupt to the core and its society in a shambles. A couple of trips to department stores, which he found bulging with products he had never dreamed of, dispelled the illusion.

He mastered the English language and was graduated at the top of his high school class. He completed his ME and MS with honours at the Stevens Institute of Technology in New Jersey and his PhD at Brown University. Ansoff joined the Rand Corporation in 1948 and Lockheed Aircraft Corporation in 1957. He went on to become vice president of planning and programmes at Lockheed Electronics and was able to develop a number of management concepts related to strategic analysis and planning.

His first book, *Corporate Strategy*, was published in 1965 when he was a professor of industrial administration at Carnegie-Mellon University. He also taught at Vanderbilt University and in 1983 accepted an appointment as Distinguished Professor of Strategic Management at the United States International University in San Diego.

In *Corporate Strategy,* Ansoff addressed the problems facing an organization in terms of the decisions it must take. He identified four standard decision types: decisions regarding strategy, policy, programmes, and standard operating procedures. The last three of these were similar to earlier ideas on policies and standard procedures – they were designed to resolve recurring issues and problems, without requiring significant management time. But strategic decisions, Ansoff said, were different because they had to be applied to new contingencies and had therefore to be freshly made each time.

Ansoff proposed a completely different classification for decisions. Decisions should be seen as 'strategic' (to do with products and markets), 'administrative' (to do with structure and resource allocation), and 'operating' (to do with budgeting, supervising and controlling). Ansoff completed what has subsequently become the well-known model of strategy-structure-systems.

Ansoff believed that previously 'concern with strategy had followed an "on-off" cycle attuned to the appearance of major strategic opportunities'. These cycles alternated between an external focus on product-markets and an internal preoccupation with operating and administrative efficiencies. These switches, Ansoff noted, often accompanied changes from one management generation to the next – they tended to be quite long-run cycles.

What concerned him, in 1965, was the turbulence of the post-war business environment. The 'deluge of technology', the dynamism of the worldwide changes in market structure, and the saturation of demand in many major United States industries were responsible for a drastic shortening in such cycles. In certain industries, for example electronics, chemicals, pharmaceuticals, plastics and aerospace, Ansoff felt that change was happening so fast that companies would have to 'continually survey the product-market environment' for new opportunities.

Today, this may sound obvious. In this new century, just 35 years after Ansoff first published his ideas, there must be few companies who are not constantly looking for new product-market opportunities. But at the time, Ansoff was trying to shake people out of their complacency, as may be judged by three additional conclusions he drew.

In this new business environment, he argued, no business 'can consider itself immune to threats of product obsolescence and saturation of demand'. Indeed, 'in some industries, surveillance of the environment for strategic threats and opportunities needs to be a continuous process'. Finally, 'at a minimum, firms in all industries need to make regular periodic reviews of product-market strategy'.

Today, these may appear self-evident, but at the time what Ansoff was proposing were new imperatives. Ansoff has subsequently been criticized, by the strategy guru Henry Mintzberg among others, for making too much of turbulence. In retrospect, Ansoff may simply have anticipated what was to come. The point is that, given the levels of satisfaction with the *status quo* (as evidenced in the writing of his contemporaries), Ansoff was trying to deliver a wake-up call to otherwise complacent managers.

Ideas into action

One of the most enduring concepts of Ansoff's 1965 book is what has become known as 'The Ansoff Matrix,' familiar to many (*see* below). The matrix relates new and existing products to new and existing markets. It is basically a simple tool for assessing the risks of strategic options. So, a strategy that involves introducing a new product into a new market carries the highest risk, and an existing product in an existing market has the least risk.

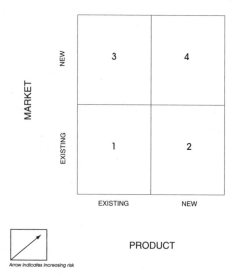

Arrow indicates increasing risk

The Ansoff matrix

Opportunities for growth can be represented as indicated on the diagram below.

Ansoff's definition of growth opportunities	Present products	New products
Present markets	Market penetration	Product development
New markets	Market development	Diversification

Source: Ansoff's definition of growth opportunities. Adapted from I. Ansoff, *Crafting Strategy*, 1965

For its time, Ansoff's book is a *tour de force*, providing tools, techniques and methodologies for deciding on objectives, synergies, growth opportunities, capabilities, levels of capital investment, diversification, integration, product-market portfolios, chosen industry characteristics and so on. Ansoff took it for granted, as everyone did at the time, that organizations had to plan. His many frameworks were designed to identify and then assist the decision-making process at multiple stages in the planning process – particularly the strategic decisions. This later led to Ansoff attracting unfair blame for all the misdeeds ever done in the name of planning. This ignored the fact that planning was already a fact of business life when he was writing. What Ansoff sought to do was to improve it.

Key text and further reading

Ansoff, I. (1965) *Corporate Strategy*, McGraw-Hill, New York.

SUCCESSION PLANNING

Succession planning is all about having able understudies in place to step into the key positions when they become vacant. Although it is often associated with senior management roles, it is a key issue running right through an organization.

In recent years it has become increasingly evident that the transfer of power from one leader to the next can have a major impact not just on morale and business performance, but on a company's share price. Traditionally, companies looked to their human resources department to ensure there were always talented managers coming up through the ranks, ready to step into the shoes of their seniors. Indeed, many believe that 'bench strength' – the talent on the bench – is an important indicator of future corporate performance. But from the HR department's point of view, succession planning has another very important role. The awareness that they are earmarked for greater things provides an incentive for the brightest managers to stick around.

Until very recently, most companies of any size created succession plans for senior posts, and development plans for key individuals in order to ensure that there was a ready supply of individuals prepared for the top jobs in the future. Usually, this involved accelerated or 'fast-track' programmes for so-called high-flyers – graduates and other high-potential recruits.

How appropriate the whole concept of succession planning is in leaner corporate structures is unclear, however. In particular, there is a question mark over the future of fast-tracking, which relies on identifying high-potential employees.

The problem with traditional succession planning – and fast-tracking in particular – is that it creates an expectation of upward progression, even though in today's leaner management structures there are now far fewer rungs on the corporate ladder. It also fails to take account of non-managerial roles – in particular, knowledge workers in creative roles, who may be vital to the future of the business. The question here is how to retain a brilliant research scientist or software designer who has no desire for promotion.

In effect, then, traditional fast-tracking and succession planning are likely to be less effective ways of retaining talent in the future. More flexible approaches will be required, customized to suit employees, their families and the changing skills-mix of the organization.

Not everyone aspires to be chief executive – or even a boss. The first step must be a clearer understanding of what career success means to the individual (*see* below).

In recent years, too, there has been considerable debate about the best way to handle the transfer of power from one CEO to the next, and that debate is only likely to get louder. It raises a number of thorny issues for HR professionals.

In the US, in particular, pressure on companies to fill senior management posts from outside the organization has been growing. Yet this flies in the face of traditional succession planning. In future, some well-known companies may have to rethink the issue.

Certain organizations pride themselves on promoting from within and have a long history of grooming insiders for the top jobs. The best scenario, they believe, is a seamless succession, where the baton is passed from one executive to the next with virtually no interruption to the momentum and style of the business.

Alternatively, it can be argued that different scenarios, or stages in a company's development, demand different types of succession. When a company is performing badly, for example, it may be dangerous to promote someone from within.

Other companies prefer a different succession strategy. Rather than anoint a new CEO in advance, they prefer a Darwinian approach, aiming to create a strong cadre of senior management from which the new CEO will 'emerge' when the time is right. Cometh the hour, cometh the man. This has its own advantages.

These companies avoid putting all their eggs (or should that be egos) in one basket, so unexpected events are less likely to derail the succession process: the person best suited to take the job when it becomes open will step in. An open race, many believe, also sharpens the instincts of the executives in the running, motivating them to higher levels of performance and commitment.

But the succession of the fittest approach also has some drawbacks. It encourages political intrigue, as senior managers jockey for power to the detriment of the business. A home-grown CEO, of course, isn't always the answer, especially when a company is in trouble. Sometimes a new broom is required. There is a school of thought, too, that says regular

Ideas into action

In the 1970s and early 1980s, succession planning was highly structured. At ICI, for example, for every job from main board director down to middle management, there was a box divided into four squares. Top left was probable successor now. Top right was possible now – in an emergency. Bottom left was probable later – the young Turks who would be coming through in four or five years' time. Bottom right was possible later – this would be a young manager in his 30s, with serious potential. 'We went through this exercise religiously every year', a former HR director explains.

But life has changed very significantly since then. Anyone who tried to plan for succession in ICI ten years ago couldn't possibly have envisaged, for example, that the company would split in two – into Zenecca and ICI.

This, combined with the high cost of developing and training high-flyers and the impact of the recession in the early 1990s, led to disillusionment with succession planning, which in turn led to the scaling down or even suspension of the fast-track approach in some companies. The pendulum now appears to be moving in the opposite direction.

The current trend appears to be that many organizations are now actively reinstating succession planning. But how appropriate such plans are to the needs of high-flyers, to other employees and to the organizations themselves is questionable.

But there are signs that succession planning is undergoing an important change. In particular, doubts have been cast recently on the ability of such plans to retain the right people. The assumption such plans are based on is that most senior management posts can be filled from within and that growing internal talent is preferable to other options. But in recent years the fast rate of organizational change has meant that many succession plans have become unworkable.

Today, it is more and more common to go outside to source senior management. While many HR professionals argue that that's no excuse for not doing succession planning, they accept that it has to be much more indicative and much less definitive than used to be the case. A messy succession can upset the carefully laid plans. The shock waves travel well beyond the boardroom. The way in which the top job is filled sends important signals to managers further down.

Traditional fast-tracking and succession planning are likely to be less effective ways of retaining talent in the future. This presents a more complex picture for HR professionals to manage.

- The first step must be a clearer understanding of what career success means to the individual.
- Not everyone aspires to be chief executive – or even a boss. HR professionals must find new ways to retain knowledge workers who are not interested in promotion.
- Sourcing the future executive population from within may be dangerous; many companies now recognize the importance of bringing in outsiders to widen the management gene pool.
- An external appointment at a senior level, on the other hand, can upset the succession plan lower down, especially if the incoming appointee brings his own team with him.
- A succession plan can help retain key individuals and allow them to be groomed for the top jobs. At very senior levels, however, nominating the crown prince in advance is likely to result in the loss of other talented managers.
- An open race sharpens the instincts of the executives in the running, motivating them to higher levels of performance and commitment, but encourages political intrigue, as senior managers jockey for power to the detriment of the business.
- The attitude of senior managers has an important influence on the way the succession issue is viewed. For some chief executives, in particular, the appointment of someone from outside to a top job is an admission of the failure of the organization to grow its own people.
- But encouraging talented young managers from below doesn't always come naturally to those at the top.
- The other side of succession planning at the very top involves persuading incumbents to go before they pass their sell-by date. But some of the greatest leaders have a blind spot when it comes to making way for others.
- A few individuals are genuinely irreplaceable.

injections of new blood are necessary to add diversity to the corporate gene pool. Either way, the solution is to bring in an outsider.

IBM's appointment of Lou Gerstner a few years back to take over from John Ackers was just such a case. The company's tradition of appointing an IBMer to carry on the famous 'IBM-way' was felt to have landed the company in trouble. Gerstner was brought in to change things – and to turn the company around. His appointment also changed the expectations of young managers joining Big Blue that the company always promoted from within.

Encouraging talented young managers from below, however, doesn't always come naturally to those at the top. Many will have had to fight off rivals on their way up the greasy pole. For them, potential successors may be perceived as a threat. As a result, it may be difficult for a new leader to emerge from the shadow of a powerful incumbent. Some people have called this effect the Thatcher phenomenon – after the former British prime minister.

The other side of succession planning at the very top involves persuading the incumbent to go before he or she passes the sell-by date. But some of the greatest leaders have a blind spot when it comes to making way for others. The best-laid succession plans can founder on this point.

An external appointment at the top, on the other hand, can drive a coach and horses through the succession plan lower down, especially if the incoming leader brings his own team with him, or slashes the management development budget. Such a short-sighted approach can leave holes in the succession plan further down the road, dooming it to failure.

But perhaps the thorniest succession issue of all involves a small group of business leaders, Bill Gates and Richard Branson among them, who are genuinely irreplaceable. These people play such a dominant role in the company that they come to be viewed as inseparable from it. The difficulty then becomes what happens to the business when they go?

Key texts and further reading

Holbeche, Linda (1998) *High-Flyers and Succession Planning in Changing Organizations*, Roffey Park Management Institute.

Rothwell, William J. (1994) *Effective Succession Planning*, AMACOM, New York.

SUPPLY CHAIN MANAGEMENT

T raditionally, the nitty-gritty of moving raw materials and products around was regarded as the truly dull side of business. Companies knew that products had to be transported, stored and distributed, but it hardly set their pulses racing. Competitiveness had little to do with whether raw materials arrived on Tuesday or Friday. If the lorry broke down, the warehouses simply filled up. A job in the warehouse was the managerial equivalent of Siberia – a step beneath manufacturing.

Today, the logistics of moving things around has become an exact science: supply chain management. Supply chain management is, at its simplest, logistics with added strategy (and a plethora of acronyms). It has been defined by Bernard La Londe of Ohio State University as 'the delivery of enhanced customer and economic value through synchronized management of the flow of physical goods and associated information from sourcing through consumption'. British supply chain expert Douglas Macbeth provides a different definition: 'The management of the two-way flows of materials and equipment, information, finance and people along the chain of customers and suppliers from raw materials through to final consumer.'

Supply chain management has emerged as being of critical importance to the modern organization for a number of reasons. First, the balance of power has shifted. In the past, manufacturers dictated terms to retailers. Now it is retailers who call the tune with sophisticated systems designed so that they get what they want when they want it. Companies such as Wal-Mart now store terabytes of information on customers. Manufacturers have to deliver to their increasingly demanding specifications.

Second, time is an increasingly important factor in overall corporate competitiveness. Laggards go out of business. Speed is of the essence whether in terms of product development, production or distribution. Competition is time-based. Late deliveries close down production lines or lead to disappointed customers all too willing to look elsewhere.

Ideas into action

At the centre of supply chain management in a modern context are speed and flexibility. The concept is founded on the image of a chain with continual links between the different stages. Other images – such as *value stream* and *supply pipeline* – have never really captured the imagination. Supply chain management fits conveniently into perspectives of organizations as a series of interlinked processes.

Supply chain management is viewed by some companies in a limited way as a means of reducing costs. It is true that elements like just-in-time manufacturing should reduce costly stores of materials or parts. Savings and efficiencies should merge in a number of ways from effective supply chain management.

More positively, supply chain management is concerned with making processes, people and material work more efficiently. It is about more than costs. More imaginatively, companies that can remove a link in the supply chain – usually through technology – can often offer improved services at highly competitive prices.

The success of the computer company Dell, for example, is built around effective supply chain management. Instead of selling through retailers, Dell chose to sell directly to consumers. It does so with impressive efficiency and sophisticated just-in-time systems which allow it to carry minimal inventories. Dell has spawned a host of imitators, lured by the apparent simplicity of mastering the supply chain. It is not that simple, as founder Michael Dell has explained. He says, 'There is a popular idea now that if you reduce your inventory and build to order, you'll be just like Dell. Well, that's one part of the puzzle, but there are other parts, too. For example, we have eleven days of inventory. The best indirect company has 38 days of inventory. The average channel has about 45 days of inventory. So if you put it together, you've got 80 days or so of inventory – a little less than eight times our inventory level.'

While it may be possible for companies imaginatively to reinvent the supply chain prevalent in their industry, this is clearly the preserve of the fortunate few. We can't all be Michael Dell. The alternative is to manage the different aspects of the supply chain in such a co-operative and efficient way that there is a feeling of true partnership. If the links in the supply chain are forged from true partnerships between manufacturers and retailers, distributors and consumers, and so on, the supply chain becomes a robust long-term competitive weapon.

> Each link in the chain is in a win/win situation with the next links in the chain. Partnerships produce the efficiencies demanded from the supply chain. The reverse is also true: supply chains founded on confrontation and a lack of trust are unlikely to yield efficiencies of any sort.

The third factor is the all-embracing expansion of information technology (IT). IT enables companies to manage the flow of goods, materials, thoughts and information in ways never previously imagined. IT enables each element of the supply chain – whether it be the manufacturer, retailer, or end consumer – to know the situation of the other. For example, if a supermarket runs out of a particular product line, technology enables it to be automatically reordered.

The final factor bolstering the standing of supply chain management is globalization. Truly global businesses require global supply chains. The right raw materials have to arrive in the obscurest of corporate outposts at the right time in the right amount. For major multinational companies, global supply chain management is a highly complex challenge but one that is critical to their competitiveness.

Key texts and further reading

Macbeth, D.K. and Ferguson, N. (1994) *Partnership Sourcing: An Integrated Supply Chain Approach*, FT/Pitman, London.

Hines, P. (1994) *Creating World Class Suppliers: Unlocking Mutual Competitive Advantage*, FT/Pitman, London.

Ford, I.D. (editor) (1997) *Understanding Business Markets: Interaction, Relationships, Networks*, Harcourt Brace & Company, London.

Farmer, D. and Van Amstel, P. (1993) *Effective Pipeline Management*, Gower, Aldershot.

Christopher, M. (1992) *Logistics and Supply Chain Management*, FT/Pitman, London.

Schonberger, R.J. (1990) *Building a Chain of Customers*, Free Press, New York.

TEAM-WORKING

Meredith Belbin is the doyen of the theory of team-working. He majored in classics and psychology at Cambridge University before becoming a researcher at the Cranfield College of Aeronautics. He worked in Paris for the Organization for Economic Cooperation and Development, with the Industrial Training Research Unit at University College, London, and in a number of manufacturing companies.

In 1967, the United Kingdom's Henley Management College introduced a computer-based business game into one of its courses. In this game, known as the Executive Management Exercise, 'company' teams of members competed to achieve the best score according to the criteria laid down in the exercise. Henley arranged to collaborate with Meredith Belbin, then with the Industrial Training Research Unit at University College, London.

Belbin was interested in group performance and how it might be influenced by the kind of people making up a group. Members engaging in the exercise were asked, voluntarily and confidentially, to undertake a personality and critical-thinking test. From his observations, based on the test results, Belbin discovered that certain combinations of personality-types performed more successfully than others. Belbin began to be able to predict the winner of the game and realized that given adequate knowledge of the personal characteristics and abilities of team members through psychometric testing, he could forecast the likely success or failure of particular teams. As a result, unsuccessful teams can be improved by analysing their team-design shortcomings and making appropriate changes.

Belbin's first practical application of this work involved a questionnaire that managers filled out for themselves. The questionnaire was then analysed to show the functional roles that the managers thought they performed in a team. This had one drawback: what you think you do is not of much value if the people with whom you work think differently. Belbin refined his methods and worked with others to design a computer programme to do the job. (His work is now available online and on CD-ROM.)

From his first-hand observation at Henley's unique 'laboratory', Belbin identified nine archetypal functions that go to make up an ideal team. They are:

- **Plant** – creative, imaginative, unorthodox; solves difficult problems. Allowable weakness: bad at dealing with ordinary people.
- **Coordinator** – mature, confident, trusting; a good chairman; clarifies goals, promotes decision making. Not necessarily the cleverest.
- **Shaper** – dynamic, outgoing, highly strung; challenges, pressurizes, finds ways around obstacles. Prone to bursts of temper.
- **Teamworker** – social, mild, perceptive, accommodating; listens, builds, averts friction. Indecisive in crunch situations.
- **Completer** – painstaking, conscientious, anxious; searches out errors; delivers on time. May worry unduly; reluctant to delegate.
- **Implementer** – disciplined, reliable, conservative, efficient; turns ideas into actions. Somewhat inflexible.
- **Resource investigator** – extrovert, enthusiastic, communicative; explores opportunities. Loses interest after initial enthusiasm.
- **Specialist** – single-minded, self-starting, dedicated; brings knowledge or skills in rare supply. Contributes only on narrow front.
- **Monitor evaluator** – sober, strategic, discerning. Sees all options, makes judgments. Lacks drive and ability to inspire others.

These categories have proved robust and are still used in a variety of organizations. The explosion of interest in team-working during the last decade has prompted greater interest in Belbin's work. He has since continued to refine and expand his theories in a series of books.

Key texts and further reading

Belbin, Meredith (2000) *Beyond the Team*, Butterworth-Heinemann, Oxford.

Belbin, Meredith (2001) *Managing Without Power: Gender Relationships in the Story of Human Evolution*, Butterworth-Heinemann, Oxford.

Ideas into action

Another more recent take on team-working was provided in 2002 by consultants Penna Change Consulting and the Cranfield School of Management. Whereas Belbin viewed teams from the perspective of a collection of individuals with the success of the team depending on the performance of those individuals, Penna and Cranfield looked at teams as a whole.

Penna's findings are the result of three years of research in conjunction with the Cranfield School of Management during which time a variety of different teams including sports teams, project and work teams, 'virtual' teams and even a jazz group were studied. The result was a model developed to assess the effectiveness of a team operating as a collective entity.

The Penna/Cranfield model identifies sixteen competencies essential for a team's success. The competencies are arranged into four groups. They are:

- **Enabling.** These are the factors which directly relate to a successful task outcome and include: *communicating* – how well the team facilitates effective communication; *integrating* – whether the team is integrated sufficiently to ensure effective task actions; *adapting* – how flexible the team is in order to meet changing task demands; *situational sensing* – the team's ability to understand the task environment and monitor changes; *evolving expertise* – the team's ability to acquire, share and develop expertise; and *creating* – the way the team facilitates creativity.

- **Resourcing.** These are the factors that lead to collective knowledge and understanding of the task and team members and include: *knowing* – collective understanding of knowledge required to complete the task successfully; *contextualizing* – the team's ability to understand organisational goals and constraints, both environmental and organisational, on team-working; and *team wisdom* – the level of knowledge relating to the members of the team, in other words, the strengths and weaknesses of individuals.

- **Fusing.** These are the factors essential to create an atmosphere conducive to effective team-working: *emotional maturation* – the ability within the team to develop an emotional understanding between team members; *bonding* – the management of social integration within the team both in and out of the work environment; *openness* – the fostering of an open environment that encourages team members to express themselves freely; and *affiliating* – this competency results in strong cohesion within the team, there is a sense of belonging to the team and team loyalty.

- *Motivating.* These are the factors relating to the team's level of motivation and include: *committing* – the means by which collective commitment is obtained; *inspiring* – how is inspiration to achieve team success achieved; and *believing* – factors that contribute to team belief and confidence that facilitate a sense of team efficacy.

THEORIES X AND Y (AND Z)

Even though he died over thirty years ago, Douglas McGregor (1906–64) remains one of the most influential and most quoted thinkers in human relations (what was known in the 1940s and 1950s as behavioural science research). His work influenced and inspired the work of thinkers as diverse as Rosabeth Moss Kanter, Warren Bennis and Robert Waterman. Most notably, McGregor is renowned for his motivational models, theories X and Y.

Detroit-born, McGregor was the son of a clergyman. He graduated from the City College of Detroit (now Wayne University) in 1932. He then went on to Harvard to study for a PhD. Following his PhD McGregor worked at Harvard as an instructor and tutor in social psychology. He then moved to MIT as an assistant professor of psychology. In 1948, he became President of Antioch College in Yellow Springs, Ohio. Antioch was renowned as a progressive liberal college. In 1954, McGregor returned to MIT as a professor of management. He became Sloan Fellows Professor of Industrial Management in 1962. At MIT, McGregor attracted some of the emerging generation of thinkers to work with him, including Warren Bennis and Edgar Schein.

Theories X and Y were the centrepiece of McGregor's 1960 classic, *The Human Side of Enterprise*. Theory X was traditional carrot-and-stick thinking built on 'the assumption of the mediocrity of the masses'. This assumed that workers were inherently lazy, needed to be supervised and motivated, and regarded work as a necessary evil to provide money. The premises of theory X, wrote McGregor, were, '(1) that the average human has an inherent dislike of work and will avoid it if he can, (2) that people, therefore, need to be coerced, controlled, directed, and threatened with punishment to get them to put forward adequate effort toward the organization's ends and (3) that the typical human prefers to be directed, wants to avoid responsibility, has relatively little ambition, and wants security above all.'

McGregor lamented that theory X 'materially influences managerial strategy in a wide sector of American industry', and observed that 'if there is a single assumption that pervades conventional organizational theory it is that authority is the central, indispensable means of managerial control.'

'The human side of enterprise today is fashioned from propositions and beliefs such as these,' wrote McGregor, before going on to conclude that 'this behaviour is not a consequence of man's inherent nature. It is a consequence rather of the nature of industrial organizations, of management philosophy, policy, and practice.' It is not people who have made organizations, but organizations that have transformed the perspectives, aspirations and behaviour of people.

The other extreme was described by McGregor as theory Y, based on the principle that people want and need to work. If this was the case, then the organization needed to develop the individual's commitment to its objectives, and then to liberate his or her abilities on behalf of those objectives. McGregor described the assumptions behind theory Y as, '(1) that the expenditure of physical and mental effort in work is as natural as in play or rest – the typical human doesn't inherently dislike work; (2) external control and threat of punishment are not the only means for bringing about effort toward a company's ends; (3) commitment to objectives is a function of the rewards associated with their achievement – the most important of such rewards is the satisfaction of ego and can be the direct product of effort directed toward an organization's purposes; (4) the average human being learns, under the right conditions, not only to accept but to seek responsibility; and (5) the capacity to exercise a relatively high degree of imagination, ingenuity, and creativity in the solution of organizational problems is widely, not narrowly, distributed in the population.'

Theories X and Y were not simplistic stereotypes. McGregor was realistic. He wrote, 'It is no more possible to create an organization today which will be a full, effective application of this theory than it was to build an atomic power plant in 1945. There are many formidable obstacles to overcome.'

The common complaint against McGregor's theories X and Y is that they are mutually exclusive, two incompatible ends of a spectrum. To counter this, before he died in 1964, McGregor was developing theory Z, a theory that synthesized the organizational and personal imperatives. The concept of theory Z was later seized upon by William Ouchi. In his book *Theory Z* he analysed Japanese working methods. Here, he found fertile ground for many of the ideas McGregor was proposing for theory Z – lifetime employment, concern for employees including their social life, informal control, decisions made by consensus, slow promotion, excellent transmission of information from top to bottom and bottom to

Ideas into action

Theories X and Y have tended to be simply interpreted as a people-oriented manifesto, with McGregor arguing that more efficient managers tend to value and trust people while the ineffective manager is cynical and mistrusts people. In fact, McGregor did not view the world so simplistically. He acknowledged that it was possible for theory X managers to be corporate dictators while still trusting people. Nor did he regard theory X managers as paragons – they could trust people and treat them fairly and still make a mess of running a business. McGregor was observing the facts of motivational life rather than prescribing the way forward. 'The motivation, the potential for development, the capacity for assuming responsibility … are all present in people. Management does not put them there,' he said.

Even so, it is worth noting that theory Y was more than mere theorizing. In the early 1950s, McGregor helped design a Proctor & Gamble plant in Georgia. Built on the theory Y model with self-managing teams its performance soon surpassed other P&G plants.

top with the help of middle management, commitment to the firm, and high concern for quality.

Key texts and further reading

McGregor, Douglas (1985) (25th anniversary printing) *The Human Side of Enterprise*, McGraw-Hill, New York.

Ouchi, William G. (1981) *Theory Z: How American business can meet the Japanese challenge*, Addison-Wesley, Reading, MA.

Waterman, Robert (1994) *The Frontiers of Excellence*, Nicholas Brealey, London.

Weick, Karl E. (1979) *The Social Psychology of Organizing*, McGraw-Hill, New York.

THOUGHT LEADERSHIP

T he term thought leadership was coined in the early 1990s by the then editor of the *Harvard Business Review* Joel Kurtzman. In an economy increasingly driven by ideas and concepts, Kurtzman observed, the ability to plant an intellectual flagpole in new territory was a potent source of competitive advantage. In key sectors, especially the consulting industry, and the business school sector, thought leadership conferred first-mover advantage on the originator.

In the early 1990s, for example, James Champy and Michael Hammer's book, *Reengineering the Corporation*, was a bestseller which established them as thought leaders. Armed with this concept, CSC Index, the consulting firm founded by Champy, came from nowhere to establish itself as a leading contender in the consulting stakes.

Kurtzman subsequently wrote a book called *Thought Leaders* in which he interviewed the leading business thinkers. The term is now generic, and denotes what has become a battleground among the leading consulting firms and the growing ranks of management gurus. The power of thought leadership is that it is a more effective way to brand and market intellectual horsepower than traditional advertising.

'Thought leadership we define as something that tells the client that we understand the problems and issues they face. It demonstrates our awareness of the issues,' says Jon Moynihan, chairman of the UK-based PA Consulting. 'That translates into a Compelling Value Proposition which demonstrates that we have the solutions. We focus very intensively on the audience we want to reach and concentrate on providing content.'

The term may be new, but as a strategy the origins of thought leadership go back much further. The traditional leader in this field is McKinsey & Company. McKinsey does not advertise. Instead, it relies on its intellectual prowess to carry the brand. It has long been the intellectual benchmark for consulting firms and, largely, continues to be so. 'The Firm', as it is affectionately known by McKinsey insiders, bolsters its brand through the *McKinsey Quarterly*, a serious, heavyweight publication that has been around for 35 years and which sometimes makes the *Harvard Business Review* appear frivolous by comparison. Intellectual vigour exudes from every page and this is exactly what McKinsey wants readers to think and experience.

Aside from the *McKinsey Quarterly*, McKinsey flexes its intellectual muscles in a number of other ways. In 1990 it set up the McKinsey Global Institute. Its objectives are characteristically bold. It aims, according to the firm, '[to] help business leaders understand the evolution of the global economy, improve the performance and competitiveness of their corporations, and provide a fact base for sound public policy-making at the national and international level.' In addition, since the McKinsey-authored *In Search of Excellence* rolled off the presses in 1982, McKinsey consultants have been churning out books with admirable dedication.

More recently, the creation of consulting businesses by the big five accountancy and auditing firms has increased competition in this area. The need to differentiate themselves from each other has raised the stakes in the thought leadership arena. In the modern era, the starting point for the branding frenzy was the operational split of Andersen Consulting from Arthur Andersen in 1989. Overnight a new giant emerged – one that needed to establish its own identity.

The top consulting firms now invest millions on thought leadership as a brand-building strategy. This strategy basically positions the brand as being intellectually superior to the competition. In an ideas business, it is a competitive advantage to have more and better ideas.

The battle for thought leadership lacks the glamour of image advertising, but it is incredibly intense. *McKinsey Quarterly* imitators have been launched by rival consulting firms. Booz·Allen & Hamilton, for example, publishes its own heavyweight journal *Strategy & Business*. Consulting firms have also been busy turning out business books which they hope will position them as thought leaders on the important emerging ideas.

Indeed, a growing section of the business book industry is given over to the thought leadership battle between competing consulting brands. Books have become highly expensive calling cards; 400-page ads to be personally inscribed to prospective clients and left in their offices. The books are expensive because often consultants pay ghost-writing firms to knock the concept into a readable shape and, in addition, often buy large numbers of the books to give away. Some have also got into trouble for buying copies in order to ensure that they reach the bestseller lists.

Inevitably, however, the success of the thought leadership strategy depends on the quality and take-up of the ideas generated. The whole concept feeds on its ability to generate more and better business concepts. It is a sign that consulting firms have started to believe their own propaganda.

Ideas into action

Most of the big strategy-based consulting firms are now involved in the thought leadership battle. 'Thought leadership is the only place for the top firms. They can't compete on price or on results. But only two firms – McKinsey and the Boston Consulting Group (BCG) – have done it consistently,' says Sam Hill of Helios Consulting (and an emergent thought leader in his own right thanks to the success of his book *Radical Marketing*). 'It is a great strategy. Ideas are the single best source of differentiation. They also mean that you can use PR instead of advertising, which is much more credible. The trouble is that it is not easy to do.' Hill should know. He was the man who led Booz·Allen & Hamilton's move into the thought leadership melée.

In many ways, Booz·Allen's strategy reaped more benefits than most. Prior to taking the thought leadership route, it was largely unheralded, a lesser light next to the intellectual beacons of McKinsey, Bain and BCG. Now, Booz·Allen is actively involved in the intellectual debate. Its consulting stars are quoted and referred to. Column inches are the payback.

Booz·Allen also publishes books in association with San Francisco-based Jossey-Bass, and sponsors the Global Business Book Awards alongside the *Financial Times*. Other consulting firms are also aggressively pursuing the thought leadership strategy. The book *Blur* by Stan Davis and Chris Meyer came out of Ernst & Young's Centre for Business Excellence. Others are following similar paths with a wide range of publishing and other activities. Arthur D. Little publishes the quarterly journal *Prism*. (Circulation of *Prism* is controlled to maintain the prestige of the publication – according to the firm, 'Subscriptions are sponsored by individual staff members as part of their continuing relationships with their clients and other business associates.') Similarly, Mercer publishes its *Management Journal* and made a great deal of the arrival in its ranks of bestselling author Adrian Slywotzky, a real thought leader.

Firms also seek to establish their thought leadership credentials through events of various sorts. Ernst & Young runs an annual knowledge management conference and the Ernst & Young Entrepreneur of the Year Award – the first winner of the national title was Michael Dell in 1989. A.T. Kearney runs an annual gathering of 50 CEOs from around the world grandly entitled the Global Business Policy Council.

Key texts and further reading

Kurtzman, Joel (1998) *Thought Leaders*, Jossey-Bass Wiley, San Francisco.

Crainer, Stuart and Dearlove, Des (1999) 'Branding consulting firms,' *American Management Review*, October.

TQM AND THE QUALITY MOVEMENT

T he quality movement is associated with the Japanese economic renaissance after World War II. Total quality management (TQM) is an approach based on the use of quality concepts developed in Japan. By the late 1970s, the diligent application of these techniques by Japanese manufacturing companies had enabled them to overtake many Western manufacturers. Ironically, however, the quality movement was originally inspired by American ideas.

Under TQM, the use of sophisticated statistical production control ensures that quality is built into production, removing the need to check quality later. The aim of TQM is to minimize waste and reworking by achieving 'zero defects' in the production process. TQM is not a single magic bullet, but rather an approach that integrates a group of concepts. These include many of those associated with lean production, such as just-in-time (*see* page 119) and *kaizen* (*see* page 124). Although process-driven, TQM is underpinned by a management philosophy that advocates continuous improvement and a 'right first time' approach to manufacturing.

The emergence of TQM can be traced to the late 1940s. During the American occupation of Japan after 1946, US engineers were instructed to help Japanese industry get back on its feet. Two Americans, Charles Protzman and Homer Sarasohn,[1] organized a series of seminars on US production techniques. In 1950, the Japanese invited W. Edwards Deming, a mathematician and expert on statistical quality control, to start some more seminars. Deming, an admirer of Walter A. Shewhart who had developed statistical control while at Bell Labs, introduced the quality circles movement into Japan. This involved small, problem-solving teams of workers, supervisors and experts (later called quality circles) with the aim of improving the efficiency and quality of work. Quality circles were instrumental in the Japanese economic miracle witnessed in the 1970s. It was largely due to the application of TQM among a highly disciplined workforce that in the space of just 25 years, Japanese companies were able to catch up with and outperform their rivals in America and Europe. By 1975, for example, Toyota had replaced Volkswagen as the US's number one car importer.

Ideas into action

TQM is no quick fix. It requires a fundamental shift in thinking and production techniques. Companies that have successfully implemented TQM confirm that it requires a culture change at all levels. That can take many years to achieve. Moreover, there is no clear consensus on the best way to apply TQM, with a great many variations on the theme. Success depends on the ability to map out and document the minutiae of production tasks. However, the basic principles of TQM are:

- A fundamental change of emphasis from quality control (checking that work already carried out meets the necessary standards) to quality assurance (whereby quality is built into the production processes so that only work of an acceptable standard is carried out).
- An adoption of the philosophy of continuous improvement. Everyone within the organization (not just managers) is responsible for trying to improve the work that is done. Improvements can include ways to reduce costs, shorten the time it takes to carry out a task, avoid wastage, make life easier for suppliers or customers or any other desirable change. The point is that everyone in the organization is continually on the look-out for such improvements. In this way, adjustments to processes are carried out on an ongoing basis rather than once-and-for-all every few years when the old way of doing it has become hopelessly out of step with the competition.
- A change to a customer-oriented approach. Under TQM, every decision starts with what the customer wants or needs and works back to the action the organization should take. The notion of customer-orientation also extends to internal customers. Every department (and every team) has a set of internal customers to whom its work is directed.
- A commitment to getting it right first time. The procedures followed by everyone within the organization are developed and documented to ensure that everything that is done is to an acceptable standard. This eliminates the wasted effort required to put right substandard work and removes the need for a quality control department checking work.
- The active participation of everyone in the organization in achieving its objectives (through quality circles). In a TQM environment, the old view of managers and supervisors overseeing the work of others is replaced by the idea that everyone is responsible

for the quality and improvement of his or her own work; the role of managers is to support them in their efforts.

- A commitment to TQM at the very highest level of the organization. Only if top management invests the time and resources that are required – including attending training themselves – will TQM deliver real benefits.
- The acceptance that it is only by finding appropriate ways to measure performance that it can be evaluated and improved over time.
- A recognition that prevention of errors is more effective than curing them later.
- A switch from the traditional adversarial management style to quality management systems which encapsulate the underlying principles of TQM.

For a while in the late 1970s and early 1980s, the Americans put the Japanese success story down to the availability of cheap labour. But when the Japanese car manufacturer Honda opened a factory in Marysville, Ohio, which used US workers paid at market rates and whose productivity outstripped the US car giants in Detroit, American companies realized that the Japanese were doing something fundamentally different in their factories.

One of the first to heed the warning was the Xerox Corporation. In the mid-1970s Xerox was obsessed with competition from its rival Kodak. At that time, Kodak had just launched some new high-price copiers, which were seen by Xerox as a direct assault on its market. Distracted by the old foe, Xerox didn't pay too much attention to the upstart Japanese competitor Canon. By the time Xerox realized the seriousness of the threat, it had already lost more than half its market share to Japanese incursions.

While other parts of corporate America clung to the notion that the Japanese success story was based not on superior process management but cheap labour costs, Xerox took a long hard look. Its partnership with Fuji made it easier to get a close-up view of the Japanese economic miracle. What Xerox quickly realized was that there was more to the superior Japanese performance than the US wanted to admit. Xerox was one of the first American companies to embrace the new Japanese management techniques that had inflicted the damage.

The company became an enthusiastic convert to the quality movement and set about introducing the 'right first time' philosophy into everything it did. In a matter of a few short years, Xerox was back. In 1983, 'Leadership Through Quality', the Xerox total quality process, was unveiled. Important lessons had been learned.

As interest in the quality movement grew, others began to write and consult on how the Western companies could adopt the approach (*see* the quality gurus box below). The best known of these Western thinkers were Joseph Juran and Philip Crosby. In time, a number of Japanese quality gurus also became better known in the West, including Genichi Taguchi, Taiichi Ohno and Shiego Shingo.

By the 1980s, TQM had become a byword for efficiency and success throughout the business world. As Japanese manufacturing companies threatened to overrun American and other Western companies, the mid-1980s were characterized by a scramble among Western companies to understand how Japanese companies were managed, and to apply TQM to their own businesses.

Indeed, such was the impact of TQM that by the end of this period it was almost possible to divide the world's top manufacturing companies into two categories: those that had introduced TQM; and those that were just about to. Reinforcing the trend was the widespread adoption of quality accreditation. International ISO 9000 standards created a global quality benchmark, although some companies complained that the bureaucracy the documentation procedures created actually undermined the improvements in competitiveness.

Key texts and further reading

Deming, W. Edwards (1982) *Out of the Crisis*, MIT centre for Advanced Engineering Study, MIT, Cambridge, MA.

Crosby, Philip (1979) *Quality is Free*, McGraw-Hill, New York.

Juran, Joseph (1964) *Managerial Breakthrough*, McGraw-Hill, New York.

Juran, Joseph (1988) *Juran on Planning For Quality*, McGraw-Hill, New York.

Feigenbaum, A.V. (1983) *Total Quality Control*, McGraw-Hill, New York.

Schonberger, Richard (1990) *Building a Chain of Customers*, Free Press, New York.

Note

1   Wren, Daniel (1994) (4th ed) *The Evolution of Management Thought*, John Wiley, New York.

The quality gurus

W. Edwards Deming

Deming is generally regarded as the founder of the modern quality movement, and regarded by the Japanese themselves as the key influence in their post-war economic miracle. Despite his stature as a guru, Deming was more active as a consultant on quality management than as a writer. His best-known book is *Out of the Crisis* (1984).

The principles underlying Deming's approach can be summarized as:

- create constancy of purpose for continual improvement of products and service;
- adopt the new philosophy created in Japan;
- cease dependence on mass inspection: build quality into the product in the first place;
- end lowest-tender contracts; instead, require meaningful measures of quality along with price;
- improve constantly and forever every process, planning, production and service;
- institute modern methods of training on the job, including management;
- adopt and institute leadership aimed at helping people to do a better job;
- drive out fear, encourage effective two-way communication;
- break down barriers between departments and staff areas;
- eliminate exhortations for the workforce – they only create adversarial relationships;
- eliminate quotas and numerical targets. Substitute aid and helpful leadership;
- remove barriers to pride of workmanship, including annual appraisals and management by objectives;
- encourage education and self-improvement for everyone; and
- define top management's permanent commitment to ever-improving quality and productivity, and their obligation to implement all these principles.

Walter A. Shewhart (US statistician)

Shewhart worked at Bell Labs and pioneered the statistical process control (SPC). His work greatly influenced Deming, and lay at the heart of the total quality management philosophy applied in Japanese manufacturing companies. Shewhart successfully brought together the disciplines of statistics, engineering, and economics and became known as the father of modern quality control. The lasting and tangible evidence of that union for which he is most widely known is the control chart, a simple but highly effective tool that represented an initial step towards what Shewhart called 'the formulation of a scientific basis for securing economic control'.

Joseph Juran

Juran began his career at Western Electric's Hawthorne Plant (famous for the Hawthorne Studies carried out there between 1927 and 1932), and worked with Shewhart. Like Deming, Juran emphasized continuous improvement, but added that this should be done in conjunction with overall corporate planning, in a long-term commitment.

Armand V. Feigenbaum

Feigenbaum was the originator of total quality control. The first edition of his book of that name was completed whilst he was still a doctoral student at MIT. His work was discovered by the Japanese in the 1950s at about the same time as Joseph Juran visited Japan. Feigenbaum was head of quality at the General Electric Company, where he had extensive contacts with such companies as Hitachi and Toshiba. His 1951 book *Quality Control: Principles, Practices and Administration* argued for a systematic or total approach to quality, requiring the involvement of all functions in the quality process, not just manufacturing. The idea was to build-in quality at an early stage, rather than inspecting and controlling quality after the fact.

Philip Crosby

Crosby started his career with the Crosely Corporation but later moved to other companies. Best known for his consulting work, Crosby focused on achieving 'zero defects' in manufacturing processes.

Taiichi Ohno

Former vice president of Toyota Motors, Ohno was inspired by the work of Frederick Taylor to introduce quality control at Toyota. He is credited with creating Toyota's famous just-in-time system. Ohno's book *The Toyota Production System: Beyond Large-Scale Production*, was the first to be published in Japan on the Toyota production system.

Shigeo Shingo

Relatively unknown in the West, Shingo's impact on Japanese industry, and less directly on Western industry, has been huge. Shingo also worked at Toyota and developed the zero-defects approach to quality manufacturing. He wrote a *Study of the Toyota Production System: From an Industrial Engineering Viewpoint*. Shingo's approach emphasizes production rather than primarily management. His motto (actually one of very many) is that 'Those who are not dissatisfied will never make any progress'. He believed that progress is achieved by careful thought, pursuit of goals, planning and implementation of solutions. Shingo died in November 1990 at the age of 81.

Genichi Taguchi

Better known in the West than Shingo, Taguchi worked for Nippon Telephone and Telegraph. Taguchi was concerned with the optimization of product and process prior to manufacture. Taguchi pushed the concepts of quality and reliability back to the design stage where they really belong. The methodology he developed provides an efficient technique to design product tests prior to entering the manufacturing phase. (It can also be used as a trouble-shooting methodology.)

In contrast with Western definitions, Taguchi worked in terms of quality loss rather than quality. This is defined as 'loss imparted by the product to society from the time the product is shipped'. This loss includes not only the loss to the company through costs of reworking or scrapping, maintenance costs, downtime due to equipment failure and warranty claims, but also costs to the customer through poor product performance and reliability, leading to further losses to the manufacturer as his market share falls.

Following his 1980 visit to the United States, more and more American manufacturers implemented Taguchi's methodology. A number of major US companies adopted his methods including Xerox, Ford and ITT.

Claus Moller

A Danish quality guru who developed the idea of personal quality, Moller sees personal quality as the basis of all other types of quality. In his book *Personal Quality*, two standards of personal quality are identified: the ideal performance level (IP) and the actual performance level (AP).

360-DEGREE FEEDBACK

T he annual appraisal was once a bureaucratic chore to be completed as speedily as possible. Every year, at an appointed hour (and often for an hour) a manager sat in an office with his or her boss. The manager's performance over the previous year was then discussed and dissected. The manager then emerged from the room and headed back to his or her desk, until next year. The traditional form of appraisal may linger on in some companies – though you have to look harder and harder to find them. In a fast-growing number, however, the annual ritual has been reinvented.

It has been reinvented by returning to first principles. Appraisal's *raison d'être* is straightforward: to improve an individual's – and, therefore, an organization's – performance. To do so, the appraisal has to be responsive to individual needs and be available to individuals throughout the organization. As a result, the modern appraisal tends to be flexible and ongoing, it revolves around feedback, involves many more people than one manager and a boss, and seeks to minimize bureaucracy. In keeping with this climate of flexibility, many companies now employ a variety of forms of appraisal.

Appraisal is now seen in the more broad-ranging context of 'performance management'. This means that it must embrace issues such as personal development and career planning, in addition to simple analysis of how well an individual has performed over the last year. Extending the range of this approach is the increasingly fashionable concept of 360-degree feedback. This involves a manager's peers, subordinates, bosses and even customers airing their views on the manager's performance – usually by way of a questionnaire.

As methods of appraisal go, 360-degree feedback is undoubtedly robust and rigorous. It is not a process designed for the faint-hearted. It takes feedback to unprecedented levels – and for those who desire even more there is 540-degree feedback, which brings even more people into the process.

The attraction of 360-degree feedback is that it gives a more complete picture of an individual's performance. Different groups see an individual in a variety of circumstances and situations and can, as a result, give a broader perspective than that of a single boss. This, of course, relies on a high degree of openness and trust – as well as perception.

Openness only goes so far. To ensure that comments are made as honestly as possible, without fear of sanction, anonymity is the almost universal rule. If people fear that critical comments about their boss will lead to reprisals, they are unlikely to venture honest opinions. Inevitably, the truth can become clouded by prejudice and politics. People can be incredibly sycophantic or completely negative. Perceptions and the objectivity of the data can also be affected by prejudices and other influential factors.

An additional danger is that if managers are being judged by subordinates their motivation will be to be liked. Good management isn't necessarily about being liked, so there is the risk of management by popularity.

Perhaps more significant is that, for traditional managers, 360-degree feedback can be a highly disturbing experience. Managers are not renowned for their willingness to contemplate their weaknesses. Indeed, the entire art of management in traditional organizations was to hide weaknesses and play to strengths. Only then could progress up the hierarchy be guaranteed. Contrast this with 360-degree feedback, which encourages managers to confront areas of weakness. The danger is that the entire experience can be demoralizing, with one negative comment after another. Counselling and support are often necessary if the experience is to be a positive one.

More mundanely, actually running 360-degree feedback programmes is demanding and time-consuming. The entire process inevitably generates a substantial amount of paperwork. Commonly it involves canvassing the opinions of six to ten people. This in itself is time-consuming. The weight of bureaucracy and the need for objectivity and impartiality mean that it is common for companies to bring in consultants to run their 360-degree feedback programmes effectively. Another side effect of the logistics of running 360-degree feedback is that it largely remains the preserve of a small number of senior managers. (One survey found that 43% of 360-degree programmes were for top managers.) The logistics of expanding the concept to others in the organization are usually not persuasive.

The final drawback of 360-degree feedback is simply that it is fashionable. Companies and managers remain anxious to keep abreast with best practice. There is, therefore, the temptation to introduce a 360-degree programme with limited awareness of the resources required, the systems necessary to make it work effectively, or of its broader objectives. This is a recipe for failure.

Ideas into action

Research at Ashridge Management College into the growth of 360-degree feedback (published as *360-degree Feedback: Unguided Missile or Powerful Weapon?*) suggests that success requires a number of factors:

- a clear strategic rationale;
- top management support and involvement;
- a culture geared towards behaviours and attitudes rather than simply on performance;
- sensitivity;
- a genuine and wide-based willingness to achieve change; and
- willingness to discuss any issue.

The central message of such criteria is that appraisal needs to be a considered and far-reaching process rather than an automatic ritual. It must embrace the goals of the organization and those of the individual in the short-term and long-term. And, above all, it must be managed effectively.

Many companies now employ a variety of forms of appraisal. The range and scale of appraisals used by Mercer Management Consulting is increasingly typical. 'We put a lot of effort and resources into the review process. But we have no qualms about that. Everything we do is about our staff's commitment and knowledge, and the change and value they deliver for our clients,' says Matthew Isotta, vice-president of Mercer's European Central Resource Group.

Mercer's appraisal process is all-embracing. There are long-established downward reviews written by partners on people working on an assignment. 'You have to sit down at the end of a project anyway,' explains Isotta, 'it is a formalized way of doing so which has become ingrained in our culture.' In addition, every six months, groups of partners spend a day analysing their personal performance. All of the partners have an adviser who takes case reviews and discusses them with the individual and with other managers. Then a one-page career review summary is produced outlining an individual's strengths, areas of growth and development objectives for the next six months. 'The review day involves 20 to 25 partners and makes the entire appraisal process transparent. The discussion is completely open, but people don't get het up because so much effort is put into the entire process.'

Finally, Mercer has an upward review process, which is currently being refined. This involves an anonymous component and the company is moving towards a survey model where everyone fills in an evaluation of people they work with every six and twelve months. The danger, warns Mercer's Matthew Isotta, is that the entire system becomes merely paper-generation. 'This process has to have bite. There is the risk of it being ignored so we feed it through to the compensation of partners. We don't have hard and fast rules but compensation is driven by a number of factors and the upward review process is key,' he says. Others seek to distance appraisal from rewards, arguing that appraisal should concentrate on development issues rather than becoming bogged down in pay negotiations.

Companies such as Mercer Management Consulting regard appraisal in the more broad-ranging context of 'performance management'. This means that it must embrace issues such as personal development and career planning, in addition to simple analysis of how well an individual has performed over the last year. 'Some organizations have almost abandoned formal appraisals,' says Angela Baron of the Institute of Personnel and Development. 'They want to escape from the form-filling mentality and, instead, want managers to talk continuously about their performance against agreed objectives, development needs and future roles.'

Key texts and further reading

Edwards, Mark and Ewen, Ann J. (1996) *360-degree Feedback*, AMACOM, New York.

Grote, Richard C. and Grote, Dick (1996) *The Complete Guide to Performance Appraisal*, AMACOM, New York.

Handy, Laurence, Devine, Marion and Heath, Laura (1996) *360-degree Feedback: Unguided Missile or Powerful Weapon?* Ashridge Management Research Group, London.

Lepsinger, Richard and Lucia, Antoinette D. (1997) *The Art and Science of 360-degree Feedback*, Jossey-Bass, San Francisco, CA.

Tornow, Walter (editor) (1998) *Maximizing the Value of 360-degree Feedback*, Jossey-Bass, San Francisco, CA.

TIME-BASED COMPETITION

D espite the fact that its underlying logic has been accepted for decades, time-based competition became a management fashion in the early 1990s, largely due to the work of the Boston Consulting Group. The chief proponents of time-based competition were two consultants with BCG, George Stalk and Thomas Hout. Their book, *Competing Against Time*, calls on companies to seek to compress time at every stage in every process. 'Time is the secret weapon of business because advantages in response time lever up all other differences that are basic to overall competitive advantage,' write Stalk and Hout. 'Providing the most value for the lowest cost in the least amount of time is the new pattern for corporate success.'

They point to Honda's triumph in the 1980s in its lengthy battle with Yamaha. Honda produced 60 new motorbikes in a year and once managed 113 new models in eighteen months. Its speed of development far outstripped Yamaha's and Honda emerged triumphant.

Time-based competition contends that organizations should be structured in the most time-efficient way. The rationale is that processes and systems that are needlessly time-consuming have a direct impact on competitiveness. Being slow costs you money. Unfortunately, traditional hierarchical organizations are not built with speed in mind. One calculation estimated that over 95% of the time products spend in an organization is wasted. Lengthy inventories as well as periods on hold during production cost money. Stalk and Hout suggest that management should focus on accomplishing three key tasks. First, they need to 'make the value-delivery systems of the company two to three times more flexible and faster than the value-delivery systems of competitors'. Second, managers of a company need to 'determine how its customers value variety and responsiveness, focus on those customers with the greatest sensitivity, and price accordingly'. Finally, managers must 'have a strategy for surprising its competitors with the company's time-based advantage'.

In general, the logic of time-based competition remains hard to dispute. Fast is undoubtedly good and being faster than competitors is clearly a route to competitiveness. However, as with many other such ideas, there is the suspicion that this is simply restating the first principles of business. Frederick Taylor's scientific management of the early twentieth century was also based on minimizing time to maximize efficiency and, therefore, profitability.

'Time waste differs from material waste in that there can be no salvage,' noted Henry Ford who had one eye on the clock and the other on costs. In this, and in many other ways, Ford was ahead of his time.

Ideas into action

To a large extent, time-based competition built from the philosophy and practice of total quality management and other Japanese-inspired quality theories like just-in-time manufacturing. These suggested that quality products could be made in large quantities if quality systems and thinking were in place. The belief in the West was generally that quality and quantity were mutually exclusive.

This, in turn, led thinkers towards the idea that became known as re-engineering. If systems and processes need to be streamlined, it may be better to start from scratch rather than tinkering at the edges.

While the need for speed coupled with quality was hardly a new idea, the pressure on companies to deliver speedy processes undoubtedly was. From being a competitive advantage, time-efficient processes became competitive necessities. From being peripheral, time to market became crucial. 'In this business, there are two kinds of people, really, the quick and the dead,' reflects Michael Dell. Announcing changes at one of its divisions, 3M stated: 'We're a 93-year-old company, and we have our own way of doing things. We couldn't keep pace.' 3M is not – and never has been – noted for its slowness. Indeed, it is routinely celebrated for its speed of innovation. Fast, but not fast enough. 'We used to take four days from getting raw material to putting the product on the truck, and now we take 25 minutes. It's still not good enough,' said the company.

Declining product life cycles and faster development cycles mean that speed is of the essence. An innovation has only a short period of opportunity before it is ruthlessly copied by the competition.

Photographic cameras, for example, have a life span as short as six months. The number of models on the market grows unceasingly as competitors avidly copy each other's innovations. Virtually any product on earth can be speedily replicated. It would be easy to assume that product copying is the preserve of the desperate, opportunistic or poor. This is not the case. The world's great corporations are engaged in a constant round of me-too developments.

In financial services, any new product – whether it is an account for the elderly or a more flexible mortgage – is copied almost instantly. There is a constant stream of products and services as old ones are tinkered with, replaced or revamped, and entirely new ones introduced. In one year the UK-based bank NatWest introduced 240 new products or improvements to existing products. There is no longer anything particularly unusual in this. Fast is good.

Also, when they seized on the idea of time-based competitiveness, Western managers did so with their usual fixation on costs. Stalk and Hout insisted that, 'Time is a more useful management tool than cost. Cost is by and large a lagging indicator, a symptom, a set of control accounts after the fact.' In practice, time-based competition was often used primarily as a means of reducing costs rather than increasing competitiveness. Shorter time cycles mean greater efficiency at lower cost. Instead of squaring the circle of quality and quantity, time-based competition provided unintentional impetus to the cost-reduction fascination of downsizing.

Key texts and further reading

Abegglen, James and Stalk, George (1988) *Kaisha: The Japanese Corporation*, Basic Books, New York.

Stalk, George and Hout, Thomas (1990) *Competing Against Time*, Free Press, New York.

Stern, Carl, Stalk, George and Clarkeson, John (1998) *Perspectives on Strategy: From the Boston Consulting Group*, John Wiley, New York.

THE TRANSNATIONAL CORPORATION

T he transnational corporation is a concept developed by Harvard Business School's Christopher Bartlett and the London Business School's Sumantra Ghoshal. (Ghoshal joined the London Business School in 1994 and was formerly professor of business policy at INSEAD and a visiting professor at MIT's Sloan School.) At the heart of Ghoshal and Bartlett's work during the late 1980s and early 1990s is the demise of the divisionalized corporation – as exemplified by Alfred Sloan's General Motors.

Their work on globalization and organizational forms came to prominence with the book *Managing Across Borders* (1989) which was one of the boldest and most accurate pronouncements of the arrival of a new era of global competition and truly global organizations.

Bartlett and Ghoshal, unlike others, suggest that new, revitalizing organizational forms can emerge – and already are emerging. Crucial to this is the recognition that multinational corporations from different regions of the world have their own management heritages, each with a distinctive source of competitive advantage.

The first multinational form identified by Bartlett and Ghoshal is the *multinational* or multidomestic firm. Its strength lies in a high degree of local responsiveness. It is a decentralized federation of local firms (such as Unilever or Philips) linked together by a web of personal controls (expatriates from the home country firm who occupy key positions abroad).

The second is the *global* firm, typified by US corporations such as Ford earlier this century and Japanese enterprises such as Matsushita. Its strengths are scale efficiencies and cost advantages. Global scale facilities, often centralized in the home country, produce standardized products, while overseas operations are considered as delivery pipelines to tap into global market opportunities. There is tight control of strategic decisions, resources and information by the global hub.

The *international* firm is the third type. Its competitive strength is its ability to transfer knowledge and expertise to overseas environments that are less advanced. It is a coordinated federation of local firms, controlled by sophisticated management systems and corporate staffs. The attitude of the parent company tends to be parochial, fostered by the superior know-how at the centre.

Bartlett and Ghoshal argue that global competition is now forcing many of these firms to shift to a fourth model, which they call the *transnational*. This firm has to combine local responsiveness with global efficiency and the ability to transfer know-how – better, cheaper, and faster.

The transnational firm is a network of specialized or differentiated units, with attention paid to managing integrative linkages between local firms as well as with the centre. The subsidiary becomes a distinctive asset rather than simply an arm of the parent company. Manufacturing and technology development are located wherever it makes sense, but there is an explicit focus on leveraging local know-how in order to exploit worldwide opportunities.

Their 1997 book *The Individualized Corporation* marked a further step forward in the thinking of Ghoshal and Bartlett. In the intervening years, they have mapped and recorded the death of a variety of corporate truisms. They insist that the questions have remained the same, but the answers have changed.

Ideas into action

Ghoshal and Bartlett conclude that, in the flux of global businesses, traditional solutions are no longer applicable. They point to the difficulties in managing growth through acquisitions and the dangerously high level of diversity in businesses that have acquired companies indiscriminately in the quest for growth. They have also declared as obsolete the assumption of independence among different businesses, technologies and geographic markets, which is central to the design of most divisionalized corporations. Such independence, they say, actively works against the prime need: integration and the creation of 'a coherent system for value delivery'.

Today's reality, as described by Ghoshal, is harsh: 'You cannot manage third generation strategies through second generation organizations with first generation managers.'[1] Even the perspectives from 'successful' companies appear bleak. 'Talk of transformation and you get the same examples,' he says, 'Toshiba in Asia Pacific, ABB, GE. If you listen to managers of those companies you will detect great scepticism about achieving victory. The battle ahead is far more complex.'

Despite such a damning critique of corporate reality, Ghoshal is not totally discouraged. 'Look at today and compare it to years ago. The quality of the strategic debate and discussion has improved by an order of magnitude,' he says. 'Third generation strategies are sophisticated and multi-dimensional. The real problem lies in managers themselves. Managers are driven by an earlier model. The real challenge is how to develop and maintain managers to operate in the new type of organization.'

The shift in emphasis is from the cool detachment of strategy to the heated complexities of people. While *Managing Across Borders* was concerned with bridging the gap between strategies and organizations, Ghoshal and Bartlett's sequel, *The Individualized Corporation,* moved from the elegance of strategy to the messiness of humanity. In so doing, they examine the factors that are likely to be crucial to the success of organizational forms of the future.

One of the phenomena they have examined is the illusion of success that surrounds some organizations. 'Satisfactory under-performance is a far greater problem than a crisis,' Ghoshal says, pointing to the example of Westinghouse, which is now one-seventh the size of GE in revenue terms. 'Over twenty years, three generations of top management have presided over the massive decline of a top US corporation,' says Ghoshal, 'yet, 80% of the time the company was thought to be doing well. Westinghouse CEOs were very competent and committed. They'd risen through the ranks and did the right things. Yet they presided over massive decline.'

The explanation he gives for this delusion of grandeur is that few companies have an ability for self-renewal. 'You cannot renew a company without revitalizing its people. Top management has always said this. After a decade of restructuring and downsizing, top management now believes it. Having come to believe it, what does it really mean?'

Ghoshal contends that revitalizing people is fundamentally about changing people. The trouble is that adults don't change their basic attitudes unless they encounter personal tragedy. Things that happen at work rarely make such an impact. If organizations are to revitalize people, they must change the context of what they create around people. 'Companies that succeed are driven by internal ambition. Stock price doesn't drive them. Ambition and values drive them. You have to create tension between reality and aspirations,' he says.

'The oppressive atmosphere in most large companies resembles downtown Calcutta in summer. We intellectualize a lot in management. But if you walk into a factory or a unit, within the first fifteen minutes you get a smell of the place.'

Vague and elusive though 'smell' sounds, Ghoshal – no touchy, feely idealist – believes that it can be nurtured. 'Smell can be created and maintained – look at 3M. Ultimately the job of the manager is to get ordinary people to create extraordinary results.'

To do so requires a paradoxical combination of what Ghoshal labels stretch and discipline. These factors do not render attention to strategy, structure and systems obsolete. Businesses can still be run by strict attention to this blessed corporate trinity. These are, in Ghoshal's eyes, the legacy of the corporate engineer Alfred Sloan, and the meat and drink of business school programmes. They are necessary, but Ghoshal adds a warning, 'Sloan created a new management doctrine. Sloan's doctrine has been wonderful but the problem is that it inevitably ends up creating downtown Calcutta in summer.'

The way out of the smog is through:

- *purpose* 'the company is also a social institution';
- *process* 'the organization as a set of roles and relationships'; and
- *people* 'helping individuals to become the best they can be'.

Key texts and further reading

Bartlett, C. and Ghoshal, S. (1989) *Managing Across Borders*, Harvard Business School Press, Boston, MA.

Bartlett, C. and Ghoshal, S. (1997) *The Individualized Corporation*, Harvard Business School Press, Boston, MA.

Note

1   International Management Symposium, London Business School, 11 November 1997.

VALUE INNOVATION

Value innovation is a concept coined by W. Chan Kim and Renee Mauborgne, based at INSEAD, the international business school. Chan Kim and Mauborgne based their ideas on their studies of high-growth companies around the world and what distinguishes them from other, less-successful firms.

Value innovation involves a paradigm shift in strategic thinking about business growth. Essentially, it is about a switch from thinking about strategy in terms of existing competitors to thinking in terms of creating entirely new markets, or redefining existing markets. Chan Kim and Mauborgne developed the idea in a 1997 *Harvard Business Review* article, 'Value Innovation: The Strategic Logic of High Growth'. They found that a key difference between companies that achieved sustained high growth and those that did not lay in the way the two groups approached strategy.

'The less-successful companies took a conventional approach: their strategic thinking was dominated by the idea of staying ahead of the competition', they wrote. 'In stark contrast, the high-growth companies paid little attention to matching or beating their rivals. Instead, they sought to make their competitors irrelevant through a strategic logic we call "value innovation".'

According to Chan Kim and Mauborgne, there are five dimensions in which value innovators typically challenge conventional competitive thinking. These are:

- *Industry assumptions*. Instead of working within them, value innovators look to leapfrog competitors by challenging the accepted rules within their industry.
- *Strategic focus*. Instead of comparing their performance with other companies, they seek to create new markets where others cannot immediately follow.

- **Customers**. Rather than trying to segment them by their differences, they look for common ground among customers, which allows them to define new market space.
- **Assets and capabilities**. Value innovators are less concerned with their existing core competencies, preferring to take a blank sheet of paper approach to the capabilities they need. In this way, they build capability to fit the market instead of defining the market to fit their capabilities.
- **Product and service offerings**. Value innovators aim to provide products and services that customers truly value even if this means moving beyond the traditional boundaries of their business.

Their ideas were refined in another *HBR* article entitled 'Creating New Market Space', where they outlined a systematic approach to value innovation by creating new market space.

'Competing head-to-head can be cut-throat, especially when markets are flat or growing slowly,' they say. 'Managers caught in this kind of competition almost universally say they dislike it and wish they could find a better alternative.'

With value innovation, Chan Kim and Mauborgne advocate a switch from strategy based on the current situation to one based primarily on innovation, by creating what they call 'new market space' – either creating brand new markets or recreating existing ones, to create superior value for customers.

'Most companies focus on matching and beating their rivals, and as a result their strategies tend to converge along the same basic dimensions of competition. Such companies share an implicit set of beliefs about "how we compete in our industry or in our strategic group" … As rivals try to outdo one another, they end up competing solely on the basis of incremental improvements in quality or cost.'

Creating new market space, however, requires a different pattern of strategic thinking. Instead of looking within the accepted boundaries that define how they compete, managers can look systemically across them. Companies can systematically pursue value innovation, they say, in six basic areas:

- looking across substitute industries;
- looking across strategic groups within industries;
- looking across the chain of buyers;
- looking across complementary product and service offerings;
- looking across functional or emotional appeal to buyers; and
- looking across time.

Ideas into action

Chan Kim is now a serious contender in the strategy guru stakes. There is a common thread to much of the new thinking. While earlier ideas on strategy were based on beating the competition at their own game, the new strategic thinkers share a more radical view. Rather than slugging it out for a couple of percentage points of market share, strategy is something that redefines the rules of the game, or creates a new game altogether.

Their emphasis is on strategy to leapfrog the competition altogether. The new thinking is all concerned with mobilizing people at the sharp-end to formulate strategy; and it is all concerned with paradigm shifts. To illustrate their point, Chan Kim and Mauborgne relate the story of Bert Claeys, a Belgian company which operates cinemas. The Belgian cinema industry was in decline from the 1960s to the 1980s. The spread of VCRs, satellite and cable television meant that over that period the average Belgian went from attending a cinema eight times a year to just twice.

By the 1980s many cinema operators were forced to close down. Those that remained competed head-to-head, turning cinemas into multiplexes with as many as ten screens and improved facilities. But in 1988 all their efforts became irrelevant when Bert Claeys created Kinepolis – the world's first megaplex. With 25 screens and 7600 seats, it offered moviegoers a radically superior service, including enough legroom that viewers do not have to move when someone passes by. By reinventing the industry, the company won 50% of market share in Brussels in the first year and expanded the market by about 40%. Today, many Belgians no longer refer to a night at the cinema but to an evening at Kinepolis.

The new thinkers also challenge the old idea of where in the organization strategy should come from. Rather than emerging from the boardroom or the planning department, they agree with Henry Mintzberg, it should come from closer to the action.

According to Gary Hamel, companies don't need leaders with big ideas. 'The next phase is to move to non-linear strategies,' he says, 'strategies that represent a quantum leap. They will not be created by the guys at the top of the company.

'Yesterday's visionary is today's straightjacket,' he says. 'Look at how Microsoft responded to the internet. Bill Gates was the last person in the company to get it.'

What companies need, he says, is to hear new voices. In many organizations the conversations about the future are the same people having the same conversations. 'Organizations need a hierarchy of imagination not of experience. They don't need visionaries they need activists.'

Key texts and further reading

Kim, Chan and Mauborgne R. (1999) 'Creating New Market Space', *Harvard Business Review*, January–February.

Kim, Chan and Mauborgne R. (1999) 'Strategy, Value Innovation, and the Knowledge Economy', *Sloan Management Review*, Spring.

Kim, Chan (1998) 'Procedural Justice, Strategic Decision Making, and the Knowledge Economy', *Strategic Management Journal*, Spring.

Kim, Chan (1997) 'Fair Process: Managing in the Knowledge Economy', *Harvard Business Review*, July–August.

Kim, Chan and Mauborgne R. (1997) 'Value Innovation: The Strategic Logic of High Growth', *Harvard Business Review*, January–February.

THE VIRTUAL ORGANIZATION

Much beloved of management theorists, the notion of the virtual organization has more than one interpretation. To some people, the virtual concept refers simply to the ability of companies to use IT to allow people in different locations, and even on different continents, to work together effectively. While for others it goes further, describing an amorphous organization made up of project teams that form to fulfil a specific purpose and disband at a moment's notice.

New organizations no longer fit into strict hierarchical pyramids, rising to a pinnacle where the all-knowing, all-seeing chief executive surveys the corporate domain. Instead, new shapes and images are emerging to describe the organization.

The organization is now described in the terminology of the new science of chaos theory. An article in the *California Management Review* describes the organization of the future as one that is 'dynamically stable', and 'capable of serving the widest range of customers and changing product demands (dynamic) while building on long-term process capabilities and the collective knowledge of the organization (stable)'. From the traditional images of machinery, the organization has become an elusive, ever-changing amoeba.

Describing the organization of the future, American writers William Davidow and Michael Malone say, 'To the outside observer, it will appear almost edgeless, with permeable and continuously-changing interfaces among company, supplier and customers. From inside the firm, the view will be no less amorphous with traditional offices, departments and operating divisions constantly re-forming according to need.' The end result is the virtual organization.

Using IT, it is argued, employees no longer need to come into the office at all and can work remotely from their homes or different offices anywhere around the globe, plugging into a virtual community that is made possible by technology.

The virtual organization is an elusive combination of technology, expertise and networks. It is a moveable feast utilizing technology to mould a changing, flexible organization, which meets the needs of customers.

In this way, companies can dismantle their cumbersome headquarters buildings, the costly bricks and mortar of the conventional business. Employees can work at home or in satellite offices when required. Linked by networks of computers, communicating by e-mail and modems, workers are freed from the burdens of commuting and the daily grind of office work. With no expensive tower blocks to support, organizations can make massive savings. The virtual organization is both life- and profit-enhancing. Virtuality creates a virtuous circle.

Other advocates of the virtual organization regard this as simply the beginning. A number of companies have found that virtual working allows the traditional structure of the organization to be discarded altogether. They advocate an organizational model which can bring together individuals or companies to work on a single project, where the virtual organization or team exists only for as long as it is required to complete the project and is then disbanded.

Virtual teams could be here today, gone tomorrow. One way to think of this is in terms of the cast of a film or play who come together to form a team for as long as the show is in production and then go their separate ways. Specialists can also belong to several virtual organizations simultaneously, ensuring that their skills are used in an optimal way.

What all the variations of the virtual organization have in common is that they start from the premise that IT now enables individuals who are geographically dispersed to work together unhindered by geographical separation. Their ability to communicate and share information also means that the patterns of decision making are fundamentally altered, with no necessity for coordination from the centre.

If we think of individual workers as dots on the organizational map, then one justification for traditional structures was to provide a framework to direct their efforts. But as soon as you can connect each dot – or computer terminal – to any other, the need for a formal structure disappears. If we go a step further and think of those dots as light bulbs connected with the power of communication, then, theoretically at least, a virtual organization can instantly light up any pattern or configuration of skills required, and can switch it off just as quickly.

For all the talk of amoebas, the concept of the virtual organization has been around for a while. Indeed, you could trace its origins back to the wishful thinking of the early seventies when people talked of the fast approaching golden age of leisure when computers would do all the work. (This was only half right: computers do a lot of work, but they unveiled vast vistas of new work which now needs to be done.) Auditors, accountants and many other professionals have been working in a virtual way for many years.

The virtual organization is well understood and a logical extension of technology. But, remorseless logic cannot fail to disguise the fact that virtual organizations are, as yet, notable by their absence. There are organizations that appear virtual to customers, but are not truly virtual in reality. Telephone banking seems more virtual than the bank down the road, but even telephone banking companies have their conventional headquarters building. Companies may relocate to cheaper alternatives, but they are still choosing to invest in reassuring concrete. If the arguments for the virtual organization are so persuasive, why are so few decision makers persuaded?

First, virtual organizations are off-puttingly fashionable. They remain terminally associated with smart and creative companies. Ad agencies, design companies and software houses are thought to be candidates for virtuality, not less esoteric manufacturers. This is a limit of perception rather than reality. A manufacturer in Dudley can benefit from organizing itself in a virtual way as much as one in Palo Alto. (Manufacturers could, for example, organize much of their administrative work virtually, and utilize technology to provide links with suppliers and customers, as well as internally.)

The second stumbling block is that the virtual organization requires a quantum leap rather than steady evolution. The virtual organization is radically different from the traditional organization. Making it work requires more than short-term enthusiasm. Senior managers, those charged with changing organizations, often have a limited appreciation of technological possibilities. Creating a virtual organization requires some understanding of the technical possibilities – as well as a harmonious and respectful relationship with corporate IT specialists.

This element is part of the third obstacle to creating the virtual organization. The virtual organization uses IT as a primary corporate resource. The trouble is that many organizations continue to regard IT as a function, a discrete and isolated budget rather than a dynamic organizational tool. In addition, the virtual organization can be seen as potentially undermining the positions of senior managers. Kings rarely start revolutions. At an individual level, in the virtual organization managers find that their old tactics and power games no longer work. They have to change the habits of a lifetime.

This list could be supplemented by the crucial fact that people, and managers in particular, remain wedded to their offices. Home-working

Ideas into action

At VeriFone – a California-based company which dominates the US credit card-authorization market – the virtual concept has been taken further than most. Talking to management writer Tom Peters, VeriFone's CEO Hatim Tyabji describes the virtual operation as like a 'blueberry pancake: independent units (blueberries) held together by a unifying medium (batter)'.

The company is highly decentralized and claims to have no head-quarters. Instead, each part – or blueberry – is expected to generate its own ideas and strategies and ultimately to make its own decisions. In the blueberry pancake model, instant communication via e-mail is an essential ingredient. Employees get a laptop before they get a desk, and internal paper mail is banned.

'The company is run 100% electronically,' says Tyabji. 'There is no paper. E-mail is the lifeblood of this company. It is direct communication, totally unfiltered. At first, some people don't think they can handle 75 e-mail messages a day, but just as you get junk mail, you get junk e-mail. It's a matter of learning to separate the important from the trivial.'

Eliminating paper, he says, creates a 'culture of urgency' which has allowed him as chief executive to break free of the manacles that keep other senior managers chained to their desks. It means he can play a more active role in the business, spending between 80% and 90% of his time on the road.

'It would be impossible for me to run a traditional company and travel as much as I do,' he says. 'All those reports and memos would pile up until I got back. Then I'd have to read them and respond. Instead of all that, wherever I am in the world, I sit down at my laptop and instantly respond. When I go back to my office, the only thing on the desk is p-mail – physical mail – usually magazines.'

Staff at VeriFone know, too, that anyone in the company – no matter how junior – is free to e-mail Tyabji direct wherever he is. 'I tell people that I don't mind being over-run with e-mail,' he says, 'in fact, I personally respond to every piece of e-mail within 24 hours.'

For most companies, true virtual working is still some way off.

may be on the increase, but it has never made the anticipated inroads simply because people do not find the idea attractive. With its social rituals, human interest and politics, office life retains a strong attraction.

Social instincts are one of the prime work-drivers. In addition, there is ease of communication – people still believe in the primacy of face-to-face communication; and control – managers feel more in control if they can see the people they manage. Also, managers like the movement and activity of office life. They believe that things are happening, even if they are not.

Given the apparent difficulties in creating truly virtual organizations, the way forward may rest with compromise solutions – such as hot-desking. Another compromise is the idea of virtual teams – groups who are accountable for the achievement of transient or short-term objectives. The groups may be temporary – specially assembled to complete a certain task or project – or permanent. The aim remains much the same as that of virtual organizations: to enable a flexible and continuously evolving fit between skills, resources and immediate needs.

Key texts and further reading

Davidow, William H., Malone, Michael S. (1993) *The Virtual Corporation*, HarperBusiness, New York.

Grenier, Raymond and Metes, George (1995) *Going Virtual*, Prentice Hall Computer Books, London.

Lipnack, Jessica and Stamps, Jeffrey (1996) *The Age of the Network*, John Wiley, New York.

Savage, Charles (1996) (Revised edition) *Fifth Generation Management*, Butterworth-Heinemann, Oxford.

Hedberg, Bo, Dahlgren, Goran, Hansson, Jorgen and Olve, Nils-Goran (1994) *Virtual Organizations and Beyond*, John Wiley & Sons, Chichester.

Goldman, Steven L., Nagel, Roger, N. and Preiss, Kenneth (1995) *Agile Competitors and Virtual Organizations*, Van Nostrand Reingold, New York.

APPENDIX

There are far too many management and business concepts to make this book anything approaching comprehensive. That is the job of a business encyclopaedia or dictionary. There are, however, some concepts that, whilst perhaps not meriting as much scrutiny as has been afforded to those we have already addressed, nevertheless deserve a mention. Here, then, are the concepts that almost made it.

Affiliate marketing

Affiliate marketing is one of the earliest marketing models used on the internet, championed by companies such as Amazon.com. The story has it that Amazon founder Jeff Bezos was at a cocktail party when a woman told him how she wanted to sell books about divorce on her web site. The result was the Amazon.com Affiliates Programme launched in July 1996. While Amazon started its programme in 1996 and filed for a patent in 1997 (it received it in 2000), several other companies were experimenting with affiliate marketing at the same time, if not before Amazon.

In affiliate marketing, the affiliate is a company that is connected to, or associated with, another company that has agreed to carry the affiliate's advertising, particularly on a web site, in exchange for a fee. The affiliate model works like this. An e-tailer sets up a web site, selling niche furniture for example, then contacts another web site, such as an interior design portal or a furniture e-store, which prospective furniture purchasers are likely to visit. The e-tailer then persuades the other web site to carry its advertising banner on its web site. In return, the affiliate receives a reward for displaying the banner. This reward could be linked to the number of surfers clicking through the banner ad, or to the number of leads produced. Alternatively, it may be linked to actual sales made, in the form of a paid commission. Through affiliate marketing, a company can build an extensive advertising network in prime positions for no up-front costs. In turn, the affiliate gets money for nothing other than giving over an unused space on its site to an advertising banner.

Setting up an affiliate marketing programme can be difficult for companies without significant marketing resources. The complexities of tracking thousands of interconnected websites and the site traffic flowing back and forth are beyond most small businesses. Therefore a number of companies offer to manage, to a lesser or greater extent, affiliate programmes on behalf of companies who cannot, or do not wish to, set up their own. These companies (including BeFree, LinkShare, and ClickTrade) plug would-be affiliate marketers straight into their affiliate network, numbering anywhere between 50,000 and 250,000 companies, and make their money, in the main, by charging commissions on affiliate earnings.

Key text and further reading

Fiore, Frank (2001) *Successful Affiliate Marketing for Merchants*, Que, Indianapolis.

BATNA (best alternative to a negotiated agreement)

The concept of BATNA or the 'best alternative to a negotiated agreement' was developed by Roger Fisher and William Ury in their book *Getting to Yes* (1981). BATNA reflects 'the course of action a party would take if the proposed deal were not possible'. It is a key factor in negotiation strategy. In order to know whether or not to accept a negotiated settlement, it is essential to know if a better outcome is obtainable by alternative means. If the settlement obtained through negotiation is better than the BATNA, then the settlement should be accepted. If a party to negotiations has a good BATNA, or even if they only perceive it to be, it will be difficult to arrive at a negotiated settlement. The better the BATNA, therefore, the stronger the negotiating position. Knowing both your own and your adversary's BATNA is crucial to successful negotiating.

As Fisher says, 'Which would you prefer to have in your back pocket during a salary negotiation with your boss: a gun or a terrific job offer from a desirable employer who is also a serious competitor of your company?'

Key text and further reading

Ury, William, Fisher, Roger (1981) *Getting to Yes: Negotiating Agreement Without Giving,* Houghton Mifflin, New York.

Career anchors

The concept of career anchors was developed by business academic Edgar H. Schein, a professor of management specializing in career issues and organizational change at Massachusetts Institute of Technology.

According to Schein, career anchors are a set of self-images and self-perceptions that govern the way people like to work. These evolve over time and tend to become stronger as people gather more life and work experience. These anchors are key to predicting which sorts of career people will find most fulfilling. Schein says he chose the metaphor of an anchor because when a work assignment did not match an individual's self-image they were unhappy and felt 'pulled back into a safe harbour'.

Schein identifies eight separate career anchors. The first four are concerned with a dominant motive or need, the next two with sense of one's own competence, and the final two with specific values:

autonomy/independence: a need to feel free and independent;

security/stability: a need for careers that provide long-range stability and security;

entrepreneurial creativity: people who define themselves by their ability to build an enterprise;

pure challenge: a need to define oneself by overcoming apparently insurmountable obstacles;

technical/functional competence: a need to become 'the best' in a specific area;

general managerial competence: people who define themselves by their ability to manage others;

service or dedication: a need to express dedication to a deeply held commitment through a career; and

lifestyle: a desire to integrate work and family/life issues.

Key text and further reading

Schein, Edgar H. (1985) *Career Anchors, Discovering Your Real Values,* Jossey-Bass/Pfeiffer, San Francisco.

Chaordic organization

In 1984, Dee Hock, founder and CEO Emeritus of VISA USA and VISA International, left VISA to pursue his interest in the evolution of organizations and management practices.

Hock coined the word 'chaord' by borrowing the first syllables from the words 'chaos' and 'order'. He uses the term chaordic to describe any system of organization that exhibits characteristics of both chaos and order, dominated by neither. In his book *Birth of the Chaordic Age,* Hock defines chaordic as '1. The behaviour of any self-governing organism, organization, or system that harmoniously blends characteristics of order and chaos. 2. Patterned in a way dominated by neither chaos nor order. 3. Characteristic of the fundamental organizing principles of evolution and nature.'

In 1993, Hock made his first speech on 'chaords' at the Sante Fe Institute. He also articulated four conditions necessary for catalysing institutional change. They were:

- creation of a dozen or more examples of new, successful chaordic organizations;
- development of visual and physical models of chaordic organizations;
- development and dissemination of an impeccable intellectual foundation for chaordic organizations; and
- creation of a global institution.

Key text and further reading

Hock, Dee (1999) *Birth of the Chaordic Age,* Berrett-Koehler Publishers, San Francisco.

Co-opetition

Co-opetition is a business concept introduced by Harvard Business School professor Adam Brandenburger and Yale School of Management professor Barry Nalebuff during the 1990s. The authors acknowledge that some companies prefer a competitive approach to business – treating business like warfare with outcomes seen in terms of winners and losers. Other companies prefer to adopt a co-operative attitude to business – embracing team and partnership approaches. Co-opetition is a combination of both the competitive and co-operative approaches. The word was originally coined by Ray Noorda, founder of the networking software company Novell, who said, 'You have to compete and cooperate at the same time'.

Incorporating elements of game theory, the concept relies on treating business as a game, then developing strategies to shape the game to suit the company. Brandenburger and Nalebuff advocate approaching co-opetition in stages. First, they suggest, construct a map, or Value Net, that identifies 'all the players in the game of business and the interdependencies among them'. The next and most important step is to 'change the game'.

Key text and further reading

Brandenburger, Adam M., Nalebuff, Barry J. (1996) *Co-Opetition*, Currency Doubleday, New York.

Corporate memory

Corporate memory is an idea introduced by American researchers and writers Art Kleiner and George Roth. It is a readily accessible fund of useful knowledge about how and why the company has done things. According to Kleiner and Roth, corporate memory aims to allow an organization to transfer experience from one generation to the next – and, more mundanely, from one office to the next. It is based on the understanding that intellectual capital is not simply a contemporary phenomenon. Knowledge is – or should be – cumulative. All of our insights come from retrospect; we just have to make the past available and then be able to put the past into perspective.

To help create and sustain a corporate memory, Kleiner and Roth suggest that companies use a tool called the *learning history* – 'a narrative of a company's recent set of critical episodes, a corporate change event, a new initiative, a widespread innovation, a successful product launch, or even a traumatic event like a downsizing'. Other techniques to organize and gather together corporate experiences are being explored. For example, technology enables databases of personal experience to be assembled.

Key texts and further reading

Kleiner, Art and Roth, George (1999) *Car Launch: The Human side of Managing Change,* Oxford University Press Learning History Library Series, New York.

Kleiner, Art and Roth, George (1999) *Oil Change: Perspectives on Corporate Transformation,* Oxford University Press Learning History Library Series, New York.

Cultural diversity

Born in Haarlem, in the Netherlands, Geert Hofstede is professor of organizational anthropology and international management in the Department of Economics and Business Administration at the University of Limburg at Maastricht, as well as director of IRIC, the Institute for Research on Intercultural Cooperation, at Tilburg University. Prior to his academic career, Hofstede worked as a sailor, factory worker, industrial engineer, plant manager, and personnel director; he also held the position of chief psychologist on the international staff of IBM.

According to *The Economist,* Geert Hofstede 'more or less invented [cultural diversity] as a management subject'. Few would deny that this is the case. The Dutch academic has exerted considerable influence over thinking on the human and cultural implications of globalization.

Each society faces some similar problems, but solutions differ from one society to another. Hofstede identified five basic characteristics that distinguish national cultures. These dimensions are:

Power distance the extent to which the less powerful members of institutions and organizations expect and accept that power is unequally distributed;

Individualism the strength of ties between individuals, ranging from loose in some societies to involving greater collectivism and strong cohesive groups in others;

Masculinity the markedness of distinction between social gender roles;

Uncertainty avoidance the extent to which society members feel threatened by uncertain or unknown situations; and

Long-term orientation the extent to which a society exhibits a pragmatic, future-oriented perspective.

In Hofstede's hands, culture becomes the crux of business. He defines it as 'the collective programming of the mind, which distinguishes the members of one group or category of people from another'. Hofstede's conclusions are based on huge amounts of research. His seminal work on cross-cultural management, *Culture's Consequences*, involved over 100,000 surveys from more than 60 countries. The sheer size of Hofstede's research base leads to perennial questions about how manageable and useful it can be.

Key texts and further reading

Hofstede, Geert (2001) *Culture's Consequences: Comparing Values, Behaviors, Institutions, and Organizations Across Nations* 2nd edition, Sage, Thousand Oaks, CA.
Hofstede, Geert (1997) *Uncommon Sense About Organizations*, Sage, Thousand Oaks, CA.
Hofstede, Geert (1995) *Cultures and Organizations*, McGraw-Hill, New York.

Delphi technique

The Delphi technique is a qualitative decision-making process developed in the 1950s by Olaf Helmer and Norman Dalkey, scientists at the RAND Corporation. It derives its name from the oracle at Delphi of ancient Greece. The process is designed to avoid conflict between, or undue influence from, individual participants in group decision making.

The process is conducted in a series of rounds. A chairman or facilitator asks each participant, often an expert in a particular field, to submit a written answer to a question or series of questions. The chairman or facilitator then considers the replies, writes a summary in the form of opinion statements, and passes the summary on to the group members. This is the end of the first round. The participants then reply to the opinion statements with a rating, usually along the lines of 'strongly agree' or 'strongly disagree'. This process continues until a consensus is arrived at or stability is obtained (each member's answer varies little from one round to the next). While the technique is especially useful where the participants are separated geographically; it can be a very slow process.

To obtain the best results, the participants must be selected according to carefully chosen criteria and not personal preference. The role of the chairman or facilitator is critical, as he has the opportunity to introduce undue influence or bias and steer the group toward a prede-termined outcome.

Diversity advantage

Diversity advantage is the supposed competitive advantage conferred by recruiting employees from diverse backgrounds. Historically, com-panies tried to recruit the same sort of people time and time again. The thinking was that people of the same sort were much easier to control. The end result, however, was more of the same people producing more of the same work. While this was acceptable in the past, the emphasis in modern business is on innovation, speed and flexibility. Managers have to be able to think differently, work with different people, and thrive on the difference.

Diversity is a competitive weapon. If companies accept difference, so the theory goes, they are likely to be more responsive to changes in their business environment. They will be more flexible, open-minded, and quicker to react. A Swiss multinational with ten nationalities on the board, including six women, and the ability to make global teams work will have a diversity advantage over an American widget maker from Cleveland with a board entirely populated by white middle-aged men who believe that Canada is the international market.

While diversity is regarded as a racial issue in the United States, in Europe it is cultural. Multicultural European role models abound – from football teams to entire countries. One outstanding European role model is Switzerland, which is highly successful, multi-ethnic, multi-lingual and multi-religious. It is notable that some of the most successful and inter-national of companies are Swiss – companies like Nestlé, Ciba Geigy and ABB appear to handle diversity more easily and more positively than others in Europe. Indeed, the Swiss-Swedish conglomerate ABB is often held up as the epitome of the modern organization and is a fervent champion of thinking global, acting local. International team-working is central to making ABB work successfully. It thrives on diversity and requires its managers to 'have an exceptional grasp of differing traditions, cultures, and environments'. ABB's supervisory board of eight includes four nationalities, while its executive committee goes one further with five. Its former chief executive Percy Barnevik argues that 'competence is the key selection criterion, not passport'.

Other multinationals are similarly diverse as they discover the twin challenges of globalization and team-working. After its merger, SmithKline Beecham boasted a management group of thirteen, which included seven nationalities.

Key texts and further reading

Jamieson, David, O'Mara, Julie (1991) *Managing Workforce 2000: Gaining the Diversity Advantage,* Jossey-Bass, San Francisco.

Fernandez, John P. (with Barr, Mary) (1993) *The Diversity Advantage; How American Business Can Out-Perform Japanese and European Companies in the Global Marketplace,* Lexington Books, New York.

Division of mental labour

Booz·Allen & Hamilton consultants Charles Lucier and Janet Torsilieri argue that a process-driven model of management has dominated our minds ever since Adam Smith. We have been engaged in maximizing the efficiency of our processes, whether we are widget makers or McDonald's. Efficient, lean processes with cost-efficient overheads have come to be regarded as the quickest route to profit heaven.

According to Lucier and Torsilieri, good intentions have not been matched by reality. 'Overhead in major corporations is not decreasing,' they note. One contributory factor to this is the rise of the knowledge worker. As Peter F. Drucker has jokingly lamented, 'knowledge workers are abysmally unproductive'.

This calls for a division of mental labour rather than an overriding emphasis on creating processes to divide physical labour. The route to this requires a number of steps. First, routine work – a depressing 80% of what we do – needs to be standardized. This means giving people more responsibility and cutting out middlemen. Second, Lucier and Torsilieri suggest that companies 'outsource the most complex (often most critical) decisions to the real experts'. 'Outsourcing the most complex decisions significantly increases both the quality of decisions and level of service,' they say. The end result will be lower costs (though only slightly). 'Companies will both eliminate expertise-driven overhead and better manage the productivity of knowledge workers,' say Lucier and Torsilieri. They fail to add the most obvious side-effect of outsourcing such work: a boon for management consultants.

As an adjunct to the idea of the division of mental labour, Peter F. Drucker argues that management's great achievement of the twentieth century was to increase the productivity of manual workers fifty-fold.

While this cannot be underestimated, it is not the great challenge of the next century. This, according to Drucker, is to increase the productivity of knowledge workers – dauntingly, he estimates that the productivity of some knowledge workers has actually declined over the last 70 years.

Key text and further reading

Lucier, Charles, Torsilieri, Janet (1999, second quarter) 'The end of overhead', *Strategy & Business*.

Early adopters

Early adopters are the second group following a technological innovation to take up the technology, after the innovators themselves. American academic Everett Rogers suggested in his book *Diffusion of Innovations* that there are several classes of adopters of technological innovation: innovators, early adopters, early majority, late majority, and laggards. Rogers documented how these classes were comprised of fundamentally different people, meaning that as a company expands its customer base, it needs also to change its marketing and behaviour. This work was built on by, among others, Geoffrey Moore in his 1991 book *Crossing the Chasm*, in which he describes the plight of one company trying to 'cross the chasm' from the early-adopter market to the mass market. Early adopters represent 13.5% of all adopters. Their role, according to Rogers, is to increase acceptance of a new idea through adoption and dissemination of a subjective evaluation of the innovation.

Key texts and further reading

Rogers, Everett M. (1962) *Diffusion of Innovations*, Free Press, New York.
Moore, Geoffrey A. (1991) *Crossing The Chasm: Marketing and Selling Technology Products to Mainstream Customers*, Harper & Row, New York.

Expectancy theory

Expectancy theory is a motivational theory proposed by Canadian Victor

Vroom, professor of management and psychology at Yale University. Vroom is one of the world's leading authorities on the psychological analysis of behaviour in organizations. His book *Work and Motivation* is a seminal work in its field.

Vroom defines motivation as 'a process governing choices ... among alternative forms of voluntary behaviour'. If a person has a choice of actions A and B, which lead to two different outcomes, then one might expect the individual to take the course of action that leads to the most desirable outcome or avoids the least desirable outcome at any given moment. Vroom, however, suggests there may be indirect motivation at work during the decision-making process.

Vroom's theory postulates that motivation is determined by three factors: the perception that effort will result in success; the perception that a successful performance will lead to a valued outcome – a reward of some kind; and that personal satisfaction will be derived from the outcome. All three elements must be present for an individual to be motivated. That motivation may be a level beyond the immediate outcome of the action. So if a person needs to achieve X sales to be top salesperson, it might be assumed that being top salesperson is the motivation. In reality, the salesperson sees top salesperson as the means to further promotion and is motivated by the desire to be promoted.

Key text and further reading

Vroom, Victor H. (1964) *Work and Motivation*, John Wiley & Sons, New York.

Guerrilla marketing

Guerrilla marketing is marketing using unorthodox methods. 'Guerrilla' was the Spanish word used to describe the irregular troops who fought with Wellington against Napoleon Bonaparte during the Peninsular War (1808–1814). Lacking professional training, the guerrillas resorted to unconventional tactics to achieve their aims. The term guerrilla marketing was coined by American marketing guru and academic Jay Conrad Levinson to describe an equally unconventional and unorthodox, but nevertheless effective, approach to marketing. One advantage of guerrilla marketing is that it can be highly cost-effective. The internet is a particularly suitable medium for guerrilla marketing campaigns. Guerrilla marketing techniques include web sites, flyers, posters, point-of-purchase materials, stunts, and many other innovative strategies.

Key texts and further reading

Rubin, Charles, Levinson, Jay Conrad (1994) *Guerrilla Marketing Handbook*, Houghton Mifflin Company, New York.

Levinson Jay C. (1997) *Guerrilla Marketing With Technology*, Addison-Wesley, Reading, MA.

Intrapreneur

If the idea of starting your own business is appealing but you don't feel confident enough to make the commitment, some employers offer an opportunity to sample the entrepreneurial life without all of the associated risk. Occasionally, companies will allow employees to start up their own ventures within the company. This halfway house is known as intrapreneuring, with the individual operating within the organization as an entrepreneur would in a separate company.

Gifford and Elizabeth Pinchot were perhaps the first to herald the arrival of the 'intra-corporate entrepreneur' back in 1978, and Gifford Pinchot is credited with coining the term 'intrapreneur'. His book *Intrapreneuring: Why You Don't Have to Leave the Corporation to Become an Entrepreneur* came out in 1985; the *American Heritage Dictionary* added the term 'intrapreneur' in 1992, and the rest, as they say, is history.

History has moved on. Intrapreneuring has grown up and become subsumed within the broader realm of 'corporate venturing'. The Centre for Business Incubation in the UK defines corporate venturing as 'a formal, direct relationship, usually between a larger and an independent smaller company, in which both contribute financial, management, or technical resources, sharing risks and rewards equally for mutual growth'. These relationships may take the form of intrapreneurial ventures, as when large companies spin off new businesses and/or technologies. However, they may also involve the provision of equity and/or non-equity investment to small, independent ventures.

Intrapreneurs have some advantages over the go-it-alone entrepreneur. They benefit, for example, from the reputation of the corporate parent, which may help foster trust in the new corporate venture. That heightened trust, rooted in the history and legitimacy of the parent organization, may make it easier for the venture to obtain financing from both internal and external sources. In addition, the longer developmental time-frame associated with corporate ventures provides an extended opportunity for the intrapreneur to develop social capital networks, thereby increasing his access to financial, technical, and other resources.

Unlike the independent entrepreneur, the intrapreneur has a bank of organizational policies, procedures, systems, and culture to draw upon, thereby freeing up time that may be more profitably devoted to core venture activities. The benefits may come at a cost, however. They may prove disadvantageous, for example, if they inhibit the new venture's flexibility and responsiveness.

Key text and further reading

Pinchot, Gifford (1985) *Intrapreneuring: Why You Don't Have to Leave the Corporation to Become an Entrepreneur*, HarperTrade, New York.

Keiretsu

Following World War II, the Allies felt that Japan's large companies should be dismantled to reduce their economic power. However, it soon became apparent that rather than a weak Japan, an industrially strong Japan was required. This was especially so as the Korean War loomed large. In a policy turnaround, the West pumped money into the Japanese economy and the partially dismantled companies reformed around the major banks, which in turn took a financial stake in those companies. The resulting network of companies was called a *keiretsu*.

The *keiretsu* is a typical organizational structure in Japan. One of its chief benefits is that it encourages the companies within the network to transact business with each other, thus promoting the interests of the *keiretsu* as a whole. Notable examples of *keiretsu* organizations include Mitsubishi and Yamaha. In the US, the term was used to describe the network of associated companies that some incubators or venture capital firms built up through start-up investment, such as venture capital firm Kleiner, Perkins, Caufield & Byers.

Key text and further reading

Miyashita, Kenichi and Russell, David W. (1994) *Keiretsu*, McGraw-Hill, New York.

Kepner-Tregoe

In the 1960s, two RAND research scientists Charles H. Kepner and Benjamin Tregoe identified three components of effective decision making: quality of the decision factors to be satisfied; quality of the evaluation of the alternatives; and quality of understanding of what alternatives can produce. This analysis was used to develop a decision-analysis methodology, the Kepner-Tregoe model. The model involves constructing a decision statement in a group environment, identifying the objectives by listing criteria that can be considered as 'musts' or 'wants', identifying the alternatives, and evaluating the consequences of the choice of outcome.

Key text and further reading

Kepner, Charles and Tregoe, Benjamin (1965) *The Rational Manager,* McGraw-Hill, New York.

Management by objectives

Management by objectives motivates the workforce within an organization by providing each level of management, and often employees as well, with specific objectives to be achieved during a specific period of time. These objectives are determined by both the subordinates and their superiors. Performance is then periodically measured against the objectives selected. The Austrian management guru Peter Drucker, in his book *The Practice of Management*, claimed that management by objectives was the best way of delegating authority in a large organization.

Key text and further reading

Drucker Peter F. (1954) *The Practice of Management*, Harper & Row, New York.

Management by wandering around (MBWA)

Management by wandering around, or management by walking about, is the practice of senior managers interacting with the workforce by visiting the shop floor or offices where the general staff work. The concept was developed and pioneered by Dave Packard and Bill Hewlett at Hewlett-Packard during the 1970s. It was then popularized in the book *In Search of Excellence: Lessons From America's Best Run Companies*, by Tom Peters and Robert Waterman, who called the practice 'the technology of the obvious'. Their research showed that those companies where managers actively engaged with employees and customers were more successful than those where the management was isolated. Not only does MBWA cut through the vertical lines of communication in a hierarchical organization structure; it also motivates the workforce by suggesting that senior management takes an active interest in them.

Key text and further reading

Peters, Thomas J. and Waterman, Robert (1982) *In Search of Excellence: Lessons From America's Best Run Companies*, HarperCollins, New York.

Mind mapping

US academic Tony Buzan developed the mind-mapping technique in the 1960s, following his research on students' note-taking techniques. The technique involves harnessing words, images, numbers, colours and spatial awareness to represent thoughts. Mind maps resemble unstructured, brightly coloured flow diagrams with pictures. Guiding principles to creating a mind map include: start in the centre of the sheet of paper; use at least three colours; use images, symbols, codes, and dimensions throughout; each word/image must be alone and sitting on its own line; lines must be connected, starting as thick lines at the centre and becoming thinner as they radiate outward; use emphasis and show associations. A mind map can be used to give an overview of a large subject, enable route planning of concepts, and promote creative thinking by highlighting new creative pathways.

Key text and further reading

Buzan, Tony (1993) *The Mind Map Book*, BBC Books, London.

One-to-one marketing

The concept of one-to-one marketing is most closely associated with US consultants Don Peppers and Martha Rogers of the Peppers & Rogers Group. It involves providing services or products to a single customer at a time by identifying and then meeting that customer's individual needs. The aim is to do this on a continuing basis with each customer. The theory is that one-to-one marketing should go beyond the sale of a product or service to the customer and permeate the organization. One-to-one marketing should become part of company culture, part of the vision driving the company. One-to-one marketing offers several benefits, including a concentration on the most profitable customers, obstacles to comparative shopping, lifetime customer relationships, the development of customer feedback and the resulting product improvement, and differentiation from competitors.

Were it not for technology, one-to-one marketing would be an impractical approach for any company other than one serving a niche market of wealthy customers. Modern technology makes it possible to provide mass-customization of products.

Key text and further reading

Peppers, Don, Rogers, Martha and Dorf, Bob (1999) *The One to One Fieldbook: The Complete Toolkit for Implementing a Tool Marketing Program*, Doubleday, New York.

Permission marketing

The term permission marketing was coined by American marketing innovator Seth Godin, former president of Yoyodyne Entertainment and former vice president of direct marketing at Yahoo! Seth Godin is a respected e-commerce pioneer, specializing in online marketing. After graduating from Tufts University in 1982, Godin went to work as brand manager for Spinnaker Software. His next stop was an MBA at Stanford Business School, graduating in 1984. At Yoyodyne Entertainment, the company Godin founded and named after the character in Thomas Pynchon's novel *The Crying of Lot 49*, he set about changing the world of on-line marketing. His idea was to persuade people to accept product pitches from companies by offering them an incentive.

Permission marketing is based on the premise that consumers will voluntarily and willingly give up valuable personal information and also grant permission for marketers to send them product information, so long as they are given sufficient incentive. A permission-marketing campaign might, for example, involve an airline offering free flights or a chance to win the trip of a lifetime, in return for which the customer would grant permission to the airline to e-mail offers of other products it thought the customer might be interested in. This model has become one of the most popular ways of marketing on-line.

The permission marketer must therefore find the appropriate incentive to persuade the consumer to grant permission. Permission marketers must be careful not to abuse the permission granted by the consumer. They also have to manage the relationship to assess whether permission is revoked or to determine if it has lapsed. There is a fine line between e-mailing product information with permission and spamming.

Key texts and further reading

Godin, Seth (2002) *Survival is Not Enough*, Free Press, New York.
Godin, Seth and Gladwell, Malcolm (2001) *Unleashing the Ideavirus: Stop Marketing at People! Turn Your Ideas into Epidemics by Helping Your Customers Do the Marketing for You*, Hyperion, New York.
Godin, Seth (1995) *Permission Marketing: Turning Strangers into Friends and Friends into Customers*, Simon & Schuster, New York.

Quality circle

A quality circle is a small group of production workers concerned with problems relating to the quality, safety, and efficiency of their product. The origins of the quality circle are unclear. Most agree that it originated in Japan during the 1960s. Others, however, argue that the practice began in the US Army in the immediate post-World War II period. Certainly, quality circles were popularized in Japan.

Key characteristics of quality circles are size (eight to twelve members); voluntary membership; natural work groups, rather than artificially created ones; autonomy in setting their own agenda; access to senior managers; and a relatively permanent existence. Commitment from senior management to the process is vital to ensure its success. An analysis of the steps to implementing a quality circle is discussed in *The*

Rational Manager, by American business writers Charles Kepner and Ben Tregoe.

Key text and further reading

Kepner, Charles and Tregoe, Benjamin (1965) *The Rational Manager,* McGraw-Hill, New York.

Single-loop learning

During the 1970s, American academics Chris Argyris and Donald Schön made a substantial contribution to the field of organizational learning, notably with their books *Theory in Practice* and *Organizational Learning.* In these books, Argyris and Schön originated two basic organizational models. Each organizational model exhibited a different attitude towards learning.

Model 1 is one in which managers concentrate on establishing individual goals. They keep to themselves and don't voice concerns or disagreements. Model 1 managers are prepared to inflict change on others, but resist any attempt to change their own thinking and working practices. Model 1 organizations are characterized by what Argyris and Schön labelled 'single-loop learning,' in which 'the detection and correction of organizational error permits the organization to carry on its present policies and achieve its current objectives'. In a Model 1 organization, any learning that takes place will only be in reference to those practices and policies already in place, rather than re-evaluating those policies (a practice which is termed double-loop learning).

In contrast, Model 2 organizations emphasize 'double-loop learning', in which 'organizational error is detected and corrected in ways that involve the modification of underlying norms, policies, and objectives'. In Model 2 organizations, managers act on information. They debate issues and respond to change, and are prepared to change. A virtuous circle emerges of learning and understanding. 'Most organizations do quite well in single-loop learning but have great difficulties in double-loop learning,' concluded Argyris and Schön.

Corporate fashions have moved Argyris's way. With the return of learning to the corporate agenda in the early 1990s, his work became slightly more fashionable.

Key text and further reading

Argyris, Chris, Schön, Donald A. (1974) *Theory In Practice: Increasing Professional Effectiveness*, Jossey-Bass, San Francisco, CA.

Spaghetti organization

The term spaghetti organization was coined by Danish businessman Lars Kolind to describe the extremely flexible organizational structure he introduced in 1991 at the Danish hearing-aid technology company Oticon, where Kolind was CEO. When Kolind took over at Oticon, the company was stagnating. He introduced a radical restructuring programme. In his concept of the perfect corporate organization, he placed the interaction, collaboration, and connectivity of people, customers, suppliers, and ideas at the company's heart. Kolind called it 'a spaghetti organization of rich strands in a chaotic network'. The key characteristics of a spaghetti organization are choice (staff initiate projects and assemble teams; individuals invited to join a project can decline); multiple roles (the project approach creates multi-disciplined individuals); and transparency (knowledge is shared throughout the organization). The organization is knowledge based and is driven internally by free market forces.

Interestingly, the company and Kolind had pulled back from the most radical implementation of the spaghetti organization sometime before his departure as CEO in 1998.

Key texts and further reading

Kolind, Lars (1990) 'Think the Unthinkable', in Morsing, Mette and Kristian (eds) (1998) *Managing the Unmanageable For a Decade*, Oticon, Hellerup, Denmark.

Lovas, Bjorn and Ghoshal, Sumantra (2000) 'Strategy as Guided Evolution', *Strategic Management Journal*, 21: 875–96.

Foss, Nicolai J. (2000) *Internal Hybrids as Sources of Competitive Advantage: A Note on the Oticon Spaghetti Experiment*, Copenhagen Business Paper Link Programme working paper.

Transactional leadership

Transactional leadership is a concept that was developed by management academics Bernard M. Bass and later expanded by Bass and fellow academic Bruce Avolio. It is based on the idea that the relationship between leaders and their followers develops from the exchange of some reward, such as performance ratings, pay, recognition, and praise. It involves leaders ensuring that wider organizational goals are met by clarifying goals and objectives and communicating to organize tasks and activities with the co-operation of their employees.

Key text and further reading

Bass, B.M. (1985) *Leadership and performance beyond expectations*, Free Press, New York.

Value chain integration

There are three distinct elements to value chain integration: the interface with the customer; the supply chain in the back room; and the connecting of the two.

ERP, or Enterprise Resource Planning, was an attempt in the early 1990s at optimizing the supply chain. Advances in software development and networking meant that companies could connect their empires and automate and co-ordinate their procurement programmes. Software manufacturers such as PeopleSoft, SAP, and Oracle provided the technologies.

ERP applications have now moved on to web-based solutions. Industry-specific procurement sites have been set up on the internet and the flexibility of the web-based approach has allowed companies to source more efficiently from a range of suppliers.

At the front end, the internet should provide an excellent way to interact with the customer. The best web sites allow customers to find what they are looking for easily and where possible to add their own specifications. Companies like Dell, for example, allow the customer to configure their own computer to a degree. Ordering, too, should be as immediate as possible. It is always surprising how many companies fail to realize the importance of getting this part of the value chain right.

The last part of the chain is the connection between the web site and the back room. It should work like this. The customer arrives at the web site and purchases a product – a set of golf clubs, say. The order is processed internally. An order is sent to the warehouse or supplier and the goods are dispatched. The software makes the appropriate stock adjustments and orders in a replacement set of clubs if required.

However, in many companies this is the least efficient part of the value chain. Often the front and back ends are processed on separate networks – frequently because of software incompatibility. Instead of overhauling the system when they introduced the front end web site, many companies patched the back end and front end together the best they could.

Only when this last part of the chain is properly addressed will companies reap the full benefits of value chain integration.

Key text and further reading

Robertson, Bruce and Sribar, Valentin (2002) *Enriching the Value Chain: Infrastructure Strategies Beyond the Enterprise*, Addison-Wesley, Reading, MA.

Viral marketing

Viral marketing is word-of-mouth advertising carried out in cyberspace, usually by e-mail. It works when one friend sends another an e-mail with a clickable link that takes the recipient through to the host web site, where the product or service is sold.

It's been a while since internet guru Michael Tchong called 'viral marketing' the buzzword of the year in 1998. The term was originally coined by venture capitalist Steve Jurvetson, who backed Hotmail. Coincidentally, Hotmail is the example most often cited by proponents of viral marketing. Spending less than $500,000, Hotmail managed to sign up more than twelve million users in less than eighteen months. How did it accomplish this prodigious feat? Every e-mail sent by a Hotmail subscriber invites the recipient to sign up for an account. It's infectious stuff. To succeed, the marketing virus must spread quickly. The most successful viruses tend to be fun or useful.

Key text and further reading

Goldsmith, Russell (2002) *Viral Marketing*, Pearson Professional Education, London.

INDEX